# American Romanticism and the Popularization of Literary Education

# American Romanticism and the Popularization of Literary Education

Clemens Spahr

LEXINGTON BOOKS
*Lanham • Boulder • New York • London*

Published by Lexington Books
An imprint of The Rowman & Littlefield Publishing Group, Inc.
4501 Forbes Boulevard, Suite 200, Lanham, Maryland 20706
www.rowman.com

86-90 Paul Street, London EC2A 4NE

Copyright © 2022 by The Rowman & Littlefield Publishing Group, Inc.

*All rights reserved.* No part of this book may be reproduced in any form or by any electronic or mechanical means, including information storage and retrieval systems, without written permission from the publisher, except by a reviewer who may quote passages in a review.

British Library Cataloguing in Publication Information Available

**Library of Congress Cataloging-in-Publication Data on File**

ISBN 978-1-7936-4954-6 (cloth : alk. Paper)
ISBN 978-1-7936-4955-3 (electronic)

♾️™ The paper used in this publication meets the minimum requirements of American National Standard for Information Sciences—Permanence of Paper for Printed Library Materials, ANSI/NISO Z39.48-1992.

*For Melanie and Benjamin*

# Contents

Acknowledgments ix

Introduction 1

1  Universal Education: American Romanticism and the Institutions of Education 17

2  Intelligent Sympathies: Conversations and the Institutionalization of Romantic Education 37

3  The Problem of Audience: Nineteenth-Century Periodical Culture and Romantic Popular Education 71

4  Public Intellectuals: The Romantic Lecture, Professionalization, and Politics 101

Conclusion 131

Bibliography 135

Index 149

About the Author 153

# Acknowledgments

This book is the product of a research project funded by the German Research Foundation (DFG, project no.: SP 1366/5). Without their financial support, none of this would have been possible. I am grateful for the support of many colleagues and friends, most notably Oliver Scheiding, Jan Stievermann, Wesley Mott, Sandra Petrulionis, Philipp Löffler, Maximilian Meinhardt, Franziska Schmid, and a host of international Romanticism experts at various pre-Corona conferences, all of whom have commented on parts of this project in its various stages. A crucial moment in the readjustment of the project occurred when I presented parts of it in the context of the Newberry Seminar in American Literature. I am particularly grateful to the seminar's coordinators, Walter Benn Michaels and Kenneth Warren, but also to Jennifer Ashton, Sarah Buchmeier, and everyone else who attended the seminar. I'd also like to thank Gregor Baszak, who has offered valuable comments on the manuscript's theoretical frame. In addition, I am grateful to the staffs at Houghton Library, the wonderful Gutman Library, and the Boston Public Library, who have guided me through the various manuscript and rare book collections I consulted.

At Lexington Books, Holly Buchanan has supported this project from the beginning. She also showed patience with the completion of the manuscript. I'd like to thank her for her professionalism and helpfulness. The anonymous reviewer has provided invaluable help with revising the manuscript.

Finally, I'd like to thank my family for putting up with yet another book project. I apologize.

Parts of chapter 3 have originally appeared as "'The Great Work of Mutual Education': Class, Popularity, and the Position of the Intellectual in Margaret Fuller's Literary Journalism," *ESQ: Journal of Nineteenth-Century American Literature and Culture* 66.3 (2020): 481–517. The text is reprinted by permission.

# Introduction

American Transcendentalism must be understood as a literary movement involved in the institutional conditions of a pre-professional nineteenth-century educational system. The Transcendentalists, the earliest representatives of Romanticism in the United States, concluded a transatlantic cultural development as much as they opened this discourse to New England's educational system. The Romantic reformers profited from a relatively unified, if contested, New England educational landscape. They employed and transformed available positions in the nineteenth-century educational field to establish their Romantic literary spaces. While the proliferation of educational institutions and practices in the 1830s and 1840s put the Transcendentalists in a position to establish their various reform projects, the field's exclusionary mechanisms contradicted their aim to enable the poetic life comprehensively for all. The more the Transcendentalists sought to expand their influence, as their universal claims eventually demanded, the more they had to confront the exclusionary mechanisms that prevented true Romantic education.

This book argues that American Transcendentalism was an attempt to institutionalize and popularize Romantic literary education. Because the Transcendentalists tried to make Romantic education "the generating Idea of society itself,"[1] self-reliance ultimately needed to become a cultural practice available to everyone. This practice could be established comprehensively only through what Margaret Fuller called "the general education of the people."[2] This comprehensive idea of education led to a popularization and professionalization of Romanticism. Popular education meant to establish alternative discursive practices to overcome "the shocking inhumanity of exclusiveness" which prevented cultural achievements from being "used for the benefit of all."[3] Studying the Romantic literary genres and their function in the context of the specific institutions of nineteenth-century education allows us to establish the history of a movement which had to acknowledge the limits of their comprehensive reform project while never retreating from its belief that cooperation and sympathetic exchange should be the fundamental principle of human interaction and social organization.

My book focuses on three Romantic educational genres and their institutional and media contexts: the conversation, literary journalism, and the public lecture. The genres discussed here illustrate the ways in which the Transcendentalists engaged nineteenth-century media and educational institutions in order to realize their projects. But the following chapters also chart a development from the semi-public conversational platforms such as Alcott's Temple School and Fuller's conversations for women in the 1830s to the increasingly public periodical culture and lecture platforms of the 1840s and the early 1850s. This expansion caused a reconsideration of the meaning and function of Romanticism. As the Romantics' attempts to institutionalize and popularize their educational ideals increasingly involved them in the institutional structures of the nineteenth-century educational field, they encountered the exclusionary mechanisms which limited educational opportunities, just as much as they had to come to terms with their own role in an educational system which recreated social privilege.

The tension between universalism and exclusion asserted itself forcefully in the writings of the American Transcendentalists. This tension is deeply ingrained in the history of transatlantic Romanticism. Just like their European predecessors, the Transcendentalists understood Romanticism as a principle of social organization. Frederick C. Beiser has demonstrated that the early German Romantics responded to the fragmentation and individualization characteristic of Western modernity through an "ethics of love" that was rooted in self-awareness: "the romantic ideal of *Bildung* reaffirmed the value of unity with oneself, others, and nature."[4] But Romantic education was not simply an ethical affair; it was also an attempt to institutionalize a communicative situation built on sympathetic relationships. Informal literary circles like those of the Lake Poets and the Jena conversational circles of the early German Romantics established a collective form of sympathetic creativity (a "Symphilosophy" and "Sympoesie").[5] Although these literary circles were often elitist, specialized groups, which carefully selected their members, the conversational principles and the educational ideas on which they were established contradicted utilitarianism and profit as organizing social principles.[6] These informal literary institutions illustrate one of the basic conflicts of Romantic education. The Romantic circles with their specialized audiences were the product of the division of labor as much as they sought to overcome it.

The conflict between specialization and universalism drove the development of American Romantic education. For the American Romantics, self-reliance was the condition for, as well as the product of, rearranging human relationships. Romantic education, however, did not automatically mean progressive reform. Alan Richardson has shown that for the British Romantic writers disseminating what they saw as "the best kind of fiction" among the masses was often supposed to function as a substitute for social and economic equality.[7] Although British Romanticism contained an egalitarian core, the moral education of the masses coincided with an attempt to control these masses. Richardson points out the Lake poets' support of the monitorial school system and "their reliance on colonialist educational metaphors, their distaste for working-class educational ventures unless rigorously controlled by established interests."[8] While Benthamites understood the education of the masses as essential for improving the working class's situation, for the Lake Poets Romantic literary education was supposed to reconcile the classes.

The Transcendentalists harbored reservations about mass education and the popularization of their Romanticism. But they became involved in the educational landscape of their time to a degree where they eventually had to link their public position to Romanticism's comprehensive reform claims. Orestes Brownson had phrased this aim pointedly in "The Laboring Classes": "No man can be a Christian who does not labor to reform society, to mould it according to the will of God and the nature of man; so that free scope shall be given to every man to unfold himself in all beauty and power, and to grow up into the stature of a perfect man in Christ Jesus."[9] For the Romantics, the dynamic yet unified nineteenth-century educational landscape promised to allow for the realization of this universal vision of self-reliance. Hence Emerson's enthusiastic claim in the *Dial* that the Transcendentalists were addressing "a new-born class long already standing waiting for this voice & wondering at its delay."[10] But as their attempts to popularize education forced the Romantics to theorize and define this class more precisely, they had to come to terms with the contradiction between their universal ideas and the social privilege their own institutions were founded on.[11] Their institutional position confronted them with the question of how to reconcile their elite position and, more importantly, their limited audience, with their comprehensive egalitarian demands. The specific realization of such a comprehensive project had to confront the problem that Romanticism in the United States was not a mass movement and that the various educational platforms were mostly restricted to a middle-class audience.

The Romantics were immensely practical figures, and accordingly assigned their literary and educational texts—ranging from fiction and poetry to journals, manifestos, and educational treatises—a pedagogical, public function. In 1837, shortly after he had graduated from Harvard, Henry David Thoreau wrote a letter to Orestes Brownson, in which he expressed his concern over education's separation from everyday life. Thoreau states that "[t]his discipline [education], which we allow to be the end of life, should not be one thing in the schoolroom, and another in the street."[12] Thoreau not only defines education as a form of practice—a claim he would reiterate in *Walden*, when he demands "so to love wisdom as to live according to its dictates a life of simplicity, independence, magnanimity, and trust." He also diagnoses a historical moment when education increasingly separated itself from "the street" and the people. Education cannot fulfill a communal function when "poverty or neglect threaten to rob the child of this right."[13] This realization affects the Transcendentalists' understanding of Romanticism. The movement sought to become increasingly popular and universal; as it did so, it encountered the limiting circumstances that are constitutive of education. Exclusion and limitation were fundamental problems for a group of intellectuals who aimed to correct the "neglect of popular education," as Fuller would put it (*SGD* 255). This book details how, in their specific institutional contexts, the Romantics established positions to realize their educational plans and, in the process of encountering the limits of such a project, had to reconsider the meaning and function of their Romanticism.

The following chapters trace how the various media and institutional contexts changed the Romantic understanding of literature and literary education. The dynamic nature of the educational field in which the Romantic educators emerged is primarily accessible through the periodicals of the time. To establish the constellation necessary for an understanding of Romantic education, my book draws on a number of periodicals which have been underexamined or studied only superficially. The nineteenth-century educational field was structured through the various discussions occurring in established journals like the *Boston Courier*, the *Boston Recorder* (*and Telegraph*), and the *American Journal of Education*. These not only reflected the discussions of the age; they were instrumental in constituting the meaning, conditions, and limits of nineteenth-century education. In fact, it is precisely the historical constellation accessible through these periodicals (its emergence in a moment when the modern educational system was still taking shape) which allows us to understand that Romanticism embodies a tradition of education significantly different from an educational system determined by competition, prestige, and profit—a tradition that needs to receive more attention today than ever before, at a time when the Humanities are under attack everywhere.

What emerges from these periodicals is the portrait of an educational system in transition. The history of Romantic education is inextricably linked to the production, reproduction, and transformation of social practices in nineteenth-century America. The Transcendentalists instituted oppositional spaces in the dynamic educational field of nineteenth-century Boston.

Conditions in the 1830s and 1840s proved hospitable to their educational ideas. While didactic rigidity often characterized the period's pedagogy, the increasing need for literacy and basic education also enabled alternative school forms, from Lancastrian industrial schools to small reform schools, and from women's academies to conversational circles and night schools. Stanley Cavell has referred to the age of the Transcendentalists as a "pre-philosophical moment," when the "professionalization of philosophy" had not yet occurred and when "philosophy and literature and theology (and politics and economics) had not isolated themselves out from one another but when these divorcements could be felt as imminent, for better or worse."[14] I will address the conditions of nineteenth-century education and intellectual labor in the next chapter in detail. But Cavell's term offers a good preliminary way to describe the emergent professionalization and stratification of education that historians and critics have identified as the determining forces of the nineteenth-century educational system.[15] The Romantic reformers encountered an increasingly differentiated, professionalized, and stratified educational system but one that was sufficiently dynamic so that they could still plausibly imagine themselves as public intellectuals.

As difficult as it was to navigate nineteenth-century media and institutions which were still taking shape, this dynamic institutional landscape allowed for Transcendentalism to become a viable institutional position. It enabled the Romantic reformers to reconnect intellectual labor and social reform through education and hence two spheres which the cultural elite tried to keep apart. In his "Discourse on the Dangers and Duties of Men of Letters" (1809), for instance, leading Unitarian Joseph Buckminster had described education as a means to create an "enlightened and virtuous community."[16] But what Buckminster meant by "community" was the intellectual elite. It is therefore logical that he cautions the young "men of letters" not to make themselves "of consequence to the people, or, rather, to some of their factions" but rather to turn to "the quiet speculations of the scholar."[17] A life of quiet speculation it is, of course, only because "the people" are largely excluded from this life. As Daniel Walker Howe has put it in his seminal study on Harvard Unitarianism in nineteenth-century Boston, when he "claimed intellectuals should be above 'factions,' in practice Buckminster equated support of conservative factions with responsible leadership."[18] Emerson, by contrast, admonishes his audience to act: "But we are not permitted to stand as spectators of the pageant which the times exhibit: we are parties also, and have a responsibility which is not to be declined."[19]

The Romantics' pedagogical writings and practices help us understand how even a non-reified, poetic educational practice is always involved in the hierarchies of the educational field that prevent this practice's universal accessibility. At the same time, American Romantic education shows that education does not simply reproduce social privilege, thereby importantly adding to sociological and historical analyses of American literature and culture. In his *Pascalian Meditations*, Pierre Bourdieu emphasizes the seminal importance of education as a field of investigation to understand social organization more generally: "It is, for example, from the social history of educational institutions [. . .] and from the (forgotten or repressed) history of our singular relationship to these institutions, that we can expect some real revelations about the objective and subjective structures (classifications, hierarchies, problematics, etc.) that always, in spite of ourselves, orient our thought."[20] Education is always, subconsciously, involved in the reproduction of social structures. While education aspires to disinterestedness, autonomy, and self-realization, these aspirations rest on exclusivist privilege.

In accordance with Bourdieu's sociology, this book analyzes the limits and contradictions of Romantic educational reform as the result of the Transcendentalists' contradictory institutional position; but it is also concerned with how the Transcendentalists openly addressed these limits, and, by doing so, were able to consciously intervene in the field of nineteenth-century education. Bourdieu-inspired scholarship often depicts educational structures as opaque to the involved individuals, something to be revealed by the sociologist. American Romantic education, however, had displayed a very clear sense of how to strategically approach the hierarchies of the educational field in order to create a true form of Romantic, poetic practice that would put everyone in a position to realize their "elevated and beautiful forms of character."[21] As strategic and political as Romantic education would become, the organizing principle remained that of poetic creativity. As Orestes Brownson had asked: "can any system of education be truly practical, which has not reference to man in his whole capacity, obligations, and destiny, as something more than a money-getting animal; which does not aim to draw out into free activity the whole faculties of his mind?"[22] It was in the name of this vision of the self that the Transcendentalists sought to popularize Romanticism.

Because they were situated in a semiprofessional educational system, the Transcendentalists occupied the contradictory position of what Lance Newman has referred to as "elite radicals."[23] While the increasingly diversified field of education put the Transcendentalists in a position to establish their various educational projects, the field's exclusiveness contradicted their aim to establish the poetic life for all. These elite radicals sought social change but had their audience largely in New England's literate public. From the outset, Amos Bronson Alcott, still misjudged as a lofty idealist, sought to strategically reconcile institutional reform and popular education. Alcott saw "Mr. Mann's influence on the interest of popular education" as "quite favorable," and gives him credit that "[h]e will do somewhat to improve existing organizations, and thus prepare the way for radical improvements."[24] But for Alcott popular appeal was essential for the project to succeed. Similarly, for Fuller, the popular press was continuous with her earlier profession as a teacher and educator of women: "Newspaper writing is next door to conversation, and should be conducted on the same principles."[25] The logic of Romantic education, then, pushed for ever larger reform efforts.

Transcendentalism was as a social, educational, and literary movement. The intellectual and educational field in which the Transcendentalists moved was what Pierre Bourdieu has called a "space of positions and the space of position-taking in which they are expressed." The Transcendentalists' use of these positions determined the direction of their movement. As Bourdieu has argued, "the network of objective relations between positions subtends and orients strategies which the occupants of the different positions implement in their struggles to defend or improve their positions."[26] The Transcendentalists were permanently involved in institutional struggles. They were idealists keenly aware of how to market their ideas, well-known public intellectuals who used their reputation and cultural capital to advocate a social organization that allowed for the realization of everyone's individuality. The progressive popularization of their reform project, from the conversation to literary journalism and the public lecture, is charted in the following chapters.

My book contributes to the ongoing reevaluation of Transcendentalism as what Wesley Mott has called an "educational demonstration."[27] By doing so, it seeks to help reinstate Romanticism as a fundamental episode in American educational history. Recent scholarship has begun the textual and archival work necessary to assess the Transcendentalists' educational writings and practices.[28] Although I seek to contribute to the ongoing establishment of the historical and contemporary relevance of Romantic education, my book is not a historical survey. The chapters trace how the various media and institutional contexts changed the Romantic understanding of literary education, and how these changes were the result of a logic inherent in Romanticism itself. This book therefore relates the Transcendentalists' educational practices to the institutions and media through which they emerged. For the Transcendentalists, even more than for the European Romantics, Romanticism was an institutionalized social practice. Most of the Transcendentalists emerged from New England's educational system and defined their literary and cultural projects in contradistinction from the rote learning and drill that dominated nineteenth-century educational practices, including those at Harvard University and various grammar schools. The practices necessary to create these spaces and the various ways in which the Romantics advocated, circulated, and critically reflected them are the subject of this book.

The diverse genre and media contexts of Romantic education display how broadly nineteenth-century education must be understood. Given its self-understanding as comprehensive practice, it may be tempting to understand Romantic education in the broad, culturalized sense of education as occurring through various socialization agencies (family, church, community, and economy), which Bernard Bailyn has influentially established. According to Bailyn, education should be understood "not only as formal pedagogy but as the entire process by which a culture transmits itself across generations."[29] Bailyn and the scholarship in his wake have importantly shown that education often occurs outside official institutions. But Romantic literary practice asserted itself quite concretely through the emergent literary and educational institutions of nineteenth-century New England. It was a conscious attempt at institutionalizing and popularizing the egalitarian principle embodied by Romantic literary practice. As such, the definition of Romantic education requires attention to the idea's universality as well as to its concrete manifestation in the context of nineteenth-century literary and educational institutions.

To gauge the parameters of these processes more precisely, it is necessary to combine the relevant fields in the study of nineteenth-century education, which still often operate largely independently from each other. Literary studies, sociology, and history have comprehensively surveyed nineteenth-century education; but they mostly limit themselves to discussing either the role of literature, questions of literacy, or institutional questions without connecting them in a meaningful way. There are, however, a number of important studies which have started to explore the relationship between literature and social reform. In *Moral Enterprise: Literature and Education in Antebellum America* (2013), Derek Pacheco has examined how the Romantics disseminated their educational efforts through the literary market.[30] From a perspective that is more interested in rhetoric and ideas, Mark Vásquez has argued that educational writings from the Great Awakening to the Transcendentalists were "synthetic discourses of authority."[31] In a similar manner, individual essays have begun to address the "material" conditions (for instance, classroom arrangement) of Romantic educational reform.[32] All of these studies have stressed the social and political aspects of Romantic literary education, just as Transcendentalism has been placed more generally in the context of social reform movements with John A. Buehrens's *Conflagration: How the Transcendentalists Sparked the American Struggle for Racial, Gender, and Social Justice* (2020).[33]

Pedagogical scholarship, in turn, has usefully made available Romantic educational ideas for twentieth- and twenty-first-century pedagogy.[34] From a different angle, sociological and historical studies, in turn, have analyzed the nineteenth century with regard to the history of American higher education and focused on the questions of literacy and access to learning in antebellum America.³⁵ They have produced indispensable institutional histories and seminal studies of the distribution of literacy and learning in the nineteenth century. Finally, any conception of Romanticism as a form of practice must take into account scholarship on the Transcendentalists' use of literary networks and the literary market. New England Transcendentalism was part of a complex literary network, and even Emerson, with his ostentatious skepticism about popular presses, was in fact known for "his work with publishers and strategic manipulation of print media to establish Transcendentalism within American culture."³⁶ The Romantics' literary networks operated both formally, as when Elizabeth Peabody provided the location for Temple School and Fuller's conversations and recruited students for both educational projects, and informally through the circulation of journals and letters, which established their positions in these networks.

Education was not only central to American Romanticism. Education was the discourse and practice through which antebellum society constituted itself. To assess the social, literary, and historical place of Romantic education it is necessary to productively synthesize these theories and methodologies. Such an approach allows us to understand Romanticism as a form of comprehensive educational practice. When the Transcendentalists circulated their literary practices through nineteenth-century media, they tapped into an educational discourse intimately connected to institutional and social politics. In April 1840 Orestes Brownson could therefore proclaim: "Education is the great problem of the age."³⁷ The social and political significance of these discussions meant that there were consequences even for challenges to institutional authority. Ralph Waldo Emerson's Divinity School Address (1838) illustrates how contested this field was, and how drastic the consequences of dissent could be. When Emerson proclaimed that teaching is "not instruction, but provocation" in front of the students and professors of Harvard Divinity School, he caused a storm of outrage (*CW* 1:80). His belief in an egalitarian relationship between teacher and learner challenged the rigid hierarchies of higher learning. In what was a rather daring manner even for an established young intellectual like Emerson, he encouraged his audience to "cast behind you all conformity, and acquaint men at first hand with Deity. Look to it first and only, [so] that fashion, custom, *authority*, pleasure, and money, are nothing to you" (*CW* 1:90). These sentences, among others, were rightly perceived as a provocation to institutional and social authority and earned Emerson an almost thirty-year ban from Harvard.

Lest someone harbored any doubts about how serious the Transcendentalist were about their rebellion, Orestes Brownson made sure to clarify his message for the establishment: "We insist upon it, that the complete and final destruction of the priestly order, in every practical sense of the word priest, is the first step to be taken towards elevating the laboring classes."[38] Emerson's address is emblematic of Romantic dissent in early-nineteenth-century America—a dissent that could range from reform to open rebellion. It is also a good example of how the Romantics pursued their projects very strategically. In 1838, Harvard was shaken by food riots, in the course of which students vehemently raged against the bad dining hall conditions, and four years earlier Harvard's president Josiah Quincy had to call "police into the Yard [. . .] to calm rioting sophomores protesting the punishment of a classmate."[39] These riots occurred at a time when Boston's standing order found itself in a crisis of legitimation.[40] Emerson must have known precisely what he was doing when he rejected authority in the temple of authority and privilege. Emerson's speech therefore illustrates how the Romantics opened the contested field of education for alternatives; and how they developed manifold strategies in order to perform, propagate, and disseminate their dissent. The complexity of this endeavor can be properly assessed only by shifting between sociological, historical, and literary analysis. The combination of these fields allows us to understand the logic of popularization that characterized Romantic education.

Romantic literary education pushed the boundaries of literature. In 1845, two years after Fuller had left New England for New York to work as a cultural critic for the *New-York Tribune*, she had settled into her new role as a journalist. In a letter to James Freeman Clarke from August 14, 1845, Fuller used the occasion to reassess the position of the public intellectual and intellectual labor: "I was pleased with your sympathy about The Tribune; I do not find much among my old friends. They think I ought to produce something excellent, while I am well content for the present to aid in the great work of mutual education in this way." Fuller goes on to declare: "I never regarded literature merely as a collection of exquisite products, but as a means of mutual interpretation. Feeling that many are reached and in some degree aided the thoughts of every day seem worth writing down, though in a form that does not inspire me."[41] The distinction between literary excellence and her work for the popular press is suggestive on numerous levels. The editors of Fuller's memoir, William Henry Channing, Ralph Waldo Emerson, and James Freeman Clarke, present the letter as evidence that Fuller's descent into popular education ultimately prevented her from creating true literary excellence "because it hindered her free action to aim at popular effect."[42] While Fuller's diction displays a similar unease about popularizing her ideas—she is "content for the present" to write in a "form that does not inspire" her—her letter simultaneously undermines the distinction between popularity and literary autonomy on which the editors insist.

Fuller's repurposing of literature, then, and her desire to aid "the general education of the people"[43] was the logical upshot of Romanticism. But it was proclamation rather than fulfilled practice. In addition, Fuller concedes that the medium of literary journalism required stylistic compromises. Popular education remained a problem but a productive one that forced the Transcendentalists to reconsider their Romanticism. The following chapters outline episodes in the institutionalization, professionalization, and popularization of American Romanticism. Professionalization and popularization drove Romanticism and reshaped it into an educational literary practice. The book treats this process not as a success story but as a problematic that emerged organically from the idea of a comprehensive Romantic education. It is for this reason that I refer to the intellectuals discussed in this group as both Transcendentalists and Romantics. The Transcendentalists were a group of rebellious intellectuals who had established themselves in nineteenth-century Boston. But they were also always Romantics because their generative principle was their inherited Romanticism. The Transcendentalists' attempt to popularize this Romanticism under the conditions of nineteenth-century New England educational landscape is the subject of this book.

The following chapters seek to establish the narrative I have just laid out, addressing various important episodes in the professionalization and popularization of Romantic education. Chapter 1, "Universal Education: American Romanticism and the Institutions of Education," locates American Romanticism in the antebellum educational field. The early nineteenth century saw an educational system in transition. The 1830s and 1840s were hospitable to comprehensive reform ideas because the characteristics of the modern educational system such as the difference between private and public education, the professionalization of teaching, and the departmentalization of academic disciplines were in the making but not yet firmly established. This dynamic field enabled the Transcendentalists to establish their educational projects. Although the increasingly diversified field of education put the Transcendentalists in a position to establish their various educational projects, the field's exclusiveness contradicted their aim to establish the poetic life for all. For the Transcendentalists, their position as intellectuals emerged as a problem as well as an opportunity. Their contradictory status as rebels profiting from the exclusionary mechanisms of the educational field forced them to reflect the possibilities and limits of Romantic education. Romantic education could not rest content with local results. The chapter delineates how the conditions of the educational system and their own contradictory situation simultaneously enabled and inhibited the Transcendentalists' reform projects.

Each of the book's subsequent chapters discusses a specific Romantic literary genre and its corresponding educational institution. By doing so, the book delineates the particular conditions which enabled and limited

Romantic reform. Chapter 2, "Intelligent Sympathies: Conversations and the Institutionalization of Romantic Education," addresses the conversational practice of Romantic education. The chapter focuses on the early days of Romantic education, when Amos Bronson Alcott and Margaret Fuller used their respective conversational experiments, Alcott's Temple School and Fuller's Boston conversational circle for women, to establish forms of education that rejected the rote learning and drill practiced at most New England schools and colleges. Conversation, as the chapter shows, was more than didactic method or polite parlor discussion. As Alcott had it, the conversationalist intends to "mould anew our Institutions, our Manners, our Men."[44] At the same time, both Alcott and Fuller were dissatisfied with the limited reach of their literary conversations and exchanged the classroom for a more public role. The chapter shows how the Romantic conversational ideal forced Alcott (and later Fuller) to adopt a more public role, and how Alcott's public defeat was the logical consequence of his comprehensive Romanticism. I show the drastic consequences which such a change in audience could bring by examining reviews of Alcott's *Conversations*. These have been incorrectly assessed and allow us to glimpse what was truly at stake with the popularization of Romantic literary education.

Chapter 3, "The Problem of Audience: Nineteenth-Century Periodical Culture and Romantic Popular Education," discusses Romanticism's ambitious yet conflicted transition into popular education. Taking advantage of the expansion of the print market in the 1830s and 1840s, the Transcendentalists carried their struggle for a creative, individualized education into the public. That journalism appeared as an opportunity to educate the public is evident from the programmatic prefaces of the *Dial*, Brownson's *Boston Quarterly Review*, and, most prominently, from Fuller's writings for the *New-York Tribune*. These periodicals reconsidered the reader as a conversational partner who did not expect instruction but provocation; a social agent whose full creative potential awaited awakening. As the chapter shows, the more the Romantics sought to popularize education, the more they had to confront the inconvenient truth that their own position was founded on the exclusionary mechanisms of the educational field. As a consequence, their literary journalism develops a class-inflected Romanticism that reconsiders both the idea of Romantic education and the intellectual's role in realizing the Romantic ideal of self-reliance and poetic social practice

Chapter 4, "Public Intellectuals: The Romantic Lecture, Professionalization, and Politics," discusses how Ralph Waldo Emerson, Henry David Thoreau, and Frederick Douglass used the lecture circuit to reach a broader audience. Lectures were a hybrid medium for the Romantics. They aimed at a particular, present audience and at a future, intended readership alike. The two audiences did not necessarily converge: the lectures were attended by an interested, literate general audience, while the printed versions were read and reviewed by professional journalists, theologians, and intellectuals. The popularization of the lecture circuit coincided with its politicization, which asserted itself most forcefully with the emergence of Frederick Douglass. In addition, the literary field was increasingly professionalized so that speakers in the lyceum circuit had to fashion their role as public intellectuals and market their literary practices. All three lecturers represent the increasing public relevance and politicization of Romantic discourse. They show how the demand that self-reliance should be possible for everyone needed to be dramatically reconfigured in antebellum America. With the increasing public prominence of the struggle against slavery, Romantic education became contingent on the abolition of slavery. In his lectures on John Brown, Thoreau therefore presented Romantic education as helping his audience understand the necessity of political action. With this politicization of Romanticism the limit case of education was reached.

In conclusion, I will address the contemporary appeal and relevance of Romantic literary education and broadly outline how this position is increasingly lost at a historical moment that thrives on corporatization. At the same time, the Romantic variety of education—the attempt to establish a form of self-reliance created through dialogue, exchange, and communication—has been a hidden substratum of progressive education, a tradition which needs to be unearthed and refunctionalized.

## NOTES

1. Elizabeth Peabody, "A Glimpse of Christ's Idea of Society," *Dial*, Oct. 1841, 227.

2. Margaret Fuller, *Papers on Literature and Art*, 2 vols. (New York: Wiley and Putnam, 1846), 2:137–8.

3. Margaret Fuller, *"These Sad but Glorious Days": Dispatches from Europe, 1846–1850*, ed. Larry J. Reynolds and Susan Belasco Smith (New Haven: Yale University Press, 1991), 88; hereafter cited parenthetically as *SGD*.

4. Frederick C. Beiser, *The Romantic Imperative: The Concept of Early German Romanticism* (Cambridge, MA: Harvard University Press, 2003), 29–31.

5. Fredrich Schlegel spoke of "collective works" created by "mutually complementary natures." Friedrich Schlegel, "Fragmente," *Athenaeum* 1, no.2 (1798), 33; my translation.

6. Friedrich Hölderlin and Friedrich Schelling argued that a revolution in interpersonal relations must be accompanied by a revolution in political affairs: "We must, then, also go beyond the state!—For every state must treat free people as a piece of machinery; and it should not do this; thus it must *come to an end*." Georg Wilhelm Friedrich Hegel, "Oldest System Program of German Idealism," trans. Andrew

Bowie, in *Aesthetics and Subjectivity: From Kant to Nietzsche, by Andrew Bowie*, 2nd ed. (Manchester: Manchester University Press, 2003), 334. The quoted manuscript is in Hegel's handwriting, but its content does not correspond with Hegel's philosophy at the time. It is therefore generally assumed that Hegel copied the text from the original drafted by Hölderlin and Schlegel.

7. Alan Richardson, *Literature, Education, and Romanticism: Reading as Social Practice, 1780–1832* (Cambridge: Cambridge University Press, 1994), 260.

8. Richardson, *Literature, Education, and Romanticism*, 270.

9. Orestes Brownson, "The Laboring Classes," *Boston Quarterly Review*, July 1840, 388–9.

10. Ralph Waldo Emerson, *Selected Letters*, ed. Joel Myerson (New York: Columbia University Press, 1997), 213.

11. While the nineteenth century not only was the time when schooling became more pervasive, it was also the time when class conditions were inscribed into this system. The revisionist school of educational history, which emerged in the 1960s, pointed out that most of this schooling was accessible only to the middle class and the elite. This view has been complicated by recent studies which have shown that, at least in towns like Newburyport, nearly "every child in Newburyport living with one of their parents" attended school, "regardless of the family's ethnic or occupational characteristics." Gerald F. Moran and Maris A Vinovskis, "Literacy, Common Schools, and High Schools in Colonial Antebellum America," *Rethinking the History of American Education*, ed. William J. Reese, John L. Rury (New York: Palgrave Macmillan, 2008), 33.

12. Henry David Thoreau, *Correspondence*, vol. 1: 1834–1848, ed. Robert N. Hudspeth (Princeton: Princeton University Press, 2013), 37.

13. Henry David Thoreau, *Walden*, ed. J. Lyndon Shanley (Princeton: Princeton University Press, 1971), 14–15; hereafter cited parenthetically as *W* with page number; *Early Essays and Miscellanies*, ed. Joseph J. Moldenhauer et al., The Writings of Henry D. Thoreau (Princeton: Princeton University Press, 1975), 60–1.

14. Stanley Cavell, *The Senses of Walden*, exp. ed. (Chicago: University of Chicago Press, 1992), viii, xiii–xiv.

15. On the professionalization and institutionalization of the school system in the early nineteenth century, see John L. Rury, *Education and Social Change: Contours in the History of American Schooling*, 5th ed. (New York: Routledge, 2016); on the professionalization of literature in the nineteenth century, see David Dowling, *The Business of Literary Circles in Nineteenth-Century America* (New York: Palgrave, 2011).

16. Joseph Buckminster, "Discourse on the Dangers and Duties of Men of Letters," *The Works of Joseph Stevens Buckminster; with Memoirs of His Life*, vol.2 (Boston: James Munroe and Co., 1839), 340.

17. Buckminster, "Discourse," 345–6.

18. Daniel Walker Howe, *The Unitarian Conscience: Harvard Moral Philosophy, 1805-1861*, 2nd ed. (Middletown: Wesleyan University Press, 1988), 179.

19. Ralph Waldo Emerson, *The Collected Works of Ralph Waldo Emerson*, ed. Alfred R. Ferguson and Joseph Slater et al., 8 vols. to date (Cambridge: Harvard University Press, 1971–), 1:141; hereafter cited parenthetically as *CW*, with volume and page number.

20. Pierre Bourdieu, *Pascalian Meditations* (Stanford: Stanford University Press, 2000), 9.
21. "Editorial," *Harbinger* 1 (1845): 16.
22. Orestes Brownson, "Education," *Boston Quarterly Review*, April 1840, 156.
23. Lance Newman, *Our Common Dwelling: Henry Thoreau, Transcendentalism, and the Class Politics of Nature* (New York: Palgrave, 2005), 72.
24. Larry A. Carlson, "Bronson Alcott's 'Journal for 1838' (Part One)." *Studies in the American Renaissance* (1993): 217.
25. Fuller, *Papers on Literature and Art*, 2:140.
26. Pierre Bourdieu, *The Field of Cultural Production* (New York: Columbia University Press, 1993), 30.
27. Wesley Mott, "Education," *The Oxford Handbook of Transcendentalism*, ed. Joel Myerson et al. (Oxford: Oxford University Press, 2010), 153.
28. See my own account of Ripley's and Alcott's writings on aesthetic education; Clemens Spahr, *Radical Beauty: American Transcendentalism and the Aesthetic Critique of Modernity* (Paderborn: Schöningh, 2011), 155–89. The most important recent works in the field are Martin Bickman, *Minding American Education: Reclaiming the Tradition of Active Learning* (New York: Teachers College Press, 2003); Monika Elbert and Lesley Ginsberg, ed., *Romantic Education in Nineteenth-Century America* (New York: Routledge, 2015); John P. Miller, *Transcendental Learning: The Educational Legacy of Alcott, Emerson, Fuller, Peabody and Thoreau* (Charlotte: Information Age Publishing, 2011); James Nehring, *The Practice of School Reform: Lessons from Two Centuries* (Albany: State University of New York Press, 2009); Franziska Schmid, *Educating New England: The Pedagogical Experiments of the American Transcendentalists* (Heidelberg: Winter, 2018). Rüdiger Schlicht's contribution is still insightful but dated because of the new critical editions and the wealth of archival material that has become available since the publication of his study. Rüdiger C. Schlicht, *Die pädagogischen Ansätze amerikanischer Transzendentalisten: Erziehungswissenschaftliche Studien zu Amos Bronson Alcott, Ralph Waldo Emerson und Henry David Thoreau, 1830-1840* (Frankfurt am Main: Lang, 1977).
29. Bernard Bailyn, *Education in the Forming of American Society* (New York: Norton, 1972), 14.
30. Derek Pacheco, *Moral Enterprise: Literature and Education in Antebellum America* (Columbus: Ohio State University Press, 2013), 7.
31. Mark G. Vásquez, *Authority and Reform: Religious and Educational Discourses in Nineteenth-Century New England Literature* (Knoxville: University of Tennessee Press, 2003), xxi.
32. See Ken Parille and Anne Mallory, "Romantic Reform and Boys: Bronson. Alcott's Materialist Pedagogy," *Romantic Education in Nineteenth-Century America,* ed. Monika Elbert and Lesley Ginsberg (New York: Routledge, 2015), 15–30.
33. John A. Buehrens, *Conflagration: How the Transcendentalists Sparked the American Struggle for Racial, Gender, and Social Justice* (Boston: Beacon Press, 2020).

34. See Bickman, *Minding American Education*; Miller, *Transcendental Learning;* Nehring, *The Practice of School Reform*.

35. Roger L. Geiger, *The History of American Higher Education: Learning and Culture form the Founding to World War II* (Princeton: Princeton University Press, 2015); Margaret A. Nash, *Women's Education in the United States, 1780-1840* (New York: Palgrave, 2005); Carl F. Kaestle and Maris A. Vinovskis, *Education and Social Change in Nineteenth-Century Massachusetts* (Cambridge: Cambridge University Press, 1980).

36. David Dowling, "Publishers," *Ralph Waldo Emerson in Context*, ed. Wesley Mott (New York: Cambridge University Press, 2014), 223.

37. Brownson, "Education," 137.

38. Brownson, "The Laboring Classes," 386.

39. Thomas J. Meyer, "The Great Rebellion of 1823." Accessed August 3, 2021. http://www.thecrimson.com/article/1982/2/17/the-great-rebellion-of-1823-pii/.

40. See Peter S. Field, *The Crisis of the Standing Order: Clerical Intellectuals and Cultural Authority in Massachusetts, 1780-1833* (Amherst: University of Massachusetts Press, 1998); Newman, *Our Common Dwelling*; Anne C. Rose, *Transcendentalism as a Social Movement, 1830-1850* (New Haven: Yale University Press, 1981).

41. Margaret Fuller, *Letters of Margaret Fuller*, ed. Robert N. Hudspeth, 6 vols. (Ithaca: Cornell University Press, 1983–94), 4:359; hereafter cited parenthetically as *L*, with volume and page number.

42. Margaret Fuller, *The Memoirs of Margaret Fuller Ossoli*, ed. Ralph Waldo Emerson, William Henry Channing, and James Freeman Clarke, 2 vols. (Boston: Philips, Sampson and Co., 1852), 2:163–4.

43. Fuller, *Papers on Literature and Art*, 2:137–8.

44. Amos Bronson Alcott, *The Doctrine and Discipline of Human Culture* (Boston: James Munroe and Co., 1836), 7.

*Chapter 1*

# Universal Education
## *American Romanticism and the Institutions of Education*

Romantic education was shaped by a fundamental contradiction: its conceptual universality clashed with its institutional exclusivity. This conflict could play out in the 1830s and 1840s because the two decades were hospitable to comprehensive reform ideas, marking a watershed moment in American educational history. The characteristics of the modern educational system such as the difference between private and public education, the professionalization of teaching, and the departmentalization of academic disciplines were in the making but not yet firmly established. In the 1830s, the dynamic educational field was still characterized by what historical sociologists have described as a "mixed private-public, non-regulated mode of education."[1] Amos Bronson Alcott, for instance, not only could establish himself as a teacher without any prior professional training but also taught at private and public schools alike. Alcott's Temple School, his most important contribution to nineteenth-century education, was a private school funded by tuition fees. In 1828, by contrast, the editor of the *American Journal of Education*, William Russell, stressed that Alcott's primary school in Cheshire, Connecticut, was an important "attempt to introduce a new system in a school supported by the *public money*, and open to the full influence of *popular* impression."[2] Russell's remarks not only show the flexibility of often temporary school models. They also illustrate how these educational efforts pointed beyond the classroom.

Education in the 1830s and 1840s was on the verge of becoming a profession. The centralization and attempted standardization of education began toward the end of the 1830s when most Transcendentalists had established themselves as intellectuals and when the movement was increasingly pushed into the public arena. In 1837, the Massachusetts Board of Education was established, and in 1839 the first normal school for teachers, which aimed at standardizing pedagogical methods, was founded in Lexington

Massachusetts. At the same time, in many ways, the educational landscape of the 1830s still resembled that of the turn of the century. As Robert Gross writes, "Urban Americans living in 1800 scarcely would have recognized distinctions between public and private in education in the first place: privately governed schools often received various forms of public funds, while schools operated by elected or appointed boards frequently depended on parental tuition payments."[3] Only in the mid-nineteenth century did the distinction between private and public schools come to dominate New England's educational system. In 1852, with the influx of Roman Catholics creating an alternative, private school system, Horace Mann and others passed the state law for mandatory school attendance. The professionalization of American education would also occur mostly from the mid-nineteenth century on.[4] Even in 1857, in an address to the National Teachers Association 1857, William Russell still demanded that teachers "make their work a profession—not just an ordinary vocation."[5]

In New England's proto-professional educational field, the Romantics hoped to realize their vision on a broad scale—to make what Russell had called a "popular impression." Upon visiting Alcott's Temple School, Emerson observed how Alcott's pedagogic vision collapsed boundaries of age and gender: "I felt strongly, as I watched the gradual dawn of a thought upon the minds of all, that to truth is no age or season. It appears or it does not appear, & when the child perceives it, he is no more a child; [or] age, sex are nothing: we are all alike before the great Whole."[6] Romantic education should encompass everyone. Such a comprehensive vision must be understood in the context of nineteenth-century educational institutions. The increasing, multifaceted need for literacy and basic education enabled alternative school forms, from Lancastrian industrial schools to small reform schools, and from women's academies to conversational circles and night schools. Education not only had a broad meaning in the 1830s and 1840s, it also reached a larger part of the population. As William J. Gilmore has demonstrated, "[i]n the half century after 1775, the emergence of a heavily commercialized rural economy and the creation of a new communications environment enabled a growing majority of all families to participate in public culture."[7] More particularly with regard to antebellum fiction, James Machor has shown that the rise of the print market, the rapid growth of the library system, and advancements in transportation "improved opportunities for people to read more and for more people to read."[8] As the Transcendentalists soon experienced, the growing print market also created more competition and fierce debates. Teachers and schools had to disseminate their ideas and practices through the print market. But first of all, it promised access to the literate public.

Social transformations, the expansion of literacy, and the increasing importance of the press combined to turn education into one of the most important discursive mediators of cultural and political discussions in nineteenth-century America. Nineteenth-century periodicals played a crucial role in channeling the energies of the field. The *Boston Courier* and the *Boston Recorder and Telegraph*, for instance, two of New England's leading newspapers, discussed various modes of education in the same pages, and along the same categories. From grammar schools to women's academies, and from conversational circles to the content of Harvard's curriculum—nineteenth-century modes of education were conjoined in the discourse about the future of a society which had recently transitioned into market capitalism and had experienced a transportation revolution that connected the country. In the *Boston Recorder*, discussions of Harvard's politics and discussions about the purposes of the lyceum, grammar schools, infant education, and women's education were printed on the same page and considered part of the same public discourse. Similarly, James Munroe, one of the most important publishers in nineteenth-century Boston, promoted Alcott's pedagogical manifestos alongside Emerson's essays, just as educational and philosophical texts were generally grouped together in advertisements (figure 1.1).

Given this situation, it is less surprising that a discussion about Alcott's Temple School, a school for children, was conducted in the major newspapers of the time and eventually turned into a political discussion about institutional authority and social order. In Massachusetts, the expansion of the school system lent the emergent educational field a larger social significance. Newspapers across the United States took notice of the Massachusetts school system. They frequently discussed it with reference to universal education. In 1842, the *Mississippian* would point out that there is "no State in the Union where education is so universally diffused." In the *North American and Daily Advertiser*, a Philadelphia newspaper, Massachusetts was equally held as the model of general education and common schools. These were questions of national significance, and many newspapers looked to New England as a model case. The *Scioto Gazette*, an Ohio-based newspaper, reported that the "system of universal education has now therefore become, to a remarkable degree, the basis of the popular character, which marks the two millions of people on New England." This narrative was not uncontested. The *Pennsylvania Inquirer* saw the origin of universal education not in Massachusetts but in Pennsylvania's public school system: "The spirit in favor of universal education, and of liberal, well-conducted public schools, which has been infused so thoroughly into the popular mind of Pennsylvania, by several of our ablest statesmen, has, as we perceive, enkindled a corresponding spirit in other sections of the Union." The *Vermont Chronicle*, in turn, described universal education not as a distinctly American form of education, but as the "Great European Movement," finding that just like Prussia the American educational system, although rightly advocating universal

> **Published by James Munroe and Company,**
> 134 WASHINGTON STREET, BOSTON.
>
> EMERSON'S ESSAYS. 1 vol. 16mo.
> NATURE. By R. W. EMERSON. 1 vol. 12mo.
> THE METHOD OF NATURE. Oration by W. R. Emerson.
> AN ORATION, delivered before the Phi Beta Kappa Society, at Cambridge, Aug. 31, 1837: by R. W. Emerson.
> AN ORATION, delivered before the Literary Societies of Dartmouth College, July 24, 1838; by R. W. Emerson.
> CRITICAL AND MISCELLANEOUS ESSAYS of THOMAS CARLYLE. Edited by R. W. Emerson. 4 vols. 12mo.
> CONVERSATIONS ON THE GOSPELS with Children. By A. Bronson Alcott. 2 vols. 12mo.
> RECORD OF A SCHOOL. By A. Bronson Alcott. 12mo.
> ESSAYS AND POEMS. By Jones Very. 1 vol. 16mo.
>
> **Published by E. P. Peabody, 13 West Street.**
>
> CONFESSIONS OF ST. AUGUSTINE. 1 Vol. 12mo.
> GUNDERODE. 16mo. Part I.
> THEORY OF TEACHING. By a Teacher. 12mo.
> METHOD OF TEACHING LINEAR DRAWING. 12mo.
> LEGEND OF ST. GEORGE, Paraphrased from Spenser's Faery Queen. 12mo.
> PESTALOZZI'S LETTERS TO GREAVES. 1 vol. 8vo.
> RELIGION AND RELIGIOUS EDUCATION; the Sequel to Hampden in the Nineteenth Century. 8vo.
> THE DIAL: a Quarterly Magazine. 3 vols. 8vo.

Figure 1.1 Advertisement of educational and philosophical books in the 1840s. In: Charles Lane, *The Law and Method in Spirit-Culture: An Interpretation of A. Bronson Alcott's Idea and Practice at the Masonic Temple, Boston* (Boston: James Munroe, 1843), 41.

education, should require children to attend school rather than present it as an option. Generally, however, educators, writers, and editors all over the United States referenced Massachusetts as the center of modern American education.⁹

The Transcendentalists tried to use the possibilities of this growing and dynamic educational field to spread and realize their vision. They wanted to put everyone in a position to realize their "elevated and beautiful forms of character."¹⁰ But because the field was expanding, debates were fierce. As soon as they stepped into the public realm, the various Romantic educational projects were linked to discussions of social and economic privilege. Alcott's Temple School became the center of a public debate; Emerson's Divinity School Address elicited reactions from all major periodicals; Orestes Brownson managed to provoke a response from the Democratic Party with his essay on "The Laboring Classes"; Margaret Fuller conceived her European literary journalism as a contribution to socialist politics; and Henry David Thoreau would heroize John Brown as the greatest Romantic. The Transcendentalists realized that education was not only affected by political decisions and social change; it also served as a discursive mediator to ask which direction the increasing need for popular education should take. Structurally and discursively, they could link themselves to a field that tended toward expansion, and to a discourse that centered on the questions of who had access to education and to which end. This affected the very way they understood their Romanticism.

## UNIVERSAL EDUCATION

The question of universal education served as a focal point for discussions about the direction and future of education. Universal education was one of the most widely used terms to link pedagogical principles, public education, and institutional reform in nineteenth-century America. Because the term was prominently used in public newspapers, often as a code for questions of social and economic privilege, it serves as a rich resource for understanding the constellation from which Romantic educational reform emerged. The idea of universal education had functioned as a vehicle for social and political questions since the early republic and therefore constituted a powerful inroad to these discussions. Republican education had addressed the broad need for basic literacy but tried to contain possible egalitarian tendencies in a vision of national unity that ultimately served economic privilege. For educators like Benjamin Rush, "to convert men into republican machines" was the best way to commit the various immigrant groups to civic virtues.[11] Rush believed that education should serve the individual as much as he understood it to be a disciplining instrument. Christian, civic virtue which secured the new republic's success, he argued, were best instilled into democratic subjects until the age of twenty-one: "Our schools of learning, by producing one general, and uniform system of education, will render the mass of the people more homogeneous, and thereby fit them more easily for uniform and peaceable government."[12] Even Thomas Jefferson, who rejected Rush's support for Christianity as the foundation of education,[13] advocated, as Edward Power has argued, "a widely available, if not universal, education for citizens, but one that was openly elitist (and one that excluded slaves)."[14]

With the market revolution, individuality and fragmentation were no longer perceived as a threat to national stability. Still, as David Labaree has argued, nineteenth-century educators in the Republican tradition had to balance individuality and civic virtue: "Too much emphasis on individual interests could turn republican community into a pluralist state that is constituted as a competition of private interests, but too much emphasis on community could turn the republic into an authoritarian state that sacrifices individual freedom to collective interests."[15] Accordingly, Horace Mann's common school movement, the most important development in nineteenth-century public education, sought to "preserve the benefits of the burgeoning market economy in the antebellum United States while ameliorating its destructive tendencies—the class differences and competing interests that threatened to destroy the civic virtue needed to sustain a fragile republic."[16] As such, however, Mann stood in a long tradition of disciplinary education. As David Hogan has argued, "[l]ike Pestalozzi, Mann was far more interested in education as a means of moralizing the poor than he was in promoting their economic mobility. Even when he used human capital arguments to drum up support for common schools, as he did in 1841, he emphasized the economic value of education to employers and the state, rather than to individuals."[17] Chris Beneke has accordingly pointed out that it "would be difficult to exaggerate the contrast between the effusive celebrations of popular, universal education in antebellum America with the dark forebodings about the dangers of rampant demagoguery and mob rule."[18] In this sense, reformers like Horace Mann could think of equality as "a limiting condition, rather than a desired outcome, of educational reform."[19]

Throughout the first half of the nineteenth century, the debate about universal education served as a catalyst for discussions about the relationship between education, socioeconomic privilege, and reform. Beneke has argued that as an idea "universal and integrated education was as popular as an expensive idea could be in antebellum America."[20] While educational reformers and the population agreed on the desirability of universal education, its principles and aims were contested. For Lancastrian schools, providing education was basically a control mechanism which disciplined the body in order to make it available as cheap, efficient labor force. The demand for universal education could advocate dramatic change while leaving class privilege untouched. On December 7, 1832, a lead article in the *Boston Courier* advocated the necessity for "universal public instruction."[21] The reader, "Humanitas," states that public education is the condition for a successful republic: "A public school, composed of all ranks and conditions in society, is a little, but just epitome of the great world upon which the pupil is to enter." Universal education is praised as the most important pillar of civic virtue: "The general dissemination of knowledge, of sound principles, of enlarged and enlightened intelligence, constitutes the very foundation of the stability of our free government." The writer demands the expansion of public schools so as to be able to do away with private school altogether in the name of universal public education: "A public school, composed of all ranks and conditions in society, is a little, but just epitome of the great world upon which the pupil is soon to enter."[22] He advocates generous spending to develop the public school system, and insists, for instance, that teachers must be well paid to secure a high standard of education. But the point here was moral education: everyone should be educated to form a sentimental bond with the republic. Social privilege was not in question, social mobility was not the aim.

Generally, in the nineteenth century universal education could be reconciled with the preservation of class privilege. But the 1820s and 1830s also saw various attempts to link the idea of universal education to social reform.[23] For George Bancroft, "universal education" was necessary to "diffuse[e] intelligence among the people; not merely the latest news about elections, the merits and rivalries of aspiring men; but the principles on which society rests and by which it is moulded."[24] Bancroft describes education as the harbinger of larger social reform: "I never will believe, that legislation must inevitably conspire with the capitalist, till the great majority of the human race are reduced to the condition of live machinery, moving for the benefit of wealth."[25] Abner Kneeland, Boston's famous radical freethinker, advocated universal education as a fundamental means of elevating the working classes prominently on every title page of his *Boston Investigator*.[26] Boston's *Working Man's Advocate* advertised its mission to advance "a system of Universal Education, which shall afford equal *means* to every child born in the State."[27] *The Emancipator*, an abolitionist newspaper, advocated the Oneida Institute as an exemplary institution, which realized the hopes of "the friends of liberty and of universal education, and the enemies of caste and privilege."[28]

Universal education in these cases entailed the struggle against the race and class conditions that restricted liberal education to the privileged. As much as the link between progressive politics and concrete social reform appealed to the Romantics, the idea of education propagated in labor periodicals was often utilitarian. Nationwide, workingman's organizations mostly defined universal education as scientific education. When they spoke of "Popular Education" they aimed at "uniting labor and science; and thus enabling students even while completing their education, to earn a living."[29] In addition, while for the Transcendentalists Romanticism constituted the philosophical principle of liberation, progressives saw universal education as primarily an anti-elitist, practical form of empowerment. The *Mechanic and Farmer*, the mouthpiece of Maine's Association of Mechanics and Farmers, advocated education as a "cheap and efficient defence of this nation."[30] The essay's author suggests that the laboring classes needed a public school system in which industrial education replaces the cultural education of the elite private schools: "Aristocratic private schools where the company is select, and the little Miss, allowed to think she studies the Latin language before she knows the parts of speech in her own because it is not so vulgar, and yanke field as must be submitted to in free schools, are our special abhorrence."[31] The Transcendentalists, by contrast, were not skeptical of higher education or the "Aristocratic" learning for "the little Miss." Accordingly, in their essays and manifestos one finds a critique of the establishment, but no populist rhetoric that vilifies liberal education.

While the Romantics could tap into these discourses, and while Kneeland frequently described working-class solidarity as Romantic friendship, the Romantic reformers had to carve out their own position in a dynamic educational field. Of all the reformers, Kneeland came closest to being a Romantic educator. Kneeland's *Boston Investigator* also offers a good example of how the literary market operated and how it was intertwined with questions of educational reform. On March 15, 1833, the *Investigator* printed a lead article which asked if new periodicals could succeed in a crowded literary market, at "a time when the public is *literally* deluged with ten times more journals, gazette's [sic], registers, magazines, &c., than any individual could read, if he were rich enough to subscribe and pay for them all, and had no other employment."[32] Acknowledging these issues, Kneeland sees journalism as the means of popular education, suggesting that "every American citizen, rich or poor, of whatever occupation, ought to subscribe for and read, at least *one* periodical work, either alone, or in company with some of his neighbors."[33] The plan was not only to educate the public on medicine, science, and history but also to recommend literary books.[34] Kneeland's programmatic remarks prefigure the history of Romantic popular education.

The universal thrust of education could be turned into an assault on hierarchies, didactically, economically, and socially. Although not immediately political in the sense that reformers such as Kneeland were, Romantic education was still a challenge to authority. Challenging the theological and pedagogical principles could call into question the cultural elite's legitimation and hence social hierarchies more generally. Emerson laid out, and simultaneously enacted, the principles of Romantic education in his Divinity School Address, when he advised Harvard Divinity School's graduates to reject tradition and authority: "Meantime, whilst the doors of the temple stand open, night and day, before every man, and the oracles of this truth cease never, it is guarded by one stern condition; this, namely; it is an intuition. It cannot be received at second hand. Truly speaking, it is not instruction, but provocation, that I can receive from another soul" (*CW* 1:80). The establishment's heated response to Emerson's speech illustrates that these literary provocations were concrete interventions in the educational system. More problematic still, Emerson evokes a universality ("every man") that projects beyond the educational system, toward a society which does not have access to, or time for, such a Romantic education of the self.

Kneeland's similarities with Emerson and the Transcendentalists were not only rhetorical; a number of Kneeland's poems could easily be classified as Romantic.[35] In addition, Kneeland was tried for atheism. It was no coincidence that Andrews Norton, the powerful voice of conservative Unitarianism, famously denounced Transcendentalism as the "latest form of infidelity."[36] Robert Burkholder has shown that "charges of atheism or infidelity implied not only an anti-establishment religious stance but also similar anti-establishment social and political views, and those who challenged accepted religious views and practices were thought to be attacking social and political stability as well."[37] Emerson's anti-systemic philosophical lectures and essays constituted a challenge to New England's tradition of rigid, structured homiletics discursively and practically. Norton, then, employed a rhetoric which threatened to have real consequences: the heretic Kneeland spent two months in prison. Given the changing nature of the educational system, discussions in newspapers and magazines were not merely struggles over moral guidance, but rather inextricably bound up with particular institutional positions of power and privilege. In this politically charged situation, alternative educational spaces could be perceived as challenges to the status quo.[38]

For the Transcendentalists, who aimed to make the poetic life available to everyone, their position as intellectuals emerged as a problem as well as an opportunity. Instead of simply assuming their own public relevance, their openly contradictory status forced them to reflect the possibilities and limits of Romantic education. Confronted with the task of how to project this educational practice into a form of public agency, the Transcendentalists developed a complex understanding of how social practice was linked to the reproduction of socioeconomic structures. In one of her Boston conversations for women, which typically discussed philosophical, religious, and literary questions, Margaret Fuller addressed the institutional conditions which prevented women from realizing their potential:

> Men are called on from a very early period to *reproduce* all that they learn— First their college exercises—their political duties—the exercises of professional study—the very first action of life in any direction—calls upon them for *reproduction* of what they have learnt.—This is what is most neglected in the education women-they learn without any attempt to reproduce.[39]

"Reproduction" is the keyword here. Sociologists such as Pierre Bourdieu and Immanuel Wallerstein have emphasized how reproduction through social practice is essential to maintain a particular form of social organization. For Wallerstein, this fact opens social structures for transformation. The system never simply remains the same but must permanently be recreated through social practices; it is therefore potentially subject to change: "The historical system within which we live are indeed systemic, but they are historical as well. They remain the same over time yet are never the same from one minute to the next."[40] For this reason, the adequate educational practice to maintain stability, conformity, and certainty was, as Harvard president Josiah Quincy argued as late as in 1845, a "thorough drilling."[41] What this meant was less corporeal punishment (which was exercised at Harvard and elsewhere, but whose necessity not even all reformers questioned) but subjecting students to a regime of discipline and rote learning, a regime that daily reproduced the practices necessary to recreate economic privilege.

As Fuller states, men, and hence those in power, are "called upon" to reproduce their knowledge and, by doing so, to recreate the everyday practices that maintain social organization. This is a typical trait of the modern educational field. In *Reproduction in Education, Society and Culture*, Bourdieu and Passeron have shown that the regeneration of knowledge usually works in the name of the status quo, as even change within the educational field is not desirable for those who come out on top of it; rather it promotes the pedagogical action which "most fully, though always indirectly, corresponds to the objective interests (material, symbolic and, in the respect considered here, pedagogic) of the dominant groups or classes, both by its mode of imposition and by its delimitation of what and on whom, it imposes."[42] But the Transcendentalists were not simply passively influenced by the conditions of education, or unconsciously adopted the habitualized practices that maintain these; they sought to engage and change these practices. It is helpful to reference Henri Lefebvre's distinction between repetitive and inventive praxis in this context because it offers a more nuanced way to think about reproductive practices. While repetitive praxis is also creative in that it recreates the rules and structures that constitute existing groups and shape individual actions, inventive praxis, by contrast, consciously tries to veer from the established standard. Since a social system is dependent on its constant reproduction through everyday practice, social change can occur by "changing the everyday" through inventive praxis.[43]

Lefebvre may assign too much importance to everyday practice; but in a situation like that of nineteenth-century New England, changes in educational practices could indeed signal larger social change. The status quo tried to contain reform efforts whenever they appeared, particularly when economic and social crises and transformations questioned their status quo. No one saw the potential threat of educational micropractices more clearly than Andrews Norton. As early as in 1825, Norton, the "Unitarian Pope," had passionately defended institutional authority against state interventions in educational institutions arguing that the resident instructors (Harvard's faculty) should be those "with whose offices all the honor due to the institution ought to be associated."[44] While state intervention could be dismissed as the transgression of non-experts into an intellectual field which should operate independently from politics, a different strategy was needed to contain the threat emerging from within the educational field when the American Romantics launched their attack on Unitarianism and its belief in authority and tradition. In his famous 1839 response to the "latest form of infidelity," as he labelled the Transcendentalists (and Emerson and Ripley in particular), Norton made it clear that institutional critique could potentially lead to undesired social change, since, as he states two years after the Panic of 1837, one of the major financial crises in the nineteenth century, "[e]verywhere is instability and uncertainty."[45]

In the wake of the Panic of 1837 social unrest and mob violence rose,[46] and Harvard's elite saw itself responsible for maintaining not only institutional authority but also the social order. In the first half of the nineteenth century, an age which has variously been captured by historians as the age of the "the market revolution," the "transportation revolution," or the "revolution in communication" and technology,[47] the social practices responsible for maintaining society's class structure were exposed to scrutiny and critique and needed to be re-legitimated discursively and practically through educational and cultural institutions. Even if the market revolution may have been more of a transition than an epochal rupture, it created a sense of instability and insecurity in which distinction and social privilege were important to maintain one's social status.[48] Norton's response must be understood in this context. Tellingly, although facing the same audience, Norton addressed not the graduates of Harvard Divinity School but its alumni (who had, symptomatically, invited him, as opposed to Emerson who was invited by Harvard's students). Any threat to Harvard's and Unitarianism's cultural authority, whether political or from rival groups within the cultural and institutional field, needed to be contained. Norton saw that Romantic education did not simply turn inward; it developed a new interiority into a structural critique of institutions and projected a vision of communal creativity.

Norton's attack signals the importance of discursive practices in reproducing social privilege. Alcott's and Fuller's conversations (particularly Fuller's later version of newspapers journalism as a form of conversation) undermined the teacher's authoritarian voice. Both understood their didactic as methods prefiguration of an egalitarian model of social interaction. On a smaller, micropractical scale, their enactment posed a threat to the rote learning and hierarchical relationships prevalent in New England's educational institutions. But in 1839, when Norton gave his speech, the Transcendentalists had already moved into the public sphere. Alcott's *Conversations* had been published in 1837/1838 and Emerson had given his Divinity School Address in 1838. Brownson's political essays were still to follow as was Fuller's major work. For Norton it was enough to see the Romantics as a threat to institutional privilege and social order.

The conservative wing of Boston Unitarianism used their periodicals to launch vicious campaigns against Emerson after he had questioned the professor's privilege and tradition in the Divinity School Address and they destroyed Alcott's reputation when he publicly advocated an egalitarian conversational method. Alcott had been relegated to the margins of public discourse in 1838 and Emerson equally found himself temporarily retreating after the heated response to his Divinity School Address. But even if the Transcendentalists challenged Unitarian authorities and the cultural elite, the question of whether these changes would ever amount to anything but a reform of methods and didactics still needed to be answered. Abner Kneeland had something the Romantics lacked: a concrete, broad audience.

## THE PROBLEM OF AUDIENCE

When Emerson, in his Divinity School Address, demanded to "cast behind you all conformity, and acquaint men at first hand with Deity" (*CW* 1:90); when Alcott demanded from teachers and students to become "an Artist of the highest order" in the spirit of Jesus;[49] and when Fuller considered her educational efforts an attempt to establish a larger "means of mutual interpretation" (*L* 6:359), these ideals emerged from, and were directed at, a society shaped by tremendous transformations. But as much as Romanticism challenged the didactic principles of nineteenth-century education and the authorities of the educational system, its reform efforts ultimately remained within the confines of the educational and intellectual field. At least initially, their literary reform projects were geared toward an educated audience rather than connected to reform movements. In addition, those participating in conversations and lyceum lectures were often part of the "middling classes," a concept that historians have used to denote the dynamic process of class formation in nineteenth-century America. Margaret Nash has stressed that these middling classes were often constituted by "nonmanual wage earners as well as farmers" who wanted to "distinguish themselves from those of both lower and higher economic status."[50] These middling classes, although interested in self-culture, were not at all interested in class politics. The link between Romantic universal poetry and everyday practice, while theoretically established, remained precarious in practice.

The Transcendentalists were involved in public debates; most of the time, however, their practice remained limited to a middle-class audience. Philosophically, they could link individuality and collectivity by proclaiming the universal validity of the individual's aesthetic experiences. As Emerson famously declared in "The American Scholar," Man Thinking, the true Romantic, "learns that *in going down* into the secrets of his own mind, he has descended into the secrets of all minds" (*CW* 1:63). Although Alcott's Temple School projected an egalitarian social model intended to prefigure an egalitarian social organization, if practically limited to the children of the upper middle class, these claims would not affect the institutional hierarchies of education. The same holds for Margaret Fuller's conversational circles with their comparatively high fees; only middle-class women would be able to participate in these discussions. In addition, Fuller's conversational circles, the Transcendentalists' essays, and their lyceum lectures required a literate audience. Popular education was a complex, contradictory, and in many ways impossible affair if it wanted to be something more than the revision of pedagogical principles.

Orestes Brownson addressed the tension between the movement's universal principles and the institutional limits imposed on its ideas in his influential essay "The Laboring Classes" (1840). The essay is a response to Carlyle's analysis of Chartism and universal education. Brownson warns his readership that if not accompanied by economic change education would in fact become an effective disguise of social hierarchies:

> Universal education we shall not be thought likely to depreciate; but we confess that we are unable to see in it that sovereign remedy for the evils of the social state as it is, which some of our friends do, or say they do. We have little faith in the power of education to elevate a people compelled to labor from twelve to sixteen hours a day, and to experience for no mean portion of the time a paucity of even the necessaries of life, let alone its comforts.[51]

Brownson links the themes and issues surrounding nineteenth-century educational reform to the Romantic intellectual position. Without addressing questions of class and exclusion, Romantic educational experiments from Alcott's Temple School to Emerson's lyceum lectures and Fuller's conversational circles would remain restricted to the American bourgeoisie and hence mostly ineffective as a means to achieve the "creation of man" that Emerson envisaged (*CW* 2:215).

As the forefather of American Transcendentalism, Carlyle serves Brownson as a foil against which he reconsiders the emergent movement's goals. Carlyle's idea of universal education illustrates a conflict that is at the heart of Romantic educational concepts. John Morrow has argued that Carlyle "promoted a system of state-supported education as a means for developing the intellectual capacities of the entire population, not merely as an instrument for reconciling the lower classes with their lot, or facilitating social control." For Morrow, "Carlyle's conception of popular education, and his promotion of an active role for the state in promoting it" was the result of a "humanistic, and, in this sense, classless and egalitarian, perspective."[52] But, as Brownson points out, if Carlyle's potentially egalitarian idea is not accompanied by economic redistribution, education remains inconsequential and incomplete. It might elevate the masses spiritually, but economic depravity would continue to render this elevation an escapist mechanism at best. Carlyle's concept does contain an egalitarian impulse, which, if followed through, would reinforce Brownson's point that education must not be a substitute for economic redistribution but complemented by it. Accordingly, Brownson objects to Carlyle's inconsequential logic: "Educate the working classes of England; and what then? Will they require less food and less clothing when educated than they do now? Will they be more contented or more happy in their condition?"[53] Brownson's point is that universal education is desirable, but it cannot be an end in itself until economic privilege is tackled. Economic redistribution must accompany spiritual elevation lest cultivation become a substitute for social reform.

The Transcendentalists increasingly sought to popularize their reform efforts. But the populace was not easy to handle. Fuller pointed to a concomitant problem: the complexity of Romanticism. In a review of Emerson's works, published in the *New-York Tribune* in 1844, Fuller chided the literate public as they were "still more injured by a large majority of writers and speakers, who lend all their efforts to flatter corrupt tastes and mental indolence." Fuller sees the public opinion as corrupted, and, as a consequence, "Literature and Art must become daily more degraded; Philosophy cannot exist."[54] Emerson becomes a vehicle for a reflection on her own writing, as Fuller's *Summer on the Lakes* was certainly not a text for popular education, nor did the complex, dense historical, and theoretical argument of *Woman in the Nineteenth Century* address a broad public. Such education was possible only through the various media available to nineteenth-century educational reform. As a consequence, in the 1840s, when they had established themselves as intellectuals and increasingly moved into the public, the Romantics made a conscious effort to popularize their literary Romanticism. This not only concerned their topics, as they were now concerned with urban poverty and abolitionism, but also affected their literary style. Fuller started working for the popular *New-York Tribune*, a newspaper founded to counter the populist press of New York, while Emerson and Thoreau increasingly used the lyceum platform for social and political talks, which forced them to make their speeches accessible. If Romanticism should truly become the organizing principle of social relations, it had to be institutionalized and popularized.

Even when using these channels to move into the public, the Romantics encountered the limits of universal education. The more they aimed at a comprehensive realization of their projects, the more they were confronted with the system's exclusionary mechanisms. The lyceum, one of the major platforms of public education, illustrated how democratic discourse did not necessarily mean access for all. The lyceum gave rise to oppositional intellectuals such as Henry David Thoreau and Frederick Douglass. The story presents itself differently, however, when looking at the general accessibility of lyceums for African Americans who did not enjoy the status of public intellectuals. As late as October 31, 1845, the *Liberator* reported that African Americans had been denied membership, allegedly for organizational reasons. The person was informed that tickets were free for purchase for nonmembers at any rate, only to be denied tickets on the grounds that he was not a member. The reader of the *Liberator* infers from this episode a remarkable critique of the lyceum's middle-class structure which links race and class:

> The Lyceum is closed against the poor, because they are poor, and the avenues to wealth and knowledge are closed by the same people who despise them on account of their poverty and ignorance! Shame, shame, on such baseness! Can men, who have signed a protest against the extension of slavery, come and lecture before such an institution?[55]

A couple of weeks later, on December 19, 1845, the *Liberator* reported how the New Bedford Lyceum had raised their fees, which was "opposed on the ground that, as the institution was a popular one, and for intellectual and moral culture, it should not be confined to the moral and cultivated, nut that those whose moral characters were not altogether correct, providing they conducted themselves with propriety, were the very class perhaps to be admitted."[56] As a consequence, Emerson and Charles Sumner declined to lecture before the lyceum.

With the increasing realization that Romanticism needed to become a popular form of literary education, the Transcendentalists were confronted with mechanisms of exclusion and stratification which were unacceptable for their Romanticism. As we will see, before they eventually became engaged in public affairs and, as in Thoreau's case, could use the lyceum to propagate political activism, they had to gain access to the literary institutions that allowed them to establish such a prominent public position. To effectively bring about such change, the Transcendentalists had to engage the pedagogical field and the literary market. Their Romanticism could unfold its universal thrust because of New England's dynamic educational landscape. Yet, drawn into these structures, the more public presence they achieved, the more they had to address the exclusionary mechanisms of the educational system they were part of. I will explore the possibilities and limits of their Romantic reform projects in the following chapters. It is important, however, to emphasize that while the Transcendentalists pursued their projects strategically and while they developed a practical understanding of Romanticism in the process, it was never in question that the aim of their educational efforts was to realize a vision of sympathetic cooperation.

## NOTES

1. Kaestle and Vinovskis, *Education and Social Change in Nineteenth-Century Massachusetts*, 12.

2. Russell's short prefatory remark serves as an introduction to one of Alcott's programmatic essays; Amos Bronson Alcott, "Primary Education," *American Journal of Education* 3, no. 1 (1828): 26 (my emphasis).

3. Robert N. Gross, *Public vs. Private: The Early History of School Choice in America* (New York: Oxford University Press, 2018), 2.

4. Damon Mayrl, *Secular Conversions: Political Institutions and Religious Education in the United States and Australia, 1800–2000* (Cambridge: Cambridge University Press, 2016), 104–10.

5. Qtd. in Mayrl, *Secular Conversions*, 106.

6. Ralph Waldo Emerson, *The Journals and Miscellaneous Notebooks of Ralph Waldo Emerson*, ed. William H. Gilman, Ralph H. Orth, et al., 16 vols. (Cambridge: Harvard University Press, 1960–82), 5:175; hereafter cited parenthetically as *JMN*, with volume and page number. In the interest of clarity, evidences of Emerson's revisions are omitted from quotations of *JMN*.

7. William J. Gilmore, *Reading Becomes a Necessity of Life: Material and Cultural Life in Rural New England, 1780-1835* (Knoxville: University of Tennessee Press, 1989), 53.

8. James L. Machor, *Reading Fiction in Antebellum America: Informed Response and Reception Histories, 1820-1865* (Baltimore: Johns Hopkins University Press, 2011), 22–23.

9. Anon., "Education in Massachusetts," *Mississippian*, March 3, 1837, 1; *North American and Daily Advertiser* Dec. 23, 1841, 1; Anon., "New England Free Schools," *Scioto Gazette*, April 11, 1832, 1; Anon., "Universal Education: The Great European Movement," *Vermont Chronicle*, Jan 31, 1838, 18; Anon., "Common Schools—Education in Philadelphia," *Philadelphia Inquirer*, April 24, 1838, n.p.

10. "Editorial," *Harbinger* 1 (1845): 16.

11. Benjamin Rush, *A Plan for the Establishment of Public Schools and the Diffusion of Knowledge in Pennsylvania; to Which Are Added Thoughts Upon the Mode of Education, Proper in a Republic* (Philadelphia: Thomas Dobson, 1786), 27.

12. Rush, *A Plan*, 14.

13. Edward J. Power. *A Legacy of Learning: A History of Western Education* (Albany: SUNY Press, 1991), 258.

14. Carl L. Bankston, III. and Stephen J. Caldas, *Public Education: America's Civil Religion. A Social History* (New York. Teachers College Press, 2009), 23.

15. David F. Labaree, "Citizens and Consumers: Changing Visions of Virtue and Opportunity in U.S. Education, 1841-1954," *Schooling and the Making of Citizens in the Long Nineteenth Century,* ed. Daniel Tröhler, Thomas Popkewitz, and David F. Labaree (New York: Palgrave Macmillan, 2011), 178.

16. Labaree, "Citizens and Consumers," 182.

17. David Hogan, "Modes of Discipline: Affective Individualism and Pedagogical Reform in New England, 1820-1850," *American Journal of Education* 99, no. 1 (1990): 34.

18. Chris Beneke, "The Idea of Integration in the Age of Horace Mann," *Inequity in Education: A Historical Perspective*, ed. Debra Meyers, Burke Miller (Lanham, MD: Lexington Books, 2009), 106.

19. Beneke, "Idea of Integration," 106.

20. Beneke, "Idea of Integration," 105.

21. Anon., "Boston Public Schools," *Boston Courier,* December 7, 1832, 1.

22. Anon. "Boston Public Schools," 1.

23. Private schools often served as alternative spaces of education nationwide. In Ohio, private schools were instrumental in providing education for African Americans, who would then go on to become educators and activists; see Nikki Marie Taylor, *America's First Black Socialist: The Radical Life of Peter H. Clark* (Lexington: University of Kentucky Press, 2013), 61–2.

24. George Bancroft, "Correspondence," *The Globe*, November 13, 1834, 2. The *Washington Globe* reprinted George Bancroft's discussion of universal education in the *Hampshire Gazette Extra*. According to Bancroft, the United States for the first time could fulfill the promise of democracy: "till the American experiment, the mass of the people have passed for nothing" (2). But even in the United States, circumstances had not yet been arranged in a way that allowed democracy to unfold its full, egalitarian potential: "For myself, my profound confidence in the benevolence of God leads me to believe that he has not doomed the largest portion of his creatures to a life of irrevocable misery; but that the gloomy result is a consequence of unjust institutions. So long as I live, I will cherish this belief; I never will relinquish the hope, that a remedy or a palliative may be found; I never will believe, that legislation must inevitably conspire with the capitalist, till the great majority of the human race are reduced to the condition of live machinery, moving for the benefit of wealth" (2).

25. Bancroft, "Correspondence," 2.

26. See, for instance, *Boston Investigator,* July 6, 1832, 1. The *Boston Investigator* was published by John Quincy Adams, which shows how diverse and complex not only the periodical market but also the discursive space of education was at the time.

27. Advertisement in the *Illinois Gazette,* Sept. 11, 1829, 3.

28. *The Emancipator*, Aug. 29, 1839, 1.

29. *Daily National Journal*, Jan. 21, 1831, n.p.

30. The article was reprinted in the St. Louis *Daily Commercial Bulletin* on Aug. 10, 1837, 2.

31. *Daily Commercial Bulletin,* Aug. 10, 1837, 2.

32. *Boston Investigator*, Mar. 15, 1833, 1.

33. *Boston Investigator*, Mar. 15, 1833, 1.

34. See the various title pages of his *Boston Investigator*, for instance *Boston Investigator*, July 6, 1832, 1; *The Emancipator*, August 29, 1839, 1.

35. Kneeland's poems praise Romantic friendship, which shall "Our hearts with love inspire: / O come! and through each bosom here / Diffuse thy generous fire," *National Hymns, Original and Selected, for the Use of Those Who Are "Slaves to No Sect"* (Boston: Boston Investigator, 1836), 7.

36. Andrews Norton, *A Discourse on the Latest Form of Infidelity* (Cambridge: John Owen, 1839).

37. Robert Burkholder, "Emerson, Kneeland, and the Divinity School Address," *American Literature* 58, no. 1 (1986): 2. Kneeland was tried and sentenced for blasphemy, but his persecutors did not hide the fact that this was also a political trial. General Attorney James Austin joined forces with conservative Unitarians in the prosecution of Kneeland, the atheist, see Rose, *Transcendentalism as a Social Movement*, 72–9. Habich has suggested that "in the Boston of the early nineteenth century threats to theological stability implied a challenge to political, legal, and social order as well." Robert D. Habich, "Emerson's Reluctant Foe: Andrews Norton and the Transcendental Controversy," *New England Quarterly* 65, no. 2 (1992): 223.

38. Peter S. Field, *The Crisis of the Standing Order: Clerical Intellectuals and Cultural Authority in Massachusetts, 1780-1833* (Amherst: University of Massachusetts Press, 1998).

39. Nancy Craig Simmons, "Margaret Fuller's Boston Conversations: The 1839-1840 Series." *Studies in the American Renaissance* (1994): 203.

40. Immanuel Wallerstein, *World-Systems Analysis: An Introduction* (Durham: Duke University Press, 2004), 22.

41. Josiah Quincy, *Speech of Josiah Quincy, President of Harvard University, Before the Board of Overseers of that Institution, February 25, 1845, on the Minority Report of the Committee of Visitation, Presented to that Board by George Bancroft, Esq., February 6, 1845* (Boston: Charles C. Little, Brown, and Co., 1845), 32.

42. Pierre Bourdieu and Jean-Claude Passeron, *Reproduction in Education, Society and Culture* (London: Sage, 1990), 7.

43. Henri Lefebvre, *The Critique of Everyday Life* (London: Verso, 1991), 535.

44. Andrews Norton, *Speech Delivered Before the Overseers of Harvard* (Boston: Cummings, Hilliard, & Co., 1825), xvii.

45. Norton, *A Discourse*, 36.

46. Mary Kupiec Cayton, *Emerson's Emergence: Self and Society in the Transformation of New England, 1800-1845* (Chapel Hill: University of North Carolina Press, 1989), 164.

47. Charles Sellers, *The Market Revolution: Jacksonian America, 1815-1846* (New York: Oxford University Press, 1991); Daniel Walker Howe, *What Hath God Wrought: The Transformation of America*, 1815–1848 (Oxford: Oxford University Press, 2007); George Taylor, *The Transportation Revolution, 1815-60* (London: Routledge, 1951); Richard R. John, *Spreading the News: The American Postal System from Franklin to Morse* (Cambridge: Harvard University Press, 1995).

48. Sellers's conceptualization of the market revolution has been criticized for its retrospective idealization of a supposedly unified, personal community predating

the market; see the essays collected in Melvyn Stokes and Stephen Conway, *The Market Revolution in America* (Charlottesville: University of Virginia Press, 1996). Nevertheless, it is still true that the market revolution introduced a sense of competition, instability, and insecurity. The 1830s were also the time of social unrest. Daniel Walker Howe has shown that "[t]he 1830s witnessed a transition in the composition of mobs from elite-led, politically motivated, and relatively restrained collective actions to impromptu violence." Howe, *What Hath God Wrought*, 433.

49. Alcott, *Doctrine and Discipline*, 9.

50. Nash, *Women's Education in the United States,* 53. In his classical study *The Culture of Professionalism* (1976), Burton Bledstein used the term "middling classes" to emphasize that the process of class formation was still underway in the first half of the nineteenth century. Particularly the professional, individualistic middle class was not yet clearly defined; Burton Bledstein, *The Culture of Professionalism: The Middle Class and the Development of Higher Education in America* (New York: Norton, 1976). But the process of class formation was clearly taking shape and the debates surrounding education show that discussion on the purpose of education were always linked to prestige and status.

51. Brownson, "The Laboring Classes," 365.

52. John Morrow, *Thomas Carlyle* (London: Continuum, 2006), 100.

53. Brownson, "The Laboring Classes," 365.

54. Margaret Fuller, "Emerson's Essays," *New-York Daily Tribune*, December 7, 1844, 1.

55. *The Liberator*, Oct. 31, 1845, 175.

56. *The Liberator*, Dec. 19, 1845, 203.

*Chapter 2*

# Intelligent Sympathies

## *Conversations and the Institutionalization of Romantic Education*

Conversation was constitutive of American Romanticism. The Transcendental Club was founded on conversational principles which were simultaneously social ones. Romantic conversation had always been much more than polite discussion. Literary conversation was a form of sympathetic exchange which, although generally limited to the cultural elite, prefigured an alternative, non-reified form of social interaction. True, the later Emerson would understand sympathy as a disposition that preceded social interaction: "It is not the circumstance of seeing more or fewer people, but the readiness of sympathy, that imports" (*CW* 7:8). In the 1830s and 1840s, however, not only for Alcott and Fuller but also for Emerson himself, sympathy was a practice that was created through conversation and interaction. By institutionalizing their conversational practice in the various spaces of education, the Transcendentalists inscribed these practices into the educational landscape of New England.

Conversations had figured prominently in the history of transatlantic Romanticism. In Jena, the early German Romantics considered their literary circles utopian communities whose conversations and collective creativity foreshadowed a golden age of the arts and sciences, and as such anticipated life after the social revolution. Not as ostensibly political in their aspirations, the Transcendentalists nonetheless meant to establish an informal bond of sympathy that signified broader social transformation. Conversation was a form of "intelligent sympathy." The term is taken from a letter that James Freeman Clarke wrote to Margaret Fuller during her time as a teacher at Greene Street School in Providence, Rhode Island. In this letter, Clarke offers a thoroughly Romantic description of their intellectual relationship as based on sympathetic exchange:

> Whatever we owe to those who give us confidence in ourselves, who make us believe we *are* something distinct and can do something special, who arouse our individual consciousness by an intelligent sympathy with tendencies and feelings we ourselves only half understand—all this I owe to you. You gave me to myself.

At the same time that Clarke believes in the visionary power of the Romantic genius ("we *are* something distinct and can do something special"), he emphasizes that interaction is needed for true self-cultivation: "What should I ever have been but for you? I am not much now, but what I am, I owe in a large degree to your influence."[1] Clarke's remarks encapsulate the principles of Romantic conversation: it is a mutual learning process between sympathetic souls.

This chapter establishes the link between pedagogical ideal, educational institutions, and the market mechanisms which needed to be addressed in order to put the conversational ideal into practice. It focuses on the conversations of Amos Bronson Alcott and Margaret Fuller, who, while received very differently by their contemporaries, were united in their belief that conversation served the cultivation of intelligent sympathies. While Fuller has been firmly reintroduced into the Transcendentalist canon, for most scholars Alcott remains the eccentric Transcendentalist, a "dreamy idealist" and an "otherworldly, Stone Age savage."[2] However, as late as 1876, William Russell's *American Journal of Education* stated that "[i]n 1837, when the Philistines where in full cry against the Temple School and its heretical teacher, Mr. Alcott was spoken of as the leader of the Transcendentalists."[3] Alcott is representative of the Transcendentalists in that he astutely knew how to use the socio-institutional conventions of nineteenth-century education.[4] Contrary to his current reputation, Alcott was a very practical person; he was permanently involved in institutional affairs, an idealist keenly aware of how to market his ideas, an intellectual respected by his peers, and a well-known public personality who used his reputation and cultural capital to bring about changes in education. His conversational model must therefore be understood as a practical intervention which sought to institutionalize a Romantic discussion forum for children that projected a vision of mutuality beyond the classroom. To achieve this aim, Alcott ultimately published his conversations in the two volumes of *Conversations with Children on the Gospels*. As we will see, these records of his school were intended to provoke the establishment and challenge the status quo. They also exemplify how the Romantics increasingly sought to distribute and popularize their literary practices.

It was no coincidence that Alcott's reform school also produced the second great conversationalist of the American Romantic era, Margaret Fuller, who started her career as a teacher at Alcott's Temple School. Fuller, whose early career was that of a teacher and conversationalist rather than the writer and public intellectual she would become after the publication of *Summer on the Lakes, in 1843* (1844) and *Woman in the Nineteenth Century* (1845), developed a complex understanding of how social practice was linked to the reproduction of socioeconomic structures and questions of social agency. Fuller's conversations were intended to free women from the "idle display" of their ornamental achievements: "The little reproduction which they are called seems mainly for the purposes of idle display. It is to supply this deficiency that these conversations have been planned."[5] Domesticity and the public display of domesticity were not only an issue for Fuller's conversational circles. Mary Loeffelholz has demonstrated that Lydia Sigourney, for instance, wrote didactic poetry to recreate but also question the "domestic-tutelary complex."[6] Fuller's and Alcott's conversations must be seen as interventions in this public discourse. It is no coincidence that the conversation that drew most of the public's ire was the one in which Alcott talked to children about labor pains. Alcott founded Temple School at a moment when the idealization of the child led to a retreat of infant schooling. By the middle of the nineteenth century, "few children under the age of five were enrolled in school," a fact that was closely linked to the idea that virtuous schooling would best occur in a domestic sphere overseen by women.[7] The nineteenth century was a catalyst in establishing the "modern cult of the child" in the United States. This image of the pure, innocent child in need of protection was "paralleled by, and linked to, a powerful movement to idealize women and confine them—especially those from the middle-class—to a women's sphere, which was defined essentially as the home and closely connected activities or environments."[8] Mothers were supposed to protect their children, lest Alcott and others corrupted them at an early stage. Alcott, by teaching children to be self-reliant, and by teaching them about the emotional depth and hardships of their mothers, contributed toward a movement that sought to reform the role of children and women alike.

Focusing on Romantic conversations as literary practices in a specific institutional context helps us understand the intellectual and educational debate of nineteenth-century America because these institutionalized Romantic literary practices exemplify concretely available positions in the intellectual field, positions that Alcott and Fuller appropriated to realize their projects. In linking these two figures, I also establish a connection that has not received sufficient scholarly attention. While Emerson's intellectual relationship with Fuller has been studied,[9] it is often forgotten that Alcott remained an important figure for Fuller during her tenure at Greene Street School. Most importantly, the connection between Alcott and Fuller allows us to understand how literary conversations established a social space in which individuals could cultivate "tendencies and feelings" they "only half understand."[10] As we will see, the fact that Alcott published his Romantic conversations as a model of social interaction was the logical consequence of his Romanticism. But this move into the public also illustrated the contradictions and limits of such a comprehensive model of education.

## THE RULE OF PRACTICE

Alcott's remarks on conversation are scattered throughout his writings. The most concise statement on conversational practice and its relationship to reform can be found in his *Doctrine and Discipline of Human Nature* (1836), a pedagogical manifesto that was republished as the preface to *Conversations with Children on the Gospels* (1836–1837). In a barely disguised self-portrait, Alcott depicts Jesus as an exemplary teacher. His means to form "the common consciousness of this age" was education: "Jesus was a Teacher; he sought to renovate Humanity."[11] It is in this context that Alcott gives his most comprehensive definition of the educational and social function of conversations:

> This preference of Jesus for Conversation, as the fittest organ of utterance, is a striking proof of his comprehensive Idea of Education. He knew what was in man, and the means of perfecting his being. He saw the superiority of this exercise over others for quickening the Spirit. For, in this all the instincts and faculties of our being are touched. They find full and fair scope. It tempts forth all the powers. Man faces his fellow man. He holds a living intercourse. He feels the quickening life and light. The social affections are addressed; and these bring all the faculties in train. Speech comes unbidden. Nature lends her images. Imagination sends abroad her winged words. We see thought as it springs from the soul, and in the very process of growth and utterance. Reason plays under the mellow light of fancy. The Genius of the Soul is waked, and eloquence sits on her tuneful lip. Wisdom finds an organ worthy her serene, yet imposing products. Ideas stand in beauty and majesty before the Soul.[12]

Jesus emerges as a Romantic teacher. He was able to achieve full self-expression in conversation with others ("his fellow man"), while at the same time stirring the "social affections" of his audience. For Alcott, conversation was a living intercourse; it was a collective endeavor, in which speaker and audience were mutually dependent on each other for the full realization of their potential. Alcott therefore wanted to restore a conversational space for children in which the "liberation of their imagination" could occur.[13]

Alcott's conversational method was not unprecedented in nineteenth-century America. Progressive educators and teachers had employed conversations as an alternative to rote learning for some time. In 1823 John Pierpont prefaced his *American First Class Book* with a note that stressed the use of exercises over the memorization of rules: "reading, like conversation, is learned from example rather than by rule."[14] Pierpont criticizes textbooks for their inability to understand reading skills as something best learned in dialogue with others; instead traditional education simply expected the memorization of rules to automatically produce these skills. Even more distinctly conversational in structure, Robert Ramble's *Table Book* (1836), a book for home schooling published in the same year as Alcott's *Conversations*, used short dialogues between a father and his son to teach the readers mathematical principles. Ramble asserts that his book differs from others by including "engravings, explanations, and conversations, such as I thought might give the pupil an insight into the meaning and use of the tables, at the same time that he should be convinced of the importance of having them very perfectly committed to memory."[15] In remarkably modern fashion, these dialogues relate mathematical problems to particular everyday situations. In most episodes, the child approaches his father with a practical problem (for instance, the conversion of shillings into dollars) which the father uses to teach his son mathematical principles and the relevance of these principles for everyday life.

Another such book was *Mind and Matter; or Familiar Conversations on the Body and Soul; Designed for Children at Home and at School* (1836). The book lacked an elaborate, programmatic preface, with the anonymous author simply stating that he felt it necessary to write a short, effective book. Its question-and-answer method resembled the conversations Alcott conducted and eventually published. These textbooks show how the conversational method was used by a number of nineteenth-century pedagogues and that Alcott, when he published his *Conversations*, could rely on an established literary genre. The teacher's and student's roles, however, were not redefined in these books. This is where Alcott differed significantly from the conversational practice of his time: he incorporated the relationship between teacher and students and thus questions of hierarchy and morality into the conversational structure itself. While *Mind and Matter* and other textbooks tried to involve the reader, even if it was in rudimentary form, Alcott presents himself as a teacher who is completely dependent on his student for the realization of his educational idea.

The published *Conversations*, however, were the culmination of Alcott's early career. To understand how these two volumes could cause a public scandal, we need to understand that Alcott meticulously established his reputation as a practitioner and one of the most progressive educators of nineteenth-century America. Alcott's strategic planning can be inferred mostly from his journal entries. These must be understood as reflections on the educational field and the literary market rather than the mere expression of individual experience. In New England's scribal culture, pages from journals circulated among literate friends and intellectuals, often with the purpose of showcasing preliminary versions of intended publications and plans for future projects. Alcott handed his journal to friends, copied pages from Fuller's journals, and explicitly stated how in this manner he hoped to establish conversational ties with others (cf. *AJ* 1:16).[16] Journals were carefully constructed semi-public exercises instrumental in establishing literary networks.[17] As such, Alcott's journal entries illustrate how diagnosis, self-promotion, and educational reform were always linked in Romantic educational texts.

An early episode in Alcott's teaching career exemplifies how his teaching practice instructed him in the hierarchies and struggles of the intellectual field. If scholarship hasn't ignored Alcott's role in the history of American literature and education altogether, it has frequently misrepresented his writings and pedagogical practices hence effectively cementing Alcott's reputation as an eccentric, selfish idealist. In 1831, when Alcott gained his first experiences as a teacher, he began to conceptualize his pedagogy as well as his position in the educational field:

I must teach in some form—at present, and perhaps hereafter, the young. Infancy seems to me the period, when most good can be done for the improvement of the character [. . .]. I am unwilling to waste my efforts upon those whose habits are fixed, and whose natures are too often sophisticated beyond the hope of reform—who are beyond the reach of human exertion. (*AJ* 1:29)

In order to be able to achieve social reform through moral regeneration, however, Alcott first had to carve out an available position in the educational field. The same entry therefore continues to promote the teacher as an alternative to the minister's moral authority. The passage is worth quoting at length for its comprehensive intellectual scope:

The minister has long preached, and what has he accomplished? Ask our penitentiaries, our prison, our jails, our almshouses, our domestic firesides; look into our civil and political codes and institutions, our periodical publications of a religious nature, our schoolrooms, our churches; count the number of various societies whose object is the suppression of some mighty vice which is preying on the heart of society—our societies for the suppression of intemperance, of war, of slavery, of oppressive governments; look into the individual life and behold the shifts of trade, of avarice, of petty prejudice, bickerings, quarrels, spites; view the low and debased forms of character which live both in high and humble life, the little regard with the precepts of Christianity seem to exert upon the lives of men. And when this mighty catalogue has been filled out, then is the answer at hand of what the minister, with all his boasted authority has done. He has done little because he has not known how. He has preached; but there have been causes operating against him more powerful than all his teachings, and he has failed. Early education is the enduring power. (*AJ* 1:29-30)

Alcott's journal entry is by no means restricted to a moralistic critique of modernity; it rather delineates the inefficacy of education in an age of social crises. The problem is not simply that the ministers are morally corrupt; they are institutionally powerless, as the habitualized practices which sustain what Alcott sees as the social vices of the age have been deeply ingrained into educational practice. Even the most progressive minister must fall prey to a system that works against him.

Alcott's attempt to carve out his intellectual position occurred in direct response to the institutional politics of the time. In her important study of Abigail and Louisa May Alcott, Eve LaPlante has suggested that Alcott's self-stylization in the passage quoted earlier may have been an envious response to the "public recognition" that Samuel Joseph May, a minister and his brother-in-law, gained in the Prudence Crandall case.[18] In Canterbury, Connecticut, Prudence Crandall had opened a home school which, once established, accepted "young Ladies and little Misses of color," as her advertisement in the *Liberator* stated.[19] Crandall was a Quaker woman who believed in the universality of education. She had set her mind on translating this universality into a form of practice. Her school caused a historical debate. John Hayward's popular *New England Gazetteer* (1839), which contained descriptions of all New England states, counties, and towns, dedicated a third of its sketch on Canterbury to Crandall's school and its public reception. As Hayward has it, although the public did not doubt "the purity of Miss Crandall's motives," it questioned "the expediency of the measure."[20] Her institutionalized attempt at liberation was ultimately unacceptable for the establishment. Canterbury's town meeting had voted against Crandall, but Crandall had already advertised her school in the *Liberator* and through this advertisement recruited twenty African American students. The state of Connecticut took legal measures against Crandall, and mobs threatened her and her students. As a consequence, Crandall eventually dissolved her school and left the town.[21]

This episode shows how the educational system tried to determine which degree of change was permissible. In this context, Alcott is often presented as dissatisfied with his own insignificance, an insignificance that shows precisely in the contrast between his idealist pedagogy and Crandall's concrete reform efforts. But Alcott had actually written his positional statement in July 1831, two years before Crandall's school became a public issue and a year prior to Crandall's first admittance of an African American student, when Crandall was still well-liked as a teacher for the town's upper-class young girls.[22] It was not written "during the Crandall controversy,"[23] and

Samuel Joseph May, of whose fame Alcott was supposedly jealous, was not yet the publicly recognized figure he would become. Alcott was at the time located in Germantown, Philadelphia, where he entertained a small school.[24] There Alcott co-taught with William Russell, former editor of the *American Journal of Education*, and it is safe to say that he learned from Russell about how to place educational ideas in the literary market. What Alcott codified in the journal entry quoted earlier was not personal resentment born out of stubborn idealism. Rather, Alcott's rhetoric draws on a familiar distinction between an old and a new school of thought which was firmly established as a distinguishing criterion of the religious and intellectual field since the days of Jonathan Edwards and George Whitefield, and which would resurface with Norton's attack on the "New School in Literature and Philosophy" in 1838. Alcott's journal entry is therefore the programmatic piece of someone aspiring to become part of a young, rebellious literary and educational movement.

We should therefore understand Alcott and Crandall as part of the same contested field. Once progressive schools were successfully established and reached beyond their institutional limits, the establishment did not shy away from taking measures even against small schools. When Alcott was a teacher at the Primary School in Cheshire, Connecticut, where he also served as schoolmaster from 1823 to 1828, he established how such changes in microsocial practices could be challenges to the status quo or, at any rate, maybe perceived as such. In 1826, six years before Emerson would break with Unitarianism and twelve years before Emerson would launch his attack on the establishment with the Divinity School Address, Alcott noted in his journals: "Those who in modern times attempt in education anything different from the old established modes are by many regarded as publick innovators on the peace *and order* of society, as persons desirous of destroying the structures which secures present happiness, and substituting in its place anarchy and confusion" (*AJ* I:5; my emphasis). In his entries of the time Alcott makes it clear that Christianity is to function as "the rule of practice" (*AJ* 1:9). This rule, however, cannot be realized without reforming the institutions responsible for the cultivation of everyday practice. Alcott declares that his teaching at infant schools is to "establish the reign of truth and reason and arrange society—our systems of education—in accordance with the laws of our nature as we find it in its incipient state" (*AJ* 1:10).

For Alcott, then, education was not simply an idea; from the outset, he considered the social and institutional conditions that needed to be addressed for his plans to be effective. Ultimately, the conditions of education and the conversational method converged in Alcott's discussion of popularity. Jesus's methods and teachings—and this means his conversations—were "*popular*. Instead of seeking formal and austere means, he rested his influence chiefly on the living word, rising spontaneously in the soul, and clothing itself at once, in the simplest, yet most commanding forms."[25] While Alcott considered his own project popular insofar as he aimed at educational reform, he was also aware of the fact that his practice was "opposed to the ruling opinions and prejudices of the age" and therefore "unpopular."[26] These remarks, however, were also part of Alcott's self-fashioning as an idealistic visionary. In fact, Alcott portrayed himself as an outcast more than he actually was. Even before he relocated to Boston in order to establish a school there, his school in Cheshire was hailed as "the best common school in the state— probably in the United States" by the *Boston Recorder and Telegraph*, an assessment that was reprinted in the *Teacher's Guide and Parent's Assistant* in 1827.[27] On May 14, 1827, the *Boston Recorder*, generally critical of the schools in Cheshire, reported a local voice that singled out Alcott as the shining example of school efforts: "There is one school of a superior or improved kind. viz., Mr. A. B. Alcott's school in Cheshire,—the best common school in this State, perhaps in the United States."[28] The *Recorder* was one of the most influential newspapers in educational politics. The mere notice of Alcott's school in such a periodical ranked him among the avant-garde of progressive schoolmasters.

Throughout his early career, Alcott established, and taught at, a number of schools, as was not unusual at the time. The journal entries of the time show just how profoundly teaching, self-promotion, and institutional reform were linked. In 1828, the *American Journal of Education* published Alcott's account of the methods he had used as a teacher at the Primary School in Cheshire, Connecticut. The editor, William Russell, stressed that Alcott's school experiment was an important "attempt to introduce a new system in a school supported by the *public money*, and open to the full influence of *popular* impression."[29] In the essay that follows these prefatory remarks, Alcott gladly underscores the public dimension of his school. He stresses the exemplary role of his teachings when he declares that his aim was to win the "public sentiment" and how consequently his classes were open to visitors. The essay shows how meticulously Alcott planned and carried out his reform project. He describes how initially he did little more than to establish new "modes of communication" while consciously avoiding the more drastic changes he would implement later. Only after the "public mind" had signaled approval did he gradually introduce further changes such as rearranging and decorating the schoolroom as well as introducing conversation as the chief pedagogical tool.[30] After his initial success, Alcott was in a position to demand more funding from the state. He used his institutional capital to successfully navigate the thin line between asking parents for further contributions and securing the district's financial support. Alcott received a higher salary, and his demands for better equipment and new textbooks were partially met. In the end, however, Cheshire was not sufficiently interested in progressive education, and Alcott eventually lost his job because student numbers declined. But he had succeeded in establishing himself as a widely received educational reformer and had access to periodicals such as the *American Journal of Education.*

Alcott saw the dynamic educational field of nineteenth-century New England as an opportunity to realize his pedagogical vision. In 1830, Alcott, intent on further establishing himself as one of the nation's foremost progressive educators, printed 1,000 copies of his educational manifesto *Observations on the Principles and Methods of Infant Instruction.* Written in 1830 when he was a teacher at an elementary school in Boston, in his book Alcott acknowledges the "comparatively free spirit of our institutions in this country." Just as in his article for the *Journal of American Education*, Alcott is again concerned with the "public mind" and its tendency "toward the study and improvement of human nature." For this tendency to manifest historically, however, institutions needed to be reshaped.[31] Through his conversations, Alcott sought to establish a Romantic discussion forum for children, which was supposed to prefigure a more egalitarian social organization. "Early education," as he writes, involves "the expansion, *direction*, and perfecting of the faculties of infant nature."[32] From the earliest stages, then, education is "infant cultivation," as it predates the corruption of institutionalized instruction: "Much systematic instruction is repulsive to the habits and feelings of infancy."[33] In *Observations*, Alcott develops a rudimentary system of methods which should help teachers establish a sympathetic teacher-student relationship. Even this early publication, then, illustrates how Alcott was invested in pedagogical practice, promotion, and larger social reform, and how he had successfully created a platform for his attempt to use literary education as a reform tool.

## PUBLIC MONSTROSITIES

Alcott's conversations were intended to create a space of mutual education; but they were also counterpublic exercises, whose pedagogical principles of mutuality and sympathy were supposed to function as principles of social organization. In October 1834, under the rubric "Causes of success," Alcott recorded in his journal that he had "secured a *reputation*" for himself.[34] Aware of the fact that he had established himself as a pedagogical authority, Alcott intended to set up a school in the contested educational landscape of Boston.[35] When Temple School opened with thirty-four students, ranging from ages three to twelve, it was not neutral ground. Institutional politics as well as the informal networks of Transcendentalism determined Temple School's educational space, and therefore any didactic effort was involved in educational politics. Through Alcott's previous educational reform work, the school was already complexly located in the various socio-institutional hierarchies of the larger Boston area.

Temple School was founded at a time of economic boom, when Boston's middle class often preferred progressive, experimental private schools over public ones. In a manner typical for private schools, Temple School was not the project of an individual; it was a collective, institutionalized endeavor from the outset, a project that shared in the cultural networks of nineteenth-century Boston. Elizabeth Palmer Peabody was not only Alcott's co-teacher; she had also helped find a location for the school and she was instrumental in recruiting students.[36] As a consequence of her support and Alcott's reputation as an exemplary teacher, Temple School initially enjoyed considerable popularity.[37] The public responded favorably to the reform school, with many newspapers praising Alcott as one of the most important educators of the time. Educational periodicals such as *Parley's Magazine* lauded Alcott's Temple School because, as an anonymous reporter wrote, "[t]here are some little boys and girls there, scarcely six years old, who know how to think and reason about things as well as most men and women."[38]

The school's reform pedagogy was also a device of public representation, promoted to cement its place among Boston's educational institutions. Temple School was prominently located right opposite Boston Common. While the school's location may have been a contingent factor, it also enabled Alcott to permanently entertain visitors in his school. In addition, the Masonic Temple's imposing architecture made a visual impression particularly on visitors, a fact that many reviewers noted (figure 2.1).

Temple School's Gothic exterior also conveniently contrasted sharply with the factory hall look of Lancastrian Schools, which, while making education accessible to the masses, operated on principles of control and surveillance.[39] Although Alcott shared some of the principles of Lancastrian education, his emphasis on collective creativity and self-reliance could not have been further from the mass education pursued at Lancastrian institutions. The building, then, became a public display of Alcott's pedagogical agenda. Similarly, Alcott used the rearrangement of the classroom and the school's architecture as to advertise his school and recruit students, a strategy that his disciple Hiram Fuller would adopt for his Greene Street School in Providence.[40] The same logic applies to Alcott's conversations.

In this context, the conversational model became more than a didactic method. Conversation was as much philosophical principle as it was an intervention in an institutional struggle for authority and power. On the opening day, Alcott asked all of his students: "what idea he or she had of the object of coming to school."[41] This question flew in the face of a teacher-centered, authoritarian educational system. Not only did Alcott assign the students an

**Figure 2.1 The exterior of Boston's Masonic Temple in 1835.** Detail of 1835 map of Boston by George W. Boynton, entitled "Plan of Boston with parts of the adjacent towns." Published by the Boston Bewick Company, 1835.

active position, he encouraged them to ponder the reason and aims of education rather than using drill and rote learning to perpetuate a supposedly evident pedagogical agenda. As Alcott had argued in *Observations on the Principles and Methods of Infant Instruction*, the teacher operates through Romantic affect and sympathy, essentially establishing an extension of the Romantic conversational circles, although he acts as more of a guide than a mere interlocutor: "Moral results can come only from moral means; and of these the teachers [sic] agency is the chief. In him the infant mind should find the object of its imitation and its love." This sympathetic interaction will achieve a "cultivation of the affections," which eventually helps develop the child's conscience, the "fundamental principle of all virtue." Alcott's pedagogy is one of affective sympathy. Knowledge and a sense of duty will arise if the child is connected "with the pure, the good, and the happy around him."[42]

Alcott's conversational practice reflects how Romantic conversation was a literary practice aimed at individual and social reform. At the same time, the educational principles of Temple School still remained firmly literary. Just as much as Alcott used the journal as a medium of self-reflection in the classroom, his conversations were first of all literary exercises. They were polite conversations which intended to help children realize a sense of self-reliance.

In his conversation on the "Integrity of the Spirit: Filial Piety," Alcott talks to Charles, a notoriously disputative, intelligent child. The discussion turns to the link between philosophy and practice:

MR. ALCOTT. *Do you see any distinction between holiness and virtue?*
SOME. *Yes.*
MR. ALCOTT. *What is virtue?*
CHARLES. *It is acting.*
MR. ALCOTT. *Virtue comes by the trial of our holiness. It is holiness brought out and represented.*
CHARLES. *Can we be virtuous unless we are holy?*
MR. ALCOTT. *Virtue is a sign of holiness; it is holiness drawn out.*[43]

Alcott's processual establishment of the meaning of virtue corresponds to the aesthetic values that were at the core of American Transcendentalism. As Lawrence Buell has shown, "Transcendentalist literary works are less aesthetic products than aesthetic processes."[44] In "The Poet," Emerson would write that beauty is something that needed to be established in conversation; the experience of beauty left the individual incomplete: "Every man should be so much an artist, that he could report in conversation what had befallen him" (*CW* 3:4). This mutual processuality is reflected in Charles's literary education.

Alcott shares this idea of conversation but explicitly insists that such a dialogue can occur only in adequate material circumstances. The Romantic conversationalist therefore intends to "mould anew our Institutions, our Manners, our Men."[45] For Alcott, the reason for the lack of proper education was twofold: "We have neither great men, nor good institutions."[46] In an unpublished journal entry of 1839, Alcott would write that Harvard "more than any other institution, in my country, of a literary character, is least friendly to reform. It is far behind the age. It mocks at the free and enthusiastic spirit of the young. It has neither faith nor hope" (*Alcott MS* 1839, 747).[47] Conversations, then, also emerge as a strategy in opposition to the habitualized, sterile practices of an institution which perpetuated the status quo.

Having successfully established Temple School in Boston in September 1834, Alcott attempted to proceed from local reform to structural change. For Alcott, conversation was part of a counterhegemonic practice he sought to establish. As Roger Bellin has suggested, we should understand Alcott's conversational method "as a discursive practice and as a kind of inquiry, one that remains both philosophical and democratic in some sense, but does not use dispute as its necessary form."[48] Alcott's attempt to locate this democratic practice in existing structures, however, was, if not intended to be disputatious, at least willing to confront the structures of education. Alcott was aware of the fact that his school was under public scrutiny. Visitors included not only William Ellery Channing, Harriett Martineau, and Emerson but also various journalists. Emerson expressed his enthusiasm about Peabody's *Record of a School* in a letter to Peabody from August 3, 1835: "It is the only book of facts I ever read that was as engaging as one of Miss [Maria] Edgeworth's fictions."[49] Alcott saw the signs: a publication of his school recordings would receive considerable attention. The publication of his *Conversations* was an important step into the public arena. Alcott wanted to make available the Romantic literary conversation as a democratic model for all education and, eventually, for all human interaction.

In 1836 and 1837, Alcott published *Conversations with Children on the Gospels*, the collection of classroom discussions that would change the course of his career.[50] Arranged as Socratic dialogues between Alcott and his students, the *Conversations* employ a Romantic conversational ideal that had long been used to create alternative spaces of education. Alcott marked out his book as a manifesto. In between the introduction and the conversations, the book features a drawing of his Temple School which visualizes how his methods went against the model of authority and discipline that the Harvard system or Lancastrian varieties of education embodied (see figure 2.2).

In addition to addressing educational practice and institutions, Alcott's *Conversations* was also an intervention in the didactics of popular

**Figure 2.2 Classroom of Alcott's Temple School.** Amos Bronson Alcott, *Conversations with Children on the Gospels*. 2 vols. (Boston: James Munroe and Co., 1836–37), 1:1.

Figure 2.3  Typical story of the Peter Parley series. Samuel Griswold Goodrich, *The Tales of Peter Parley About America*. Rev. ed. (Philadelphia: Thomas, Cowperthwait & Co., 1847), 6–7.

nineteenth-century educational textbooks. At the time, the textbook market was dominated by Abbott's *The Little Scholar Learns to Talk* (1835), with its instructive stories about Rollo, Samuel Griswold Goodrich's Peter Parley books, with their traditional adventures that sought to instruct children in geographical and historical knowledge, and the sentimental Romanticism of Lydia Sigourney's *Poems for Children* (1835)[51] (figure 2.3).

In stark contradistinction to these, readers could find conversations on labor pains in the *Conversations*, discussions which in their printed version were located at the intersection of spiritual development, institutional reform, and social reform: "And a mother suffers when she has a child. When she is going to have a child she gives up her body to God, and He works upon it in a mysterious way, and, with her aid, brings forth the child's Spirit in a little Body of its own; and when it has come she is blissful."[52]

Alcott's *Conversations* drew on, and transformed, a number of influential educational genres and conventions of the literary market in order to propagate an egalitarian conversational model and to address topics usually deemed inappropriate for children and adults alike. This concrete involvement with nineteenth-century education and the book's announcement that there would be a second volume disturbed the establishment, since Alcott could present his reform school as a successful transformation of dominant curricula (math, grammar, rhetoric) into a radically democratic and antihierarchical conversational model. Temple School in itself, as a relatively small experiment, did not elicit much of a response from the standing order, although, as we have seen, it did receive attention from educational reformers. This changed, however, once Alcott used his reputation and the powerful literary institutions of the time to disseminate his ideas as a voice of the New School to publicly challenge tradition and authority. At the time that Alcott published his *Conversations with Children on the Gospels* in 1836 and 1837, he was seen as part of a movement: 1836, the year that Perry Miller famously referred to as Transcendentalism's *annus mirabilis*, saw the publication of Emerson's *Nature*, Ripley's *Discourses on the Philosophy of Religion*, and the formation of the Transcendental Club.[53]

The move from a local institution to a text that translated this local experiment into general claims for educational and social reform came at a time of instability and change when such challenges needed to be contained, especially since the book was culturally authorized by the publication through James Munroe, one of Boston's influential publishers. Munroe had published books and pamphlets by the Harvard Law School, influential sermons, and Emerson's *Nature*. Many of these texts were advertised and reviewed in law journals, the *North American Review*, and, importantly, the *Christian Examiner*. Alcott meticulously traced his publisher's endeavors to circulate his book: "Some weeks since my publishers, James Munroe & Co, sent, by my direction, copies of the 'Conversations' to the editors of the 'Daily Advertiser' and the 'Boston Courier.' These papers circulate more widely than other papers of this metropolis; and are conducted with more ability."[54] It was the *Courier*'s editor, who, pressed by his reader's outraged response, eventually wrote: "The *Conversations on the Gospels* is a more indecent and obscene book (we say nothing of its absurdity) than any other we saw exposed for sale on a bookseller's counter. Mr. A. interrogates his pupils on subjects which are universally excluded from promiscuous companies of men and women."[55]

The question was, of course, why to address such an obscene absurdity at all. A reviewer in the *Christian Examiner* noted that he was actually supportive of some of the principles that Alcott presented and would have happily ignored its alleged follies; but, as the reviewer writes, "[a]s all the monstrosities of this book have been *given to the public*, we may be pardoned if we make some extracts to prove this assertion of ours."[56] Interestingly, he chides Alcott for his "very inadequate *practice* of this great and true method of education,"[57] although this practice had been lauded by educational reformers of the time. In fact, Alcott had acquired a reputation for being a successful practitioner; but this was precisely the point: on a philosophical and theoretical level, Alcott's *Conversations* could be tolerated; as an alternative practice that undermined rote learning and discipline, they needed to be contained. The intellectual elite ultimately responded vehemently to a book about a small reform school in Boston, launching an unprecedented campaign against Alcott. His peers Emerson and Peabody rushed to his defense, and James Freeman Clarke, the editor of the *Western Messenger*, compared Alcott to Socrates, stating that "[w]e also are pledged to these principles in theory, and we shall aim as far as in us lies to uphold and protect their practical application."[58] But the school's patrons started to turn their backs on Alcott. First attendance dropped in the aftermath of the *Conversations*, from forty students in 1834 to ten students in 1837. The economic crisis of 1837 did its part to end the project in 1838.

The most instructive example of what was truly at stake in the reception of Alcott's *Conversations* (and his conversational model) is Joseph T. Buckingham's review in his influential *Boston Courier*. The review is frequently cited for its famous condemnation of Alcott as "half-witted."[59] The editorial politics of Buckingham's statement, however, reveals the true issue at stake: namely that Alcott challenged the hierarchies of the intellectual field. The editorial comment was printed below the letter of an outraged parent. Although the parent frankly admits to having only read excerpts of the *Conversations* in the *Daily Advertiser*, he feels obliged to address the *Courier*'s readership in time so as to prevent that the "public feeling should tolerate" a third installment of the *Conversations*.[60] In the final section of his subsequent short remark, Buckingham establishes a connection between Alcott and freethinker Abner Kneeland, who was accused of atheism in a series of trials in front of the state supreme court between 1834 and 1838. Kneeland was officially on trial for his atheism, but his supposed heresy was perceived as a challenge to the social order. The trial against Kneeland exemplified a larger campaign of the conservative forces to impose order and hierarchy. Church and state cooperated: attorney general James Austin employed religious arguments while conservative Unitarian forces gladly accepted the help of political institutions to fight religious dissenters.[61] The Unitarian orthodoxy equally perceived Emerson, Theodore Parker, and Brownson as a threat to the social order.[62] It is no coincidence, therefore, that Buckingham concludes his letter by stating that Alcott's "friends ought to take care of him without delay," implicitly urging Emerson and his peers to exclude Alcott from their circle lest his actions fall back on them. What is even more, the *Courier*'s editor threatens to help with this process: "Has the honorable Judge of our Municipal Court examined these 'Conversations?' We have a copy which we will lend him with pleasure."[63]

Buckingham's response is a blatant attempt to contain the radical direction of a movement that was beginning to establish itself. In another editorial from May 11, 1837, Buckingham felt obliged to correct the *Christian Register*'s supposed misrepresentation of the *Courier*'s alleged support for

Alcott, stating that an approving letter was printed in the name of ideological diversity, but that it was prefixed with an editorial remark which clearly signaled disapproval of both Alcott and the supportive letter. Buckingham's editorial piece has become famous for citing a Unitarian minister (supposedly Andrews Norton) who stated that of the *Conversations*' "one third was absurd, one third was blasphemous, and one third obscene." But the review is actually important because it reveals the mechanisms at work in the establishment's response to Alcott. The factual correction is accompanied by Buckingham's statement that "many gentlemen of great reputation for learning and piety are in raptures of delight with these 'Conversations,' and have labored mightily, in season and out of season, to extend their fame and their circulation." Alcott's *Conversations* had become part of a struggle over authority in the intellectual field. The book no longer only represented Alcott's individual challenge to authority. Because of the furious attacks and passionate defenses alike, the *Conversations* had become emblematic of a larger movement that challenged the field's hierarchies.[64]

The campaign against Alcott succeeded. Alcott's response was to aim for broader reform. In an unpublished manuscript he writes: "I closed my School, in anticipation of entering upon my ministry of education, wherein I hope to demonstrate the principles of human culture in a popular form. I shall have more freedom of action" (*Alcott MS* 1838, 267). Shortly before his school was closed, Alcott noted in his journal:

> It were better, so far as popular effect is concerned, that the school should be continued. Yet, as for the final success of my doctrines, the school has but little to do. These will spread and find acceptance, though the school were given up. Through the "Conversations," and the course of action which I shall pursue, these will be kept before the public; and whatever of good they may contain, or promise in their extension, will be ascertained. Better were it, however, that I should present, from under my own guidance, specimens of character exemplifying these principles, in living form. I trust that I shall be sustained in this effort, & thus continue to spend a part of my time in the practical duties of an instructor. To these, I wish to add, other modes of action.[65]

Alcott remained dedicated to establishing Romanticism as a conversational, egalitarian practice. Temple School is usually cited as an admirable didactic effort, whose pedagogical merits are undeniable, but which failed because of Alcott's organizational ineptitude: "Alcott's failure to understand the oral tenor of his time had already seeded the origins of a public uproar. He little realized how few of his contemporaries thought it appropriate to ask six-year-olds to interpret of the word of the Lord, as opposed to telling them exactly to think about the scriptures."[66] The archive suggests the opposite: Alcott meticulously planned the popularization of his teachings by carving out his position in the educational field.[67]

Alcott pushed his Temple School into the public, where he encountered the institutional limits of Romantic reform. The vehement responses to Alcott's *Conversations on the Gospels with Children* were in fact very perceptive about how the changed teacher-student relationship ultimately questioned the authority of the teacher and therefore a small, educated elite's claim to be the arbiters of knowledge and truth. But the challenge remained institutional. James Nehring has rightly pointed out that Temple School was not a representative school at the time, nor could it figure as a model for urban schools: it "easily outstrips the dank and leaning rural schoolhouses in Massachusetts but also the Boston primary schools" of the time.[68] Alcott never considered the class conditions which prevented comprehensive education in the first place. Temple School was not an attempt to shake the foundations of the educational field. But Alcott was instrumental in making Romantic literary education an increasingly public affair and in establishing Transcendentalism as an educational reform movement. Consequently, Alcott emphasized the necessity for public reform in 1838, even after the fall of his Temple school: "My books must in time find readers, and my methods be adopted as models of culture, both in domestic, and public instruction" (*Alcott MS* 1838, 268).

Alcott himself would never achieve the popular reform he desired, although he had a lasting influence on other educators. In England, James Pierrepont Greaves founded Alcott House, a utopian community and progressive school. Alcott's books were ordered and read abroad, and he was frequently invited as a lecturer. In 1877, the *American Journal of Education* would write that Alcott's "ideas in education" were "now almost universally received."[69] Two years before Emerson's Divinity School Address, which would elicit a similarly vehement response from the establishment, Alcott had publicly challenged the educational field's authorities and helped connect Romantic literary education to institutional politics.

## GREENE STREET SCHOOL

Margaret Fuller's position as a woman intent on leaving the orbit of domestic education and ornamental representation is particularly helpful in framing the conditions of conversational practice. Fuller's Boston conversations for women, conducted between 1839 and 1844, established an educational space where women could redefine their social roles. Fuller's aim was to "ascertain what pursuits are best suited to us in our time and state of society, and how we may make best use of our means for *building up the life of thought upon the life of action*" (*L* 2: 87; emphasis added). Christina Zwarg has demonstrated that for Fuller "conversation became central to her larger feminist orientation, particularly the revised theory of pedagogy and reading so vital to her later work."[70] In a letter to Sophia Ripley, one among many women of Boston's cultural elite who would attend Fuller's conversations, Fuller announced that the participants of her conversational circles would become schooled in a form of practice: "I am so sure that the success of the whole depends on conversation being general that I do not wish any one to join who does not intend, *if possible*, to take an *active part*" (*L* 2: 88). Conversations were supposed to create a space in which women could collectively find a sense of self-reliance. They were particularly powerful instruments in "a democracy that valued oratory as the main vehicle for shaping collective values."[71]

Fuller's pedagogical career commenced in 1836 as an assistant teacher at Amos Bronson Alcott's Temple School, where she replaced Elizabeth Palmer Peabody. When Alcott's Temple School started declining, Fuller took up a position as a teacher at Hiram Fuller's Greene Street School in Providence, where she stayed from June 1837 until December 1838. From her early days as a teacher, conversation was a means to realize a sense of self-reliance that was repressed by traditional education. The problem for women in the nineteenth century was not that of public visibility; they were very much publicly visible. But they were visible through their display of politeness and restriction, in which they were thoroughly schooled. As Mary Ryan has demonstrated, women in nineteenth-century America had "multiple points of entry into the public life"; but they "hardly found a commodious, legitimate or powerful place in the polity."[72] Even in the relatively progressive *Boston Recorder*, schools for young women were advertised as dedicated to "the higher branches of an English education," including music, drawing, and painting as well as "plain and ornamental Needle Work." Readers also suggested that it was necessary to complement the ornamental arts with a more "useful female education." Economy, cooking, style, and politeness were required. Needle work, one reader cautions, should equally not become too ornamental, lest it lose its domestic function. This emphasis on domestic practicality, the reader asserted, was to be at the core of female academies. Although female academies had been widely established, from boarding schools to private institution that operated by way of subscription, they mostly continued to teach ornament and household economy.[73]

The importance of Fuller's school experience as a pedagogical training ground for her Boston conversations has been thoroughly studied.[74] But Greene Street School also helped Fuller understand the mechanisms of the educational field in a way that prefigured her own career. In a historical constellation that considered alternative practices a potential threat to the social order, even a comparatively small school could become contested ground, as the vehement responses to Alcott's *Conversations with Children on the*

*Gospels* demonstrated. Opened in 1837, at the very moment when Alcott's Temple School was failing, Hiram Fuller's Greene Street School was inspired by Alcott's Temple School and shared Alcott's vision of an alternative, institutionalized space of education. Hiram Fuller's link to Alcott was explicit, as he often used Alcott's *Conversations on the Gospels with Children* as a textbook.[75] Their aim and strategy were fundamentally similar. Annie Russell Marble captures how a typical Transcendentalist skepticism about tradition was reflected in the school's educational methods: "In both [Temple and Greene Street School] the aim was to emancipate education from traditional fetters,—to stimulate high and free thought in place of mere memorizing, to nourish the heart by cordial relations between teacher and pupil, and to educate the senses by surroundings of art and beauty."[76] Just like Alcott's Temple School, Greene Street School was a small, but prestigious school, with the building's architecture modeled on a Greek Temple. The school's outward appearance had established it prominently in Providence's social geography: "The school's new building, supported by Providence's literary elite, had opened [. . .] with great fanfare."[77]

But Hiram Fuller, who was not related to Margaret, was more pragmatic and much more eclectic in his pedagogical principles than Alcott. In a letter to Peabody from July 8, 1837, Margaret Fuller captured this difference: "Mr. Fuller is as unlike as possible to Mr. Alcott. He has neither his poetic beauty nor his practical defects" (*L* 1:291). Fuller's remark points to the question of how practical Romanticism could become. This question posed itself clearly and urgently with Greene Street School's inaugural speech. Originally, Alcott had been requested as the opening day speaker, but in the wake of the public assault on his *Conversations*, he refrained from giving the speech. Alcott's replacement was Ralph Waldo Emerson. On June 10, 1837, anticipating the critique of tradition and convention that would earn him notoriety with his Divinity School Address a year later, Emerson criticized the "dead form in the schools, in the state, in the church."[78] In front of a large audience, Emerson, by then a leading voice in criticizing how "denominational pluralism transformed religion in New England into a commodity to be selected by different consumer markets,"[79] sketched the role of education as a catalyst in a social system in which "Men are subject to things."[80] This condition also affects the intellectual class, who has become a mere bystander: "At times the land smells with suicide. Young men have no hope. The educated class stand idle in the streets. No man calleth them to labor." Emerson then demands the reestablishment of "public instruction," although he remains vague about the precise nature of his intended reform: "The great object of education should be commensurate with the object of life."[81]

Emerson's speech displays the complicated relationships between message, audiences, and the mechanisms of the literary market. Whether or not intended as a provocation or simply the result of the reviewers' by then common assumptions about Emerson, the lecture's content hardly mattered to newspaper correspondents. Of course, Emerson played with expectations to a degree where he threatened to obliterate his own message. As much as Emerson rejected education as a form of competition, and as much as he criticized individuals for being affected by the "fever of the market," he cultivated his status as a rebellious intellectual when he declared that his views may be deemed "too abstract and purely theoretic."[82] The address's universalist critique as well as Emerson's supposed obscurity stage Emerson's trademarks as an intellectual, and thus seek to cement his position in the literary field. Reviewers picked up on Emerson's hint and pointed out the lecture's supposed unintelligibility, although the lecture, while vague in its suggestions for reform, was not at all obscure in its argument or style. Emerson's self-fashioning, a suspicious audience, and the actual educational ideals that were at stake clashed in the speech's reception. As Fuller remarked in a letter to Alcott a few days later, Emerson's remarks fell "on stony soil" (*L* 1:286). At the same time, Fuller hoped that others would help circulate the message: "Yet there is always comfort in the thought that, if such seed must not fertilize the spot for which it was intended, the fowl of the air may carry it away to some more propitious clime" (*L* 1:286). Fuller certainly hoped that she could be "that bird" (*L* 1:286). But her remarks capture precisely the problem that Fuller would continue to come to terms with: Emerson was essentially preaching to a lonely bird.[83]

The question of audience would become much more important for Fuller in her literary journalism. Greene Street School was as much a haven as Temple School initially was. Fuller was the third female teacher that Hiram Fuller hired. Georgianna Nias and Frances Aborn, however, were examples of an older generation that taught girls "decorum and rectitude," whereas it was Fuller's role to teach them self-reliance and rhetorical abilities. Her teaching was guided by the idea of a sympathetic, collective conversation. Fuller created "an intimate and non-competitive association between classmates that was a manifestation of growing feelings of sorority and kinship between women; and the fusion of these into a particular academic environment composed of physical, social, and cognitive elements."[84] Her classes did not only promote a progressive form of women's education. They also went against the market's demand for education in household economy. Fuller introduced Romanticism thematically and institutionally whenever possible, whether in her selection of English Romantic poetry or when she urged her students to cultivate their own rhetorical style rather than following an established formalism. As Charles Capper has it, "[i]f nothing else, we can at least be sure Fuller's students were some of the youngest people in America trying to grapple with Transcendentalist philosophy."[85]

Fuller continued a tradition of rebelling against rote learning that was on the one hand indebted to her Romanticism, and, on the other hand, to a tradition exemplified by Susanna Rowson who saw that rote learning reproduced the status quo.[86] Mary Ware Allen, one of Fuller's students, who was eighteen when she entered Greene Street School, captures this practice in her journal:

> One of the class asked if we were to get our lessons *by heart*—Miss Fuller said she never wished us to get our lessons by heart, as that expression is commonly understood, [. . .] for nothing could be farther from getting it by heart—it was oftener only getting it by body—the heart had nothing to [do] with it. No, she wanted us to get our lessons by *mind*—to give our minds and souls to the work. If there were any who thought they could not do this, who did not feel an interes[t] in it, who did not feel willing to answer her questions, and to open their minds to her, she wished them to leave the class—it would not displease her, she wished they would do it, even if there were only two left who really felt interested.[87]

The text's subtle rhetoric revolves around the phrase "learning by heart." The phrase appropriates a key Romantic term for a thoroughly anti-Romantic purpose. True learning occurs through the Romantic work of "minds and souls" in conversation with each other.

Mary Ware Allen's journal is in many ways a key to understanding the practices of Greene Street School. Mary was the daughter of Joseph Ellen Allen, the Unitarian Minister of First Church in Northborough, Massachusetts, and Lucy Clark Ware, the daughter of Henry Ware, Sr. As part of the cultural elite of the time, she was not only educated, but steeped in the controversies of the time, as her father's election as Hollis Chair at Harvard in 1805 had initiated the schism between traditional Calvinists and liberal Unitarians. In addition, her parents established a small boarding school, as was not unusual at the time. Mary Allen, in short, arrived with a suitable conception of the nineteenth-century educational landscape and was thus able to appreciate what Fuller was trying to achieve at Greene Street School. It is small wonder that other younger and more inexperienced students would be less susceptible to Fuller's rhetorically challenging, often sarcastic remarks.

It is also Allen's remarks which allow us to understand that even in her early days as a teacher Fuller was confronted with the problem of audience. Allen's thoughts were recorded in a journal, which students received on their first day of school. The journal played an important role in the school's didactics as well as for its institutional politics. Inspired by Alcott, Hiram and Margaret Fuller used them as literary tools of introspection. Allen was initially skeptical of the fact that Hiram Fuller also read from the journals as inspiration to other students, but eventually overcame her skepticism because she saw its value for self-reliance and rhetorical refinement:

> I have overcome my repugnance to writing a journal, and find it, what I did not expect, a pleasant, as well as useful exercise. It has, as Miss Fuller said to me the other day, when she saw what I had written on the first page, all the advantages of writing a composition without the danger of acquiring a stiff and formal manner of expressing oneself, which is usually seen in common school compositions.[88]

As Granville Ganter and Hani Sarji have argued, "[a]lthough Allen herself clearly identified with women's gender roles, her journal accounts regarding her developing literary identity show that she borrowed from a variety of rhetorical traditions."[89] Allen's journal illustrates the predicament of Fuller's Romantic education. Just like Emerson, she was caught between various networks and audiences. Allen could very much appreciate Fuller's education to self-reliance; but she was part of an elite who could afford such education and therefore retained a distance from Fuller's more critical social comments: "Some things that were said about Women's Rights were good, hut others went farther than I would go, inasmuch as they advocated loudly her speaking in public."[90]

The defenders of the status quo were certainly eager to respond to the challenges posed by Greene Street School. It soon became a thorn in the side of traditional education. Just as with Alcott, measures were taken to push the school out of the educational system. As Charles Capper writes, "[b]y the fall, plans were afoot, among a group of Calvinist and some non-Calvinist citizens, to 'break up the school' by building a competing one nearby, which they would do by the spring."[91] This and other problems made Hiram Fuller vacate his position a year later. At this point, Margaret Fuller had already resigned from Greene Street School. Evelina Metcalf, one of Fuller's students, recorded in her journal: "Our dear Miss Fuller has gone after giving us words of kindness and love which shall never, never forget, words which may govern our present and future conduct."[92] Although Fuller apparently often dominated her classes, even her monologues were well liked by her students.

Teaching as cooperation and voluntary exchange remained a fundamental educational principle for Fuller. But despite her initial enthusiasm, Fuller remained conflicted about her school experience in Providence, where she worked on the fringes of the reform movement. Although popular among her students and sincerely dedicated to her teaching, in one of her final letters from Providence, addressed to William H. Channing, she writes that she does "not wish to teach again at all" (*L* 1:354). Fuller states that she was ready to leave Providence and to "do so with unfeigned delight [. . .] because I have here been always in a false position and my energies been consequently much repressed" (*L* 1:353–4). Yet, while she was bothered by the daily requirements of the school, she also considered it a lesson in practicality, as she wrote to Emerson: "My time here has been full of petty annoyances, but I regret none of them; they have so enlarged my practical knowledge" (*L* 1:295). As she wrote to Frederic Hedge, Greene Street School ultimately was a testing ground for larger plans: "My plan grows quietly and easily in my mind; this experience here will be useful to me, if not to Providence, for I am bringing my opinions to the test, and thus far have reason to be satisfied" (*L* 1:292).

## BOSTON CONVERSATIONS

Although Fuller's educational experiments were also conducted for financial reasons, mainly because she had to provide for her family after her father's death in 1835,[93] they offered her enough room to develop her conversational method. Her proclamation that she was not without "dreams and hopes as to the education of women" (*L* 1:354) remained relatively vague, as Fuller had neither the institutional nor the financial means to establish herself as an educator, let alone as a writer. After her tenure at Greene Street School had come to an end, Fuller even considered moving to Cincinnati for a new beginning, "more independent of *aristocratic patrona[ge]* than in any of the great Eastern cities" (*L* 1:355). Fuller's remarks testify to her personal exhaustion; but they also exemplify the tension between public appeal, promotion, and the wish to remain autonomous, which characterized Romantic education.

These tensions intensified as Fuller's teaching efforts became more organized. Instead of escaping the educational system, Fuller ultimately returned to it. Starting in 1839, Fuller's Boston conversations broadened her conception of education not only thematically but also organizationally as she was now responsible for location and financial support. Elizabeth Palmer Peabody made available the parlor of her house and bookstore in Boston at 13 West Street. She simultaneously considered Fuller's circles an occasion to advertise the not-yet-open bookstore to her future audience. Classes ran for thirteen weeks, two hours each, and tickets were fairly expensive at $20 for ten conversations. Even her participants found that a high price, but then again these were not conversations for the masses. The participants were educated women: "almost none of these families were connected with Boston's new, politically conservative industrial wealth." At the same time, "beyond class, status, and education, the most salient feature of the group as a whole was the strong ties many of the women had, like Fuller's friends in general, to various social reform movements."[94]

In this reform-oriented context, Fuller could seek to transcend the thematic limits of the field but she also had to confront the problem of her elite status and the concomitant question of her limited audience. It is important to consider the semi-public nature of Fuller's conversational circles and how these conversations were enabled by the literary institutions of Transcendentalism, however parochial these remained. Critics have pointed out how Fuller transformed the European salon model into a space for women's education.[95] With her conversations, Fuller saw the opportunity to redirect the reproduction of social structures. In a letter to Sophia Ripley, who would participate in these meetings, Fuller imagined a "point of union to well-educated and thinking women in a city which [. . .] boasts at present nothing of the kind" (*L* 2:86). If her plan would not work in Boston, she "could hardly hope that such a plan could be brought to bear upon general society in any other city in the U.S." (*L* 2:87). Fuller hoped that "what is invaluable in the experience of each might be brought to bear upon all" (*L* 2:87). Experience is therefore located in a collective space.

This small conversational circle of like-minded women was the perfect testing ground for Fuller's Romantic project. As the Transcendentalist most thoroughly familiar with German Romanticism, Fuller was aware of the comprehensive claims of early German Romanticism and their conversational circles.[96] But she had to confront the question of who had access to a potentially universalist form of education in the first place. After Emerson had initially been allowed to the conversations and somewhat obnoxiously dominated them, the conversations were restricted to women, and the topics were chosen so as to reconsider the social position of women. Accordingly, Fuller introduced a notion of beauty in her conversations that was very different from the mere display of erudition or ornament taught at most women's academies. As Emerson remarks in the *Memoir*, Fuller "sympathized with all the sensible people who were tired of hearing all the young ladies of Boston *sighing like furnace after being beautiful*."[97] In one of the meetings, Fuller asked all of the participants to bring a written definition of "beauty" to class. One of Fuller's students brought an essay which stated: "We could never see it all if we had it not within us."[98] As the student—the recorder to the conversations—explains, Fuller seemed to approve of this idea, and indeed, it was the realization of her fundamental pedagogical principle. In "Likeness to God" (1828), William Ellery Channing had taught his parish: "We see God around us, because he dwells within us."[99] Fuller turns this principle into a form of practice that is refracted through socio-institutional conditions. Beauty expresses a person's potential; but to realize the poetic life, it is necessary to overcome existing restrictions imposed on universal beauty.

Fuller did not only seek to transcend the limits of the field thematically, but ultimately attempted to confront the problem of her elite status and the concomitant question of her limited audience. Her Boston conversations were careful attempts to use the literary conversation as a form of self-authorization for women. As Charles Capper has suggested, Fuller's conversations "initiated the growth of a countercultural tradition in American women's culture."[100] However, if Fuller's conversations pursued a "clear feminist reform agenda,"[101] structurally and thematically, this agenda was not yet refracted through the class conditions on which the educational system ultimately rests. Fuller strove to reinstate women as Women Thinking, as intellectuals who could establish themselves in the field of education and potentially reach beyond it, but her cultural reform efforts left the class conditions of intellectual autonomy unchallenged. Fuller's early educational efforts remained largely cultural and were a far cry from her later political radicalism. Yet, they still created alternative discussion platforms and helped Fuller build her reputation as a public intellectual, thereby preparing the ground for her increasingly public role.

With the institutionalization of Romanticism through conversational practice, literary expression became a semi-public practice, involved with the politics of the educational field. Both Alcott's and Fuller's schoolroom reform was directed at a middle-class audience. After the campaign against his school had succeeded, Alcott insisted that "the institutions of education have been, to some degree, modified thereby. Abroad, also, they have been made a subject of inquiry" (*AJ* 1:268). Indeed, the mutuality practiced in the classroom pushed for more comprehensive reform and for a reconceptualization of education as popular education. While not yet a form of public critique, the institutionalization of literary conversations moved Transcendentalism into an institutional position from which to develop their more comprehensive reform projects.

For Alcott this prospect ended with Fruitlands, the ambitious but ultimately failed utopian community. Fuller fulfilled Alcott's aspirations with her move into newspaper journalism and away from New England. It is fitting that Fuller's transition to the popular press eventually occurred through one of the informal networks so important for the institutionalization for Romantic education. One of the women attending her conversations was Mary Greeley, who, enthusiastic about the conversations, recommended Fuller to her husband as a reviewer for the *New-York Tribune*.[102] This propelled her into the realm of popular education, which for her soon would become inextricably linked to a class-based understanding of education and intellectual labor. But it was the literary conversation which helped established the link between literary practice and institutional reform that would drive the Transcendentalist reform project.

# NOTES

1. James Freeman Clarke, *The Letters of James Freeman Clarke to Margaret Fuller*, ed. John Wesley Thomas (Hamburg: Cram, De Gruyter, 1957), 129.

2. Megan Marshall, *Margaret Fuller: A New American Life* (Boston: Houghton Mifflin Harcourt, 2013), 96; Charles Capper, *Margaret Fuller: An American Romantic Life*, 2 vols (New York: Oxford University Press, 1992, 2007), 1:195.

3. Anon., "A. Bronson Alcott," *American Journal of Education* 6 (1877): 233.

4. Scholarship still tends to denigrate Alcott's *Conversations with Children on the Gospels* (published in two volumes in 1836 and 1837) as a school record that sounds "as if it had been written by a particularly relentless dramatist of the absurd." Barbara Packer, "The Transcendentalists," *The Cambridge History of American Literature*, vol. 2: 1820–1865, ed. Sacvan Bercovitch (Cambridge: Cambridge University Press, 1995), 329–604. In addition, Alcott is often described as a flawed inspiration for Emerson, whose value consists largely of showing Emerson the dangers of hyperidealism. While Emerson is presented as the balanced Man Thinking, Alcott abandoned "the world of sensation and secondary causes—and with them, the realms of art, nature, friendship, work." Joseph Urbas, *Emerson's Metaphysics: A Song of Laws and Causes* (Lanham: Lexington Books, 2016), 146. If for Frothingham and others, Alcott was a public intellectual in 1837, it is irritating that in the twenty-first century these assessments have been all but forgotten. In 2013, it is possible to describe Alcott in 1836 as the "aging faun of the Transcendentalist inner circle" and a potential "charlatan." Marshall, *Margaret Fuller,* 99. Wonderment at whether Alcott was "aging" at age thirty-six aside, the point here is the ease with which these verdicts are passed. Thus, scholarship which mentions Alcott in passing can rest content stating that "[o]utside his immediate circle of sympathetic but more practical friends, he became something of a joke." Kyle Gann, *Charles Ives's Concord: Essays After a Sonata* (Urbana: University of Illinois Press, 2017), 211. Such false assessments not only ignore that Alcott influenced English school reformers and was publicly visible to the degree where a reviewer stated that Alcott was the author of Emerson's *Nature*. This repeats a sentiment of Alcott's own time—but ignores how that sentiment was tied to a larger attempt to contain a prominent voice of group of young reformers that challenged institutional authority. In the nineteenth century it was for a long time possible to seriously argue that Alcott was among the leading Transcendentalist. He was admired by Channing and Emerson, and Frothingham stated that "[i]n 1837 Mr. Alcott—not Mr. Emerson—was the reputed leader of the Transcendentalists, none being more active than he in diffusing the ideas of the Spiritual Philosophy, and none being so uncompromising in his interpretations of them." Octavius Brooks Frothingham, *Transcendentalism in New England: A History* (Philadelphia: University of Pennsylvania Press, 1972 [1876]), 257–8.

5. Simmons, "Margaret Fuller's Boston Conversations," 203.

6. Mary Loeffelholz, *From School to Salon: Reading Nineteenth-Century American Women's Poetry* (Princeton: Princeton University Press, 2004), 4.

7. N. Ray Hiner, "Children in American History," *Rethinking the History of American Education*, ed. William J. Reese, John L. Rury (New York: Palgrave Macmillan, 2008), 169.

8. Hiner, "Children in American History," 169.

9. See David Dowling, *Emerson's Protégés: Mentoring and Marketing Transcendentalism's Future* (New Haven: Yale University Press, 2014).

10. Clarke, *Letters*, 129

11. Amos Bronson Alcott, *The Doctrine and Discipline of Human Culture* (Boston: James Munroe and Co., 1836), 7–8.

12. Alcott, *Doctrine and Discipline*, 10.

13. James Nehring, *The Practice of School Reform*, 33.

14. John Pierpont, *The American First Class Book, or, Exercises in Reading and Recitation* (Boston: William B. Fowle, 1823), 3.

15. Robert Ramble, *The Table Book: Comprising the Tables Necessary to Be Committed to Memory at an Early Age* (Philadelphia: Desilver, Thomas & Co., 1836), 5.

16. Despite the important archival work of Odell Shepard, Joel Myerson and Larry Carlson, all of these resources have been thoroughly understudied. Alcott's journals have been published in excerpts by Odell Shepard in 1938. Shepard's edition has been supplemented by Joel Myerson's and Larry A. Carlson's transcription of the complete diaries of 1836–1838 in *Studies in the American Renaissance* in the 1970s and 1980s. In addition, the journals of Alcott's formative educational years up to 1834 have been made available only in the rudimentary form provided by Shepard. This lack of attention particularly to his early journals has obscured how thoroughly Alcott was involved in the intellectual networks of the time.

17. Alcott sent out his journals for 1834 and 1835 to Emerson, who read them while working on *Nature* (see *AJ* 1:45, fn. 4). As Emerson writes in his journal: "*I have read with interest Mr. Alcott's Journal* in MS for 1835. He has attained at least to a perfectly simple & elegant utterance. There is no inflation & no cramp in his writing" (*JMN* 5: 170). Later, Alcott sent out individual pages of his journal to Margaret Fuller. Alcott understood the semi-public nature of his journals, as he often revised earlier entries in the journal in order to revisit his position on pedagogy and social affairs. He unequivocally embraced the public character of his journals when he published a large portion of it in the *Dial* in April 1842. Amos Bronson Alcott, "Days from a Diary," *Dial*, April 1842, 409–37.

18. Eve LaPlante, *Marmee & Louisa: The Untold Story of Louisa May Alcott and Her Mother* (New York: Simon and Schuster, 2012), 66.

19. *Liberator*, April 13, 1833, 59.

20. John Hayward, *The New England Gazetteer: Containing Descriptions of All the States, Counties and Towns in New England*. 6th ed. (Concord, NH: Israel S. Boyd and William White, 1839), n.p.

21. See LaPlante, *Marmee & Louisa*, 64.

22. In his *Memoir*, Samuel Joseph May's relates that Prudence Crandall received "a bright young colored woman of fine character as a pupil" in 1833. Samuel Joseph May, *Memoir of Samuel Joseph May*, ed. Thomas James Mumford (Boston: American Unitarian Society, 1876), 148.

23. LaPlante, *Marmee & Louisa*, 66.

24. Odell Shepard, *Pedlar's Progress: The Life of Bronson Alcott* (Boston: Little, Brown, and Co. 1938), 140.

25. Alcott, *Doctrine and Discipline,* 9; my emphasis.

26. Alcott, *Doctrine and Discipline,* 10. Alcott writes that Jesus's methods and teachings—and this means his conversations—were *"popular.* Instead of seeking formal and austere means, he rested his influence chiefly on the living word, rising spontaneously in the soul, and clothing itself at once, in the simplest, yet most commanding forms" (9, my emphasis).

27. *Teacher's Guide and Parent's Assistant,* vol.1, ed. J. L. Parkhurst (Portland: Shirley and Hyde Printers, 1827), 192.

28. Qtd. in Frank B. Sanborn, *Bronson Alcott: His Life and Philosophy,* vol. 1 (Cambridge, MA: John Wilson and Son, 1893), 75–6.

29. Amos Bronson Alcott, "Primary Education," *American Journal of Education* 3, no. 1 (1828): 26; my emphasis.

30. Alcott, "Primary Education," 27.

31. Amos Bronson Alcott, *Observations on the Principles and Methods of Infant Instruction* (Boston: Carter and Hendee, 1830), 3.

32. Alcott, *Observations,* 4; my emphasis.

33. Alcott, *Observations,* 4, 12. Alcott's emphasis on order has also been discussed as a historical residue that shows even in Alcott's progressive pedagogy. Karen Sánchez-Eppler has argued that Alcott's emphasis on play in "Observations on the Principles and Methods of Infant Instruction" is still characterized by a suspicion about play as play. As a consequence of a "culture's general view of leisure as besmirched by infant depravity and original sin." Karen Sánchez-Eppler, *Dependent States: The Child's Part in Nineteenth-Century American Culture* (Chicago: University of Chicago Press, 2005), 153. Alcott makes sure to grant children's play a "designed purpose." Alcott, *Observations,* 5. Yet, while Alcott's early writings are indebted to a Protestant spiritualism that constantly seeks to deemphasizes matter, and the bodily enjoyment of children (which he nevertheless prominently discusses), Alcott actually emphasizes that play should be channeled into "active duty, and expressed in character" (7); it should become a reflected form of everyday practice.

34. Amos Bronson Alcott Papers, MS Am 1130.12, Houghton Library, Harvard University, 1834, 130. hereafter cited parenthetically as *Alcott MS,* with year and page number. In some places of Shepard's excellent yet incomplete edition one could get the sense that Alcott's schools were rejected for pedagogical reasons. In April 1834, when he still kept a school in Philadelphia, Alcott reports that two pupils would be withdrawn from his school by their mother (*AJ* 1:42). In fact, however, the decision was purely practical since the mother needed a school at which her children "could remain during the day" (*Alcott MS* 1834, 109). Alcott's school simply could not provide this service. To be sure, Alcott was quite unforgiving as he explained that these children would be "sacrificed to their mother's indisposition" (109). The "shortsight" of their parents (112) had propelled the two boys into the arms of a restrictive, unimaginative educational system, into a school "where cunning, (as is almost always the case in our institutions of education,) was made the usual motive of action" (120). The "good convictions of his mind, will die away" (111). But Alcott's lack of understanding for the mother's pragmatic decision should not obscure the fact that the decision in fact had nothing to do with his pedagogical methods, but with the lack of resources of Temple School.

35. In 1829, Alcott already aimed to link himself to Boston's intellectual elite. Alcott was particularly fascinated with William Ellery Channing, but included Emerson, George Ripley, James Russell Lowell, and Octavius Frothingham in his list of intellectuals with whom he would like to establish, or maintain, ties: "To be favored with the acquaintance of such men as these is a privilege which I am desirous to obtain and secure" (*AJ* 1:19).

36. On the importance of Peabody in establishing Transcendentalism's literary network, see Bruce Ronda, *Elizabeth Palmer Peabody: A Reformer on Her Own Terms* (Cambridge, MA: Harvard University Press, 1999).

37. See Shepard, *Pedlar's Progress*, 177.

38. Anon. "About Mr. Alcott's School," *Parley's Magazine* 4 (1836): 131.

39. For the best discussion of Alcott's pedagogical theories, see Schmid, *Educating New England,* 65–126.

40. Elizabeth Peabody points out the influence of the environment on the mind in her *Record of a School*: "Believing that the objects which meet the senses every day for years, must necessarily mould the mind, he felt it necessary to choose a spacious room, and ornament it, not with such furniture as only an upholsterer can appreciate, but with such forms as would address and cultivate the imagination and heart." Thus the exterior had to be remodeled so as to allow for the drawing out of the individual's potential—a thought that could easily be applied to larger social issues. Elizabeth Palmer Peabody, *Record of a School: Exemplifying the General Principles of Spiritual Culture* (Boston: James Munroe, 1835), 1.

41. Peabody, *Record of a School*, 2.

42. Alcott, *Observations*, 8–10.

43. Amos Bronson Alcott, *Conversations with Children on the Gospels*. 2 vols. (Boston: James Munroe and Co., 1836–37), 1:262.

44. Lawrence Buell, *Literary Transcendentalism: Style and Vision in the American Renaissance* (Ithaca: Cornell University Press, 1973), 100.

45. Alcott, *Doctrine and Discipline*, 7.

46. Alcott, *Doctrine and Discipline*, 14.

47. Alcott writes down these thoughts after the Transcendental Club "had some general conversation on the present state and prospects of Harvard University. Nearly every member of our circle had graduated at this college, and was quite familiar with the spirit of the institution" (*Alcott MS* 1839, 747).

48. Roger Bellin, "Argument: The American Transcendentalists and Disputatious Reasons." PhD diss., Princeton University, 2011.

49. Ralph Waldo Emerson, *The Letters of Ralph Waldo Emerson,* ed. Ralph L. Rusk and Eleanor M. Tilton, 10 vols. (New York: Columbia University Press, 1939–1995), 7:245.

50. The first meeting of the Transcendental Club was held on September 8, 1836. The first volume of *Conversations* was published on December 23, 1836.

51. Sigourney saw poetry as a "most valuable adjunct, in moral and religious instruction" which "enwraps the new-born existence,—as the song of the bird breaks the slumber of morning." Lydia Howard Sigourney, *Poems for Children* (Harford: Canfield & Robins, 1836), 5, 7.

52. Alcott, *Conversations*, 1:229.

53. The first meeting of the Transcendental Club was held on September 8, 1836. The first volume of *Conversations* was published on December 23, 1836.

54. Larry A. Carlson, "Bronson Alcott's 'Journal for 1837' (Part One)." *Studies in the American Renaissance* (1981): 94.

55. In: Nehring, *The Practice of School Reform*, 40.

56. "Alcott's *Conversations on the Gospels*," *Christian Examiner* 5, no. 2 (1837): 252; my emphasis.

57. *Christian Examiner*, November 1837, 260; original emphasis

58. James Freeman Clarke, "Mr. Alcott's Book and the Objections Made to It," *Western Messenger* 3, no. 4 (1837): 683. For a closer examination of the reactions to Alcott's views, see Larry A. Carlson, "Those Pure Pages of Yours': Bronson Alcott's *Conversations with Children on the Gospels*," *American Literature* 60, no. 3 (1988): 451–60.

59. Buckingham, Postscript to "To Fathers and Mothers," *Boston Courier*, March 30, 1837, 1.

60. Anon., "To Fathers and Mothers," *Boston Courier*, March 30, 1837, 1.

61. Anne C. Rose, *Transcendentalism as a Social Movement,* 72–9.

62. See David M. Robinson, "'A Religious Demonstration': The Theological Emergence of New England Transcendentalism." *Transient and Permanent: The Transcendentalist Movement and Its Contexts*, ed. Charles Capper and Conrad Edick Wright (Boston: Massachusetts Historical Society, 1999), 49–72.

63. Buckingham, Postscript, 1.

64. Joseph T. Buckingham, "Alcott's Conversations on the Gospels," *Boston Courier*, May 11, 1837, 1.

65. Carlson, "Bronson Alcott's "Journal for 1837" (Part One)," 98.

66. Frank Matteson, *The Lives of Margaret Fuller: A Biography* (New York: Norton, 2012), 122.

67. As early as in 1830, in a letter to Roberts Vaux (July 27, 1830), a Philadelphia lawyer active in the abolitionist movement, Alcott described the complicated web of publishing relations: "I have thought best to publish the Essay in the Christian Examiner—one of our most liberal periodicals—and after its appearance in that form, to have a few hundred copies struck off, for more individual distribution. This can be done at a trifling expense; and, in the carefulness of our Booksellers here, about what they publish, seems all that I can venture to do." Amos Bronson Alcott, *The Letters of A. Bronson Alcott*, ed. Richard L. Herrnstadt (Ames: Iowa State University Press, 1969), 17–8.

68. Nehring, *The Practice of School Reform*, 110.

69. Anon., "A. Bronson Alcott," 230.

70. Christina Zwarg, *Feminist Conversations: Fuller, Emerson, and the Play of Reading* (Ithaca: Cornell University Press, 2018), 3.

71. Sandra M. Gustafson, "Choosing a Medium: Margaret Fuller and the Forms of Sentiment," *American Quarterly* 47, no. 1 (1995), 34–65.

72. Mary Ryan, *Women in Public Between Banners and Ballots, 1825-1880* (Baltimore: Johns Hopkins University Press, 1990), 4. Charles Capper explains

that while secondary schools for women were established on a large scale, these schools were "intended to prepare young women for only two occupations: that of wife and mother or, in the case of middle- or lower-middle-class single girls, teaching." Charles Capper, "Margaret Fuller as Cultural Reformer: The Conversations in Boston," *American Quarterly* 39, no. 4 (1987): 510.

73. Nancy Beadie has shown that the institutionalization of women's education went hand in hand with the attempt to put their existence on a secure financial basis. Nancy Beadie, *Education and the Creation of Capital in the Early American Republic* (Cambridge: Cambridge University Press, 2010), 21, 32. Equally, women educators tried to secure "guarantees of permanent institutions" by seeking funding from the state or local government, just like men's academies. Barbara Miller Solomon, *In the Company of Educated Women: A History of Women and Higher Education in America* (New Haven: Yale University Press, 1985), 18.

74. See Laraine R. Fergenson, "Margaret Fuller in the Classroom: The Providence Period," *Studies in the American Renaissance* (1987): 131–42; Frank Shuffelton, "Margaret Fuller at the Greene Street School: The Journal of Evelina Metcalf," *Studies in the American Renaissance* (1985): 29–46.

75. Capper, *Fuller* 1:209.

76. Annie Russell Marble, "Margaret Fuller as Teacher," *Critic* 43 (October 1903), 339.

77. Granville Ganter and Hani Sarji, "'May We Put Forth Our Leaves': Rhetoric in the School Journal of Mary Ware Allen, Student of Margaret Fuller, 1837–1838," *Proceedings of the American Antiquarian Society* 117 (2007): 68.

78. Ralph Waldo Emerson, *Selected Lectures*, ed. Ronald A. Bosco, Joel Myerson (Athens: University of Georgia Press, 2005), 47.

79. Cayton, *Emerson's Emergence*, 180.

80. Emerson, *Selected Lectures,* 46.

81. Emerson, *Selected Lectures,* 45–50.

82. Emerson, *Selected Lectures,* 45–6.

83. For Fuller, the speech also constituted an occasion to position herself as a teacher and intellectual. Fuller sent Emerson a leaf from her journal "to give Mr Alcott" (*L* 2:136–7), just as she sent Alcott a copy of a leaf from her journals which discussed Alcott's teaching method (*L* 2:143). Alcott was not only a lasting didactic influence on Fuller; he also emerges as a figure of cultural authority that authenticated Fuller's emergent public persona. In a letter to Alcott from June 27, 1837, in which Fuller reported the responses to Emerson's speech, she underlined her status as an independent intellectual by stressing how she had become a successful teacher on her own: "Particularly do I feel the importance of your attempts to teach the uses of language and cultivate the imagination in dealing with young persons who have had no faculties exercised except the memory and the common" (*L* 1:287). As Frank Shuffelton usefully points out, "this is one of Fuller's first letters to Alcott, and she clearly wished to impress him as a correspondent." Shuffelton "Margaret Fuller," 30.

84. Judith Strong Albert, "Margaret Fuller's Row at Green Street School: Early Female Education in Providence, 1837-1839," *Rhode Island History* 42 (1983): 43–4.

85. Capper, *Fuller,* 1:232.

86. Rowson's *Spelling Dictionary* (1807) features a programmatic preface in which Rowson demands that children must be "early habituated to connect ideas with words." Instead of only memorizing the words, thereby naturalizing their meaning and function, Rowson asks students to commit words to their memory while at the same time understanding that the truly important linguistic operation is that words signify ideas. Rowson's demand that children must be taught to "associate ideas" goes against the dominant educational practice of rote learning. Instead of being subjected to this "very serious ill," consisting of a routine of memorization and recitation, children must be educated in the conscious use of words. But for Rowson this technical pedagogical question is connected with the mechanical, routinized reproduction of social hierarchies. Rote learning is "a mechanical kind of reading" consisting in the repetition a "string of words." Susanna Rowson, *A Spelling Dictionary* (Boston: John West, 1807), iii–iv.

87. In Ganter and Sarji, "May We Put Forth" 87.

88. In Ganter and Sarji, "May We Put Forth," 88.

89. Ganter and Sarji, "May We Put Forth," 64.

90. In Ganter and Sarji, "May We Put Forth," 83.

91. Capper, *Fuller* 1:249.

92. In Shuffelton, "Margaret Fuller," 44.

93. Catherine C. Mitchell, ed., *Margaret Fuller's New York Journalism: A Biographical Essay and Key Writings* (Knoxville: University of Tennessee Press, 1995).

94. Capper, *Fuller* 1:292.

95. Christel-Maria Maas, *Margaret Fullers transnationales Projekt: Selbstbildung, feminine Kultur und amerikanische Nationalliteratur nach deutschem Vorbild* (Göttingen: Universitätsverlag Göttingen, 2006), 106.

96. In 1840 Fuller translated Schlegel's speech "Über das Verhältnis der bildenden Künste zur Natur" (1807). Schlegel's speech was intimately connected to the founding of an institution of which Schlegel was to become part, the Bavarian Academy of Fine Arts. In Athenaeum fragment no. 125, August Wilhelm and Friedrich Schlegel address how in the sphere of arts and sciences cooperation would realize the Romantic spirit: "Vielleicht würde eine ganz neue Epoche der Wissenschaften und Künste beginnen, wenn die Symphilosophie und Sympoesie so allgemein und so innig würde, daß es *nichts Seltnes mehr wäre*, wenn mehre sich gegenseitig ergänzende Naturen gemeinschaftliche Werke bildeten." Schlegel, "Fragmente," 33.

97. Fuller, *Memoirs,* 2: 155.

98. Simmons, "Margaret Fuller's Boston Conversations," 209.

99. William Ellery Channing, *The Works of William E. Channing, D. D.*, 2nd ed. 6 vols. (Boston: James Munroe and Co., 1843), 3:235.

100. Capper, *Fuller,* 1:306.

101. Tiffany K. Wayne, *Woman Thinking: Feminism and Transcendentalism in Nineteenth-Century America* (Langham: Lexington, 2005), 18.

102. See Hans Bergmann, *God in the Street: New York Writing from the Penny Press to Melville* (Philadelphia: Temple University Press, 1995), 37; Daniel Walker Howe, *Making the American Self: Jonathan Edwards to Abraham Lincoln* (Oxford: Oxford University Press, 1997), 224.

*Chapter 3*

# The Problem of Audience

*Nineteenth-Century Periodical Culture and Romantic Popular Education*

It is hard to overstate the importance of periodicals for both American Romanticism and nineteenth-century educational discourse. In the 1830s and 1840s, "technological innovation in print production and distribution soared in response to surging demand brought by growing literacy rates and an increasingly sophisticated urban populace."[1] Seizing this opportunity, the Transcendentalists carried their struggle for a creative, individualized education into the literate public. Periodicals served a twofold function. On the one hand, the print market was the place where most educational discussions occurred. On the other hand, periodicals also established intellectuals themselves as authorities in the educational discourse. Gaining access to periodicals, then, promised to advance the Romantic educational project by establishing a public platform from which the Romantics could speak to a wider audience.

That the Transcendentalists considered journalism an opportunity to educate the public shows in the programmatic prefaces of the *Dial*, the *Boston Quarterly Review*, and, most prominently, in Fuller's comments on her work for the *New-York Tribune*. For these periodicals, the reader was not a passive recipient of instructions, but a social agent whose full creative and critical potential awaited realization. They addressed, as Emerson had it, "a new-born class long already standing waiting for this voice & wondering at its delay."[2] The periodical market promised to bridge the gap between institutional education and the literate public. The expansion of print culture was supposed to ignite a revolution in everyday practice: "What rebellion has been nurtured within us by the ugly confinements to which artificial life and education have accustomed us!", John Sullivan Dwight exclaims in July 1840 when he programmatically declares the importance of aesthetic education in the *Dial*'s first issue.[3]

The Romantic educators had to redefine intellectual labor and the position of the intellectual as part of a broader public yet to be created. But the more the Transcendentalists tried to move into broader political discussions with their periodicals—first with Brownson's *Boston Quarterly Review*, then with the influential *New-York Tribune*—the more they had to confront the limits of education. Not only did questions of exclusion and opportunity figure prominently in their educational debates, the medium of the periodical also forced them to question their own relationship with their implied audience. Was the readership really "standing waiting for this voice"? In his "Conversations with a Radical," a fictive dialogue published in the *Boston Quarterly Review* in January 1841, Orestes Brownson described the situation of the progressive as that of a misunderstood, marginalized prophet:

> He who has the misfortune to think in advance of his contemporaries, and to desire a good for mankind beyond that already attained, is necessarily unpopular. If he venture to translate his thoughts into words, and his hopes into actions, he will be branded a jacobin, an agrarian, a leveller, an anarchist, or at best, a visionary, who, though he may mean well, is to be pitied, not trusted.[4]

Brownson cultivates an outsider rhetoric that only partially reflects the Transcendentalists' position in the field. While facing backlashes from the establishment, they had become an established group with their own access to publication venues, cultural institutions, and with their own pedagogical system and tradition in 1840. Still, the question was how to transcend the limits of the educational system and how to systematically disseminate Romantic educational ideas through the mass media of the time.

The question of popularity and outreach became increasingly significant for the Transcendentalists' future. In the second half of the 1830s, the movement had gained access to literary institutions and had to consider how to use them. Fourierism, Associationism, and other forms of early socialist and communalist theories were intensely received by the Romantics.[5] In the early 1840s, many New England intellectuals joined reform projects and utopian communities like Brook Farm. These communalist theories demanded a reconsideration of what education meant. As a 1846 lead article, "Education," in the *Harbinger*, states: "Does it [the state] throw open the doors of its academies, its universities, and say to all, 'Enter freely,' The knowledge, the culture, you long for is yours!' By no means."[6] In a way that continues Alcott's collective, conversational education, the members of Brook Farm considered their school and their utopian community an experiment in "integral education": the whole man, Emerson's figure for the individual who has transcended modern alienation, is "bearing his true part with others who are naturally dependent, each the complement of all the rest, and they all of him."⁷ But while Brook Farm enacted a successful school project and asked important questions about privilege and accessibility, it also remained a local project. Nineteenth-century periodicals promised to overcome the limited influence of local educational experiments. Practiced in the field of nineteenth-century periodical culture, Romantic education not only became a public literary practice but also increasingly confronted its own contradictions and limits.

## THE CRITIQUE OF PRIVILEGE: THE *BOSTON QUARTERLY REVIEW*

Orestes Brownson was the first Romantic reformer to address the limits of education. Brownson, a member of the Transcendental Club, was sympathetic of Romantic reform efforts, but stressed the class limitations of educational reform. He supported his fellow Transcendentalists' educational efforts while at the same emphasizing that education cannot become universal in a class society. For Brownson, the various calls for "universal education" were justified, but blind to the category of class and hence restricted to the middle class rather than truly universal. In "Union and Progress" (1838), Brownson emphasizes that "the perfection and happiness of entire [*sic*] Humanity" can only occur by parting with tradition: "The press, the lyceum, the pulpit have been all held in servile bondage to the taste of the past."⁸ Of course, Brownson's generalization does not address the fact that the periodical landscape wasn't simply dominated by "the press," but was sufficiently diverse to allow for a variety of niche and avant-garde periodicals such as his own, the *Boston Quarterly Review* (1838–1842). Nevertheless, Brownson's point was clear: Romanticism needed to become more rigorous and radical in its demands.

Brownson's career illustrates the intersection of educational reform, literary market, and political institutions. He not only founded and edited the *Boston Quarterly Review*, a journal for literature, philosophy, religion, and politics, but was also frequently its sole contributor. As George Ripley writes in the *Dial*, Brownson's journal "stands alone in the history of periodical works. It was undertaken by a single individual, without the cooperation of friends, with no external patronage, supported by no sectarian interests, and called for by no motive but the inward promptings of the author's soul."⁹ As quixotic as such an effort may have initially seemed, the periodical not only established Brownson's position in the intellectual field; he also managed to elicit a fiery response from the Democratic Party when he demanded radical reform. As the speculative bubble of Jacksonian America burst in 1837, banks failed and unemployment rate dramatically increased. The result was a depression that lasted into the 1840s. In response to the crisis, Brownson published "The Laboring Classes." In the two-part essay, first published in the *Boston Quarterly Review* and later as a single pamphlet, he argued that if the class antagonisms of modern capitalism were not overcome, class warfare was inevitable. To prevent this scenario, Brownson demanded a radical, partially Jacksonian program of redistribution.

Brownson's *Boston Quarterly Review* was one of the major journals of the 1830s and more widely circulated than, for instance, the *Dial*. In his seminal study of Transcendentalist periodicals, Clarence Gohdes has pointed out that "no figure stood out more prominently before the eyes of the educated public in New England than the singular Orestes A. Brownson, whose *Boston Quarterly Review* aroused discussion, and opposition, in the pages of many of its fellow journals."[10] A prolific writer, with a vast array of interests, Brownson came to the group from the outside, constantly navigating the lines between intellectual discourse and working-class politics.[11] Brownson had established his reputation with a number of politico-philosophical treatises, including *New Views of Christianity, Society, and the Church* (1836), consecrated by Perry Miller as part of the Transcendentalists' annus mirabilis. In *A Discourse on the Wants of the Times* (1836), Brownson had clearly laid out the socialist position he would adhere to until his conversion to Catholicism in 1844: "We are, indeed, levellers, but *we would level upward, not downward*. We see no one too high, too great, too learned, too refined, or too good, and the extent of our radicalism is to bring up the low, and place every man, if possible, in such a position, that he can fulfil the great end of his being."[12]

The *Boston Quarterly Review* helps us understand the possibilities and impasses of nineteenth-century popular education and the concomitant problem of audience structure. A look at the comprehensiveness of Brownson's *Boston Quarterly Review* illustrates the multiple contexts in which popular education was discussed and located. In "American Literature," an essay which reviews Emerson's oration at Dartmouth College in 1838, Brownson argues that popular education is predicated on the speaker's or writer's ability to communicate in universally understandable terms:

> [The scholar's] own attainments cannot far outrun the capacity of the masses to comprehend and relish his speech. It follows from this, that the first requisite to the scholar's success, in this country, is to make the whole nation a nation of readers, and to secure to the great mass of people the leisure necessary to attend to the subjects on which the scholar discourses.

The piece is an essay on American literature, and therefore Brownson relates the question of art and aesthetic experiences to the question of who has access to them. He explicitly addresses the class conditions which underlie the intellectual field: "Now in this country the whole people must constitute the audience, the public. The scholar here must speak not to a clique, a coterie, but to the entire nation."[13] Brownson calls for universal education; but he also draws attention to the fact that the Romantics were often preaching to the converted.

Brownson's periodical is particularly helpful in framing the conditions of popular education about whose dangers he warns from an egalitarian perspective. In one of his "Literary Notices," a regular column in the *Boston Quarterly Review*, Brownson reviews Catherine Maria Sedgwick's *Means and Ends: Or, Self-Training* (1839). Sedgwick's self-help manual for young women was sanctioned by the Massachusetts Board of Education and published in its "Juvenile Series." Sedgwick seeks to instill a sense of religious, moral duty in her readers. This religious self-reliance is supposed to help women "attain your own rights, and the firm and independent position for which Providence destined you." As opposed to Alcott, who relied on children's agency, Sedgwick sees self-help as a guided effort to interest "[y]oung persons" who have "nothing to say" on the subject of education.[14] Brownson singles out this exemplary model of New England educational writing to engage in the same dialectic critique that characterizes all his writings on education: he stresses the potential universality of education, while pointing out its role in the reproduction of class privilege. Consequently, he lauds Sedgwick's comments on education but criticizes her book for its "tendency to overrate moral and religious education as distinct from intellectual education."[15] For Brownson, this is a symptom of all "popular writers on education." "The rage is for what is called the education of the heart," he writes. Sheer sentimentalism, although widely popular, is a form of withdrawal that contributes neither to the individual nor to social progress. Sedgwick is therefore "not truly democratic," just like popular education in its present state is not truly popular for Brownson.

The popularization of educational reform proved problematic if, as in Sedgwick's case, popularity did not coincide with the critique of economic privilege. Brownson voices a similar objection to Alcott, but simultaneously acknowledges that Alcott's uncompromising, systemic critique was much closer to an egalitarian popular education. Brownson's main contention is with Alcott's pantheistic tendency to equate God with his creation, rather than as distinct from it. For Brownson this pantheism necessarily leads to a form of individualism. From his theological perspective, Brownson's objection may be sound; but he fails to see how, practically, Alcott's pantheistic education occurred in a collective space. Instead of reading Brownson's essay as an accurate assessment of Alcott's theory and practice (which Brownson himself admits is not his aim), it is more important to see that he criticizes Alcott for a perceived form of mysticism and an overemphasis on spontaneity and intuition for the same reason that he rejected Sedgwick's sentimentalism.[16] But Brownson also acknowledges that Alcott "will never sacrifice what he holds as truth, virtue, manhood, independence, to popular opinion, to a sickly taste, or a heartless conventionalism." Although he fails to discuss how Alcott always situates the individual in a collective, conversational space, he rightly points out that Alcott's emphasis on the individual produces the demand for institutional change: "he thinks that the aim of our systems of education, whether private, public, domestic, or social, is too low."[17]

Just like Alcott, Brownson proposed and circulated an uncompromising vision of spiritual equality. But Brownson introduces class politics as necessary to realize this vision. His most famous essays were the two installments on "The Laboring Classes." A review of Thomas Carlyle's *Chartism* (1840), the first essay is an eerily prescient proto-Marxist manifesto and a socioeconomic diagnosis of the nineteenth-century United States. But it is also a text on education. Brownson admonishes his reader that the revolution needs careful preparation, lest it slide into chaos: "We are not ready for this measure yet. There is much previous work to be done, and we should be the last to bring it before the legislature. The time, however, has come for its free and full discussion. It must be canvassed in the public mind, and society prepared for acting on it."[18] In this context, Brownson establishes that Carlyle's thought is characterized by a structural contradiction: on the one hand, Carlyle rightly advocates the necessity for universal education in order to improve humanity. On the other hand, he views the masses as immature and in need of control. Brownson shows that the category of "universal education" may easily be used to obscure the educational field's exclusionary mechanisms and its stabilizing function for the status quo. Universal education is a desirable aim, but it is not a "sovereign remedy for the evils of the social state as it is." Instead, true universal education can only be realized when the social ills have been corrected so as to provide the opportunity for education for everyone: "We have little faith in the power of education to elevate a people compelled to labor from twelve to sixteen hours a day, and to experience for no mean portion of the time a paucity of even the necessaries of life, let alone its comforts."[19]

The idea that education is the solution to economic problems is at best misguided, and at worst intentionally employed in the name of preserving social hierarchies: "A swarm of naked and starving urchins crowded into a schoolroom will make little proficiency in the 'Humanities.'"[20] The swarm here evokes a threat and a potentially transformative force alike. As Scott Henkel has shown, the swarm was a widely used metaphor in nineteenth-century American literature. Whether meant to denigrate the masses as politically immature and in need of control or as a powerful democratic force, the phrase signaled that "a writer has judged that a swarm of people, protestors, or picketers has sufficient power not just to be noticed, but to be dealt with in some way."[21] Brownson taps into this discourse in order to establish the laboring classes as a political agent, and in order to strip the middle class of the illusion that they represent a universally valid position. The middle-class intellectual does, however, exemplify a creativity that should be universally available—not in the sense that everyone should become a professional intellectual but in the sense that everyone is free and economically secure to a degree where they can consider realizing their creative potential. The point of "The Laboring Classes" is that the educated middle class "has done nothing for the laboring population, the real *proletarii*."[22] For Brownson, education can establish "the bonds of brotherhoods" and elevate the laboring classes; but it remains incomplete as long as the economic system remains unchanged.

How explicitly Brownson introduced class as a determining category of education becomes evident when contrasting his program with William Ellery Channing's reform Unitarianism. In "The Laboring Classes," Brownson explicitly references Channing's "Address on Self-Culture" (1838). In his lecture, Channing addressed the "working classes,"[23] with the lecture room attended mostly by artisans, mechanics, and laborers.[24] Channing was indeed dedicated to helping the laboring classes.[25] In the early 1830s, he had sided with the Workingmen's movement to fight imprisonment for debt. In his lecture, Channing rhetorically links himself to the concerns of his audience by stating that he "belong[s] rightfully to the great fraternity of working men." But this rhetorical figure establishes precisely the false universalism which Brownson criticized, particularly when Channing seems to define hardships rather cynically as occasions for self-culture: "Hardships are not on this account to be sought for. [. . .] But when God sends them, they are noble means of self-culture, and as such, let us meet and bear them cheerfully. Thus all parts of our condition may be pressed into the service of self-improvement." Channing, however, is aware of the workingmen's struggles, and thus chooses to finish his speech on a critical, even rebellious note: "Were I, on visiting a strange country, to see the vast majority of the people maimed, crippled, and bereft of sight, and were I told that social order required mutilation, I should say, Perish this order."[26] While appealing to his audience's class status, he ultimately avoids discussing the class conditions of education. Symptomatically, rebellion is imagined in a "strange country," far away from the concrete social contradictions of nineteenth-century Boston. It is such an idea of self-culture as false universality which Brownson rejects: "Self-culture is a good thing, but it cannot abolish inequality, nor restore men to their rights."[27]

In "The Laboring Classes," Brownson shows that any popularization of education must reconnect the educational field to its economic and social conditions. Only thus is it possible "to draw out into free activity the whole faculties of his mind," as he had it in his essay on education.[28] Brownson's project introduces class into the public discourse not only as a category of political analysis, but also as the underlying basis of education. Brownson sees first signs for the establishment of universal education in the United States: "Genius has come out of the cloister and the university, and creates in the ship-yard and the smithy, reasons on 'change, and sings in the music of the axe, the hammer, and the loom, giving dignity to labor and the empire of the world to the laborer."[29] But this change must remain incomplete as long as the class system that maintains and produces the structures of the educational field prevents the realization of the principle of self-reliance. With his *Boston Quarterly Review* Brownson conceptualizes the divide between the universal idea of education and a class society.

Brownson used the literary market in a way that allowed him to become a prominent voice on literary, educational, and political affairs. He was a successful public provocateur in Emerson's sense, an intellectual and activist who challenged the orthodoxies of the liberal readership that dominated the literary market and nineteenth-century periodicals. "The Laboring Classes" was also a form of political practice, as it intervened in an ongoing political debate. Brownson advised the workingman to vote for Martin Van Buren, whom he saw as the most hopeful candidate to ameliorate their lot. As Merrill D. Peterson has shown, the Whigs readily took up "The Laboring Classes" as "a disclosure of the true 'class war' doctrine of the Democratic party, and Van Buren allegedly blamed the Brownson pamphlet for his defeat."[30] In a close presidential race between Van Buren and William Henry Harrison, the Whigs eventually "distributed the article in hopes that the Democrats would hand themselves with their own words."[31] This was not what Brownson had intended, and it is symptomatic of the problem of reaching, and educating, an audience, which characterizes the entire Romantic project. At the same time, the history of Brownson's essay also shows how influential and political Romanticism had become. All of Brownson's political interventions, however, occurred in the name of his Romantic idea: to reform society "so that free scope shall be given to every man to unfold himself in all beauty and power, and to grow up into the stature of a perfect man in Christ Jesus."[32]

## IMAGINED AUDIENCES: THE *DIAL*

In many ways, the *Dial* was a catalyst for the Transcendentalists' educational endeavors. The *Dial* was instrumental in the institutionalization and marketing of the informal literary network that Transcendentalism had been before. It was a medium that channeled their individual writings and diffuse set of cultural practices, which ranged from published treatises to educational reform and lyceum lectures, into a collective public display of the movement. In his classic study of the Transcendentalists' periodicals, Clarence Gohdes has pointed out that the *Dial* was instrumental in showcasing the group's works: "so far as literature is concerned, the closest approximation to concerted activity upon the part of the people who were known as transcendentalists in their own day, was attempting to bring their views before the public by means of periodicals."[33] Before the *Dial*, the group had not spoken as a group. True, Brownson had tried to establish a collective mouthpiece and to define the movement's public role with his *Boston Quarterly Review,* whose first issue appeared in January 1838, one and a half years before the *Dial* was published. But the *Boston Quarterly Review* was hardly a collaborative effort; Brownson was the main contributor to his journal, which was consequently seen as the periodical of someone affiliated with the Transcendental Club, but not as the platform of a movement.

Brownson himself saw the need for a collaborative Romantic periodical. In October 1839, he had suggested to broaden the scope of the *Boston Quarterly Review* to include the other Transcendentalists. Alcott, Fuller, and Emerson, however, feared that the magazine, while generally respected and one of the most important periodicals in nineteenth-century New England, would not be inclusive enough to accommodate all writers affiliated with the new school of philosophy and literature.[34] Instead, they decided to found a new periodical, the *Dial*. Emerson was supposed to edit the journal, mostly because he was the most famous Romantic writer at this point. When Emerson refused to become the editor, and after a series of coincidences, Fuller assumed the editorial duties.

Such an ambitious project required a reconsideration of target audiences. The *Dial* was confronted with the problem of audience from the outset because of its diverse content. The *Dial*'s first editorial, written by Emerson, distinctly outlines the magazine's aims and the conditions of educational reform. Emerson proclaimed the periodical's intention to give voice to

> the strong current of thought and feeling, which, for a few years past, has led many sincere persons in New England to make new demands on literature, and to reprobate that rigor of our conventions of religion and education which is turning us to stone, which renounces hope, which looks only backward, which asks only such a future as the past, which suspects improvement, and holds nothing so much in horror as new views and the *dreams of youth.*

Speaking for Fuller and himself, he states that the "revolution" that was taking shape in New England cut across "different classes": "Those who share in it have no external organization, no badge, no creed, no name." Not only did the *Dial* represent a diverse group of young, rebellious voices; these voices also intended to speak to a readership that shared in the dream of a young, rebellious multitude. Hence the declaration that the *Dial* "cannot now prescribe its own course"; the editors think that "[a]ll criticism should be poetic; unpredictable; superseding, as every new though does, all foregone thoughts, and making a new light on the whole world."[35] This programmatic statement captures the core belief of the young, rebellious Romantics, just as much as it realistically assesses that its readership still needed to be identified.

Emerson's editorial delineates an ideal discursive situation, in which mutual education is conducted as an open, ever evolving process, comparable to the literary conversations which projected a universal participatory culture. But Emerson also addresses how this situation first needs to be established through literary practices. The *Dial*'s first editorial accordingly revolves around the question of group membership and audience. Emerson's editorial makes concrete reference to the conflict between tradition and youth, which gained currency in the 1840s,[36] thus underscoring the magazine's rebellious avant-garde character. But as much as Emerson stressed the periodical's iconoclastic character, the *Dial*'s democratic ideals were, as Adam Tuchinsky has argued, "articulated in a cultural vacuum, with an audience that would remain, as it was rendered in the first number, a fantasy."[37] It is true that Emerson's conception of the *Dial* uneasily wavered between a commitment to educating a broad public and the assumption that the journal existed for a select few. In a letter to Margaret Fuller of April 1840, Emerson discussed his plan for the periodical's strategy:

> With the old drowsy Public which the magazines address, I think we have nothing to do;—as little with the journals & critics of the day. If we knew any other Journal, certainly we should not write this. This Journal has a public of its own; its own *Thou* as well as I; a new-born class long already standing waiting for this voice & wondering at its delay.[38]

This is not a concrete analysis of available audiences. Emerson here simply presupposes an audience which still needed to come into being. At the same time, however, this fictional audience is understood as a "class" in the making. This imagined class, of which the Transcendentalists are supposed to be but the harbingers, shaped Emerson's and Fuller's editorial strategies.

The *Dial* can be understood as a project of literary education that was supposed to turn the fantasy of a young, rebellious audience into reality. In the pages of the *Dial*, literature, in its broad Romantic definition as a dialogue that cuts across genres, was understood as an occasion to converse with the literate public. In his "Orphic Sayings," published prominently in the *Dial*, Alcott propagated his ideal of the teacher as someone defending "his pupils against his own personal influence."[39] Interaction needed to be made the fundamental principle of Romantic education. This was true for the schoolroom, the lecture platform but also, as we have seen in Emerson's editorial, for the periodical.

Elizabeth Palmer Peabody articulated the fundamental Romantic educational concept in the pages of the *Dial*: "As long as Education is made the object of an Institution in society, rather than is the generating Idea of society itself, it must be apart from life."[40] But the more universalistic and comprehensive the idea of education was understood, the more urgent the question of the *Dial*'s audience became.[41] The *Dial*'s own contributors saw the problem of an avant-garde magazine trying to reach a broad audience. After the *Dial* was first published in 1840, the Transcendentalist periodical quickly built a reputation as a lofty, idealist philosophical magazine which primarily catered to a privileged elite. In his caricature "Moral Influence of the Dial" (c. 1840–1844), Christopher Cranch humorously depicts what to many readers appeared the periodical's solipsistic tendencies (figure 3.1).

The caricature portrays the philosophy of contemplation and self-culture as an excuse for self-indulgence. It shows a male character who is waiting for inspiration—or, more problematically still, perhaps has already found it as evidenced by his reclining posture and his presumably wine-induced contentment. Meanwhile, his wife is cleaning the boots that literally allow him to walk, although the character does not seem inclined to leave his retreat in the foreseeable future. Instead of heeding the *Dial*'s call to perpetual improvement, the man has abandoned reading and learning altogether: he has put aside his copy of the *Dial*, which rests comfortably under the bed.

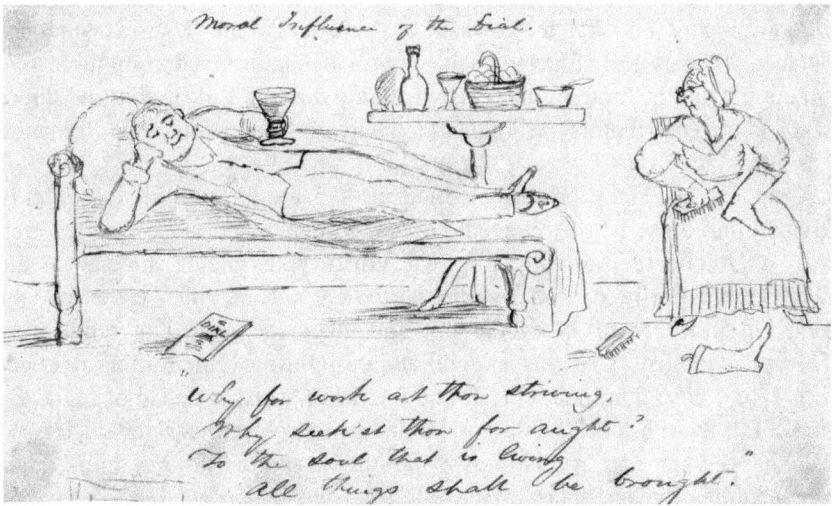

**Figure 3.1  Caricature of the Transcendentalist as impractical idealist.** Christopher Cranch, "Moral Influence of the Dial." MS Am 1506 (2), Houghton Library, Harvard University.

Apparently, the Emersonian maxim that "in going down into the secrets of his own mind [the scholar] has descended into the secrets of all minds" (*CW* 1:63) conveniently justifies privilege.

Cranch's caricature captured the possible excesses of Romantic education and the priority of the self.[42] In doing so, Cranch pointed to a tension inherent in the *Dial*'s editorial politics. Did not the *Dial*, with its avant-garde habitus, which deliberately sought distinction from popular periodicals, contradict Romanticism's universalist, egalitarian thrust? But the caricature is also significant because of its publication history, or rather, the lack thereof. Cranch's caricature did not appear in print but can be found only in his private notebooks, which may have circulated among friends but which were not meant for the literate public. Cranch insisted that these sketches "were really for the private amusement of [James Freeman] Clarke and myself and a few other Emersonians; and there was never any intention that they should be known to the public. I always took pains to repudiate any Philistine idea that anything like ridicule was here attempted."[43] Cranch was himself affiliated with the Transcendental Club. He filled in as the editor of James Freeman Clarke's *Western Messenger*, and his poems, most notably "Correspondences," were in fact published in the *Dial*. The fact that Cranch never published the sketch suggests that he was too much aware of what was at stake with the *Dial* to risk public ridicule. This was a justified expectation as his sketches would have easily been instrumentalized by the journal's vocal critics. For Cranch as for others it was clear that their own careers as well as the future of American Transcendentalism, the avant-garde "new school" in philosophy, religion, and literature, to a large degree hinged on the success of the *Dial*. Cranch's withholding of his sketch shows how strategically the Transcendentalists pursued their project. Emerson's ideal of a dynamic, open communicative situation could be brought into existence only through a clear editorial direction and the contributors' willingness to share in the creation of the Romantic position.

Cranch's hesitancy proved justified, as the literate public was quickly divided into those who embraced the *Dial*'s agenda and those who rejected it as an intellectual abomination. The vitriol and ridicule directed at the *Dial* was partially caused by the periodical's sometimes esoteric content, but much more so by the role the magazine played in reinforcing Transcendentalism's role as a social and cultural movement in an intellectual field whose dominant elite found itself in permanent need of legitimation. Matthew Philpotts has argued that "a literary journal is characterized by what we can identify as its own 'common habitus,' the defining ethos which unites the members of its 'nucleus' and which acts as 'a unifying and generative principle' for their cultural practice."[44] The most important generative principle to emerge from the *Dial* was that of collaboration:

a collectively produced magazine by an avant-garde movement, which emphasized conversation and exchange. As an intervention in the literary market, the periodical displayed and institutionalized an elusive cultural movement. The *Dial* codified a collective form of Romantic authorship. It enabled the group to position themselves in the literary market and to respond effectively to the often harsh criticism leveled at individual figures such as Emerson and Alcott.

The *Dial*'s role and reception remained relatively consistent throughout the five years of its publication. Initial reception varied between praise, particularly in Horace Greeley's *New-Yorker*, and fervent, often polemical criticism. Major periodicals such as the *Christian Examiner*, the *New-York Review*, and the *Knickerbocker* ignored or ridiculed the periodical, but in the larger Boston area, the *Dial* was relatively well received.[45] Some of the criticism focused precisely on the lofty tendency that Cranch had highlighted in his sketches. A Harvard graduate simply referred to the *Dial* as "trash."[46] It quickly became evident that the responses addressed the position of the movement rather than individual authors, as the most fervent criticism often included the claim that an essay or poem was "too transcendental." It is true that Alcott's "Orphic Sayings" were often singled out for their esoteric otherworldliness and supposed unintelligibility.[47] While scholarship still tends to represent Alcott as the contributor that singlehandedly disgraced the *Dial*, it is important that these responses cannot be easily linked to individual authors. Emerson's poetry was as much the aim of ridicule as Alcott's "Orphic Sayings." Conversely, while Alcott was frequently criticized as otherworldly dreamer, Christopher A. Greene, editor of the Providence-based *Plain Speaker*, criticized everyone else in the *Dial* for not being practical enough: "Save A. Bronson Alcott, none that I know, of the 'Dialists' are actively engaged in the Great Reforms of the day."[48] The subject under discussion was not simply Emerson or Alcott or Fuller—it was the group as such.

The *Dial* understood itself as part of the Romantic educational mission. But, more importantly perhaps, it laid the ground for further educational projects by making visible the group as such. With its disappearance from the print market in 1844, it may have seemed that the journal's critics had rightly predicted its futility. This assessment still resounds in contemporary scholarship. Critics tend to emphasize the radically innovative content of the *Dial*, which, while important for intellectual history, "was too radical and outré for most of the intellectual establishment and yet too scholarly and esoteric for the masses" so that the *Dial* supposedly "spoke primarily to its own coterie."[49] Despite the groundbreaking work that has been done by Clarence Gohdes, Joel Myerson, and others, the *Dial* is still often viewed as a mildly interesting, complimentary source for scholarship on American Romanticism, a journal with esoteric tendencies, representative of, and limited to, a relatively small group of Boston and Concord intellectuals; a journal, that is, without any lasting influence outside New England's literary market. In one of the most important studies of Romantic periodicals in the United States, Adam Tuchinsky has argued that Margaret Fuller's real entry into the literary market occurred when she became the literary editor of the *New-York Tribune* in 1844. Tuchinsky contrasts the *Tribune*'s cosmopolitan, populist editorial politics with what he considers a delusional form of populism at work in the *Dial*, which Fuller had edited prior to her engagement with the *Tribune*: "The *Dial*'s populism, mixed with a curious elitism, was of an imagined and symbolic sort; a perspective and not a practice, it was a counterculture in which disaffected elites identified with the 'manual' classes as a kind of literary protest against commercial materialism and bourgeois respectability."[50]

While it is true that the *Dial* operated on a symbolic level different from the *Tribune*'s more immediate political agenda, it was in fact very much a form of social practice. The *Dial* represented a relatively small segment of the cultural elite, but its audience was larger than is usually assumed. The periodical had up to 300 subscribers. In addition, it was sold through Elizabeth Palmer Peabody's bookstore, by then a central cultural location in New England. Perhaps most significantly, the journal was widely reviewed and discussed in influential Boston and New York newspapers and magazines from the *Christian Examiner* to the *New-Yorker*, with excerpts from the *Dial* frequently reprinted in these periodicals. When approaching the *Dial* for its role in the constitution of a movement through the literary market, it achieves an eminently practical function. Theodore Parker, himself affiliated with the Transcendentalists, retrospectively described the periodical as that of "the movement party": "The movement party established a new quarterly, the *Dial*, wherein their wisdom and their folly rode together on the same saddle, to the amazement of lookers-on."[51] What is significant here is that Parker not only captures the literate public's response to the *Dial*—that it was situated somewhere between esoteric folly and deep philosophical insight—but that he defines it as the mouthpiece of a movement.

The *Dial*'s numbers were not spectacular nor was its influence if compared to Brownson's *Boston Quarterly Review*. But assessments which judge the *Dial* solely based on its subscription numbers and longevity (or lack thereof) neglect its true influence. The *Dial* helped establish an intellectual position (that of the Transcendentalist) in the literary market, which made publicly visible both the group and its Romanticism. As opposed to the *Christian Examiner*, it did not propagate the universal authority of the minister over moral and social affairs. Instead, it featured aphoristic pieces like Alcott's which were supposed to inspire the reader to self-cultivation, and, later, political writings such as Margaret Fuller's seminal feminist treatise "The Great Lawsuit" (1843). It is true that "[i]n practice, the *Dial*'s elite aesthetic and radical cultural politics were irreconcilable and ultimately it struggled to close the gap between its populist pretensions and its avant-garde marginality."[52] But by accepting this struggle as part of the Romantic reform project, the *Dial* positioned Romantic education in the public realm. Fuller's engagement with the popular *New-York Tribune* can be seen as the logical next step in the evolution of Romantic education.

## POPULAR EDUCATION: THE *NEW-YORK TRIBUNE*

In 1844, Margaret Fuller took a leap into popular journalism. Two years before she would embark on the journey to Europe that would eventually turn her into a political radical, Fuller accepted a position as the literary editor of the *New-York Tribune*, whose editor, Horace Greeley, had been a champion of the *Dial* throughout. Greeley had printed one of the final reviews of the *Dial* on the *Tribune*'s front page on April 27, 1844. Greeley's eulogy was a celebration of the *Dial*'s cause: "'The Dial' holds the same relation to our current periodical literature that the Poet or Prophet does to the money-getting, pork-producing characters of everyday life [. . .]. We know no magazine more valuable to a strong mind, more fascinating to a refined one, than that before us." Greeley then humorously relates how someone supposedly stole the *Dial* from his desk because it was in such high demand in his office, and how he therefore has to quote from memory. The point, however, is made clearly: "If this work should close now, they must be heard and felt through other channels."[53] Greeley concludes his article by offering to backorder copies from the *Dial* for his readership. As a major figure in the New York publishing market, who had already helped popularize Emerson's works, Greeley's promotion of the *Dial*, and consequently of Transcendentalism as a movement, was an important step forward in popularizing Romanticism.

Fuller's journalistic essays for the *Tribune* were concrete interventions, written with reference to specific social and political situations for one of the most popular newspapers in the United States. Fuller's move to the *Tribune* was a logical extension of her previous educational work. In "American Literature," published in her *Papers on Literature and Art* (1846), Fuller underscores the conceptual continuity between her Boston conversations and her literary journalism: "Newspaper writing is next door to conversation, and should be conducted on the same principles."[54] But conversational circles and print media had different audiences, and consequently Fuller asserts that "the most important part of our literature, while the work of diffusion is still going on, lies in the journals, which monthly, weekly, daily, send their messages to every corner of this great land, and form, at present, the only efficient instrument for *the general education of the people.*"[55] Fuller's "mutual education" was not a refutation of her earlier educational efforts; it was her large-scale attempt to realize what Alcott had established at Temple School: an empowering, collective Romantic practice that helped individuals realize their creativity.

Fuller's turn to journalism forced her to address what she saw as a "neglect of popular education" (*SGD* 255). Her earlier pedagogical activities, from her positions at Amos Bronson Alcott's Temple School and Hiram Fuller's Greene Street School to her Boston conversational circles for women, although comprehensive in principle, were limited to the middle class.[56] When Fuller moved to Horace Greeley's *New-York Tribune*, she was forced to reconsider her conception of literature and literary conversations. Greeley's *Tribune* was not a niche periodical like the *Dial* or many other nineteenth-century avant-garde periodicals. An influential figure in the New York print market, Greeley had successfully established a progressive alternative to New York's sensationalist newspapers: "The Tribune, as it name imports, will labor to advance the interests of the people and promote their moral, social, and political well-being." To maintain a broad readership, he encouraged his writers to appeal to a general audience. His aim was to reach not only a politically interested audience but also the "welcome visitant at the family fireside."[57]

One of the most influential nineteenth-century newspapers, the *Tribune*'s editorial policy forced Fuller to address the gaps in how she conceptualized education. Working with a relatively benevolent editor whose agenda combined literary style and mass appeal, Fuller saw the newspaper as the perfect occasion to make an uncompromsing version of her Romanticism more broadly available.[58] In her early *Tribune* essays, written during her time in New York, she began to link literary essay, cultural critique, and social diagnosis. As David Robinson has demonstrated, in these years, "Fuller became much more disquieted by the social injustices arising from class divisions, and much more concerned about practical ways to redress those inequalities."[59] Similarly, Jeffrey Steele has argued that she "shifted attention to the *collective* existence of urban dwellers."[60] In the process, Fuller also redefined her understanding of literature as an educational tool. During her time in New York, Fuller met Georgiana Bruce, a social reformer who had lived at Brook Farm. Bruce showed her the journals of women imprisoned in Sing Sing. As Robert N. Hudspeth has demonstrated, Fuller was impressed with the results: "In her own mind what she had accomplished in Boston was being repeated at Sing Sing. What she saw in Providence was political, public, abstract, anonymous. What she found at Sing Sing was deeply personal, very concrete and human."[61] Morever, the use of journals as a reform tool for prisoners reinforced Fuller's growing conviction that literary expression should serve a social function.

Fuller's own reports on New York's tenements forced her to consider questions of poverty more directly. In "Our City Charities," an essay that was prominently placed on the *Tribune*'s title page, Fuller outlines how the unsolved social issues corrupt the promise of natural beauty: "The aspect of Nature was sad; what is worse, it was dull and dubious, when we set forth on these visits. The sky was leaden and lowering, the air unkind and piercing, the little birds sat mute and astonished at the departure of the beautiful days which had lured them to premature song." The Romantic promise of beauty forces the observer to address poverty: the pauper establishments "admonish us of stern realities, which must bear the same explanation as the frequent blight of Nature's bloom. They should be looked at by all, if only for their own sakes, that they may not sink listlessly into selfish ease, in a world so full of disease."[62] The essay displays moral outrage but lacks the systemic social diagnosis that characterizes Fuller's later dispatches. It ultimately advocates political measures and a form of charity but does not address the possibility of economic redistribution. As Judith Mattson Bean and Joel Myerson have observed, "living in New York increased Fuller's interest in theories of economics and social class and convinced her of the need for a literature that mediated between classes."[63] "Mediate" is a key term as Fuller essentially advocates class reconciliation. She does not yet regard class as an analytical category; consequently, she portrays the intellectual's authority as unaffected by, and dissociated from, social struggle: "we longed and hoped for that genius, who shall teach how to make, of these establishments, places of rest and instruction, not of degradation."[64] As much as she sought to connect her Romanticism to social reform, her New York reform writings remain indebted to what Monika Elbert has termed "communal mothering."[65]

Fuller would struggle with questions of inequality, social reform, and public appeal throughout her New York years. Perhaps the most important step toward structurally incorporating class into her concept of intellectual labor and education occurred in a Christmas 1844 column that once again appeared on the *Tribune*'s title page. The essay is also Fuller's most complex reflection on how to make Romantic ideals available to the public before her time in Europe. Mirroring her analysis of the New York tenements, Fuller presents education as a system of mutual relations that transcends, rather than questions, class distinctions. Teachers should teach according to the maxim "what they have they must bestow." In this sense, teaching would foster a voluntary redistribution of cultural but not economic capital: "If a girl for instance, who has only a passable talent for music, but who, from the advantage of social position, has been able to gain thorough instruction, felt it her duty to teach whomsoever she knew that had such a talent, without money to cultivate it, the good is obvious."[66] As Paula Kopacz has suggested, "Fuller argues for a form of education that is natural, charitable, and generous—the responsibility for all to share what they have learned."[67] Fuller refers to this exchange as a form of "justice"; but justice here, perhaps fittingly for a column concerned with the potential meanings of Christmas, is located in a "utopia not so far off." This utopia is not yet mediated through the class relations from which it emerges, but rather transcends them, leaving in place the exclusionary mechanisms that prevent access to Romantic education.

Fuller's conception of how class impacts education and intellectual work remained ambivalent before her journey to Europe, but the necessary parameters to recalibrate Romantic education were firmly established. Her New York essays illustrate what is at stake in the concept of popular education. The rift between an exclusive creativity and its egalitarian pedagogical potential would lead Fuller to realize that the reformist intellectual's work is contingent on others for its final realization. Her political transformation, which had been shaped by Greeley's impact, the influence of the Young America movement, and her journalistic forays into the slums of New York, was aided by the various ties she formed in Europe. Rebecca and Marcus Spring, Fuller's traveling companions, were Quakers supporting abolitionism and the struggle against poverty. In Paris, she encountered socialism and the Saint-Simonists. The Polish poet Adam Mickiewicz was favorably disposed toward the Transcendentalists and proved a lasting influence.[68] The most important influence was certainly Giuseppe Mazzini, who shaped Fuller's view of the Italian revolution and the educational measures required to achieve equality. These cultural and political influences led her to reconsider the relationship between Romanticism and education and the intellectual's role in popularizing Romantic ideals. Her true radicalization, however, occurred with the acceptance that social class is inevitably tied to the intellectual's position and that before Romantic education could succeed, it needed to confront the fact that the majority was excluded from the Romantic life.

Fuller wrote her *New-York Tribune* dispatches between 1846 and 1850 during her stay in Europe. These dispatches are densely crafted yet accessible literary essays.[69] To understand how Fuller repositioned the intellectual in these dispatches, we must bracket her personal life and closely observe the formal strategies through which she decentered her own individuality into structural questions. Fuller uses the popular travelogue genre for a self-reflexive meditation on the class underpinnings of Romantic education.[70] This formal strategy appears in her first European dispatch, written in August 1846 and published in Greeley's *New-York Tribune* a month later. That the piece reflects the mid-century state of Romanticism rather than simply records the author's experience is evident when we compare the published text to the corresponding notes in Fuller's letters. In a letter to her mother from August 16, 1846, she had complained that the voyage to Europe was truly dispiriting: "I enjoyed nothing on the sea," she complains; only the "sight of land delighted" her (*L* 4:225). In the dispatch, by contrast, Fuller's malaise ultimately leads to an inspiring, Romantic sight: "In the evening, when the wind was favorable, and the sails set so that the vessel looked like a great winged creature darting across the apparently measureless expanse, the effect was very grand" (*SGD*, 39). Fuller's published account includes only retrospectively the elation that the sea allegedly produces; this retrospective narrativization adds a social symbolism to her personal experience, turning the text into a meditation on how an individual must work to achieve Romantic elation. When she states that "for such a spectacle one pays too dear; I far prefer looking out upon 'the blue and foaming sea' from a firm green shore" (*SGD*, 39), she refers not only to the unsettling passage but also to the bewildering social privilege that she had observed on the ship.

Fuller builds this first dispatch around the tension between social privilege and the experience of beauty and grandeur, which precedes her discussion about the necessity to popularize Romanticism. The dispatch's structure reflects this tension. As she does in many dispatches, Fuller starts with general observations on nature's beauty then discusses social and cultural conventions in Europe before revisiting her initial, aesthetic observations based on her analysis of social and institutional structures. Before resuming the discourse about the experience of beauty when she describes the "highly romantic" and "charming" sights that Europe offers to her "trans-Atlantic eyes" (*SGD*, 48), she paints a complex portrait of England as both progressive and poverty-ridden, which symbolically illustrates the tensions that prevent true beauty from being realized. Fuller is particularly interested in how these conditions affect art and culture. In England, she claims, there is a strong tendency to understand art as practical engagement. Francis Legatt Chantrey's paintings, for instance, exemplify how the artist is "engaged with his fellow-citizens in practical life"; they display "a fine conception of an individuality which might exist, if it does not yet" (*SGD*, 48). She envisions the artist as an exemplary teacher involved in a public cultural exchange. Only popular Romanticism, the essay suggests, can fulfill the movement's aspirations to realize the poetic life for everyone.

In this initial dispatch Fuller redefines the role of the intellectual as an engaged yet distant observer while simultaneously expanding education beyond the safe borders of the middle class. Given the author's use of her public persona as a vehicle for these discussions, the dispatch must also be understood as an assessment of her career up to this point. When Fuller shows herself impressed by the reach of the Liverpool's Mechanics' Institute—a Benthamite night school for working-class adults—she is particularly pleased with the fact that the director refers to an essay on "self-improvement" that the *Dial* had published. Fuller's use of the *Dial* in this context signals both the continuity of her earlier Romantic efforts with the dispatches and her enthusiasm about the practical expansion of the magazine's small readership into the reform project that the Benthamite night school for the working class represented. Although she fully links theory and practice only later, her first dispatch carefully addresses the tensions between intellectual work, social reform, and social reality, displaying a consciousness of the obstacles to universal education. Fuller presents Romanticism not as a grand experience—as Emerson had done when he describes himself becoming a "transparent eyeball" (*CW* 1:10)—but as the promise of such an experience, a promise which Ian Balfour has called "a call oriented toward a present that is not present."[71]

Fuller's dispatches link her reconsideration of Romanticism as a popular, practical reform effort to a critical assessment of the intellectual's role in this transformation. This reflection becomes particularly obvious when she uses European intellectuals as mirror images through which she can redefine her own role. In a dispatch published on January 5, 1847, Fuller introduces preacher and political figure George Dawson as an "educator of the people" and as a "friend of the people, in the sense of brotherhood, not of social convenience or patronage" (*SGD,* 85). A public figure in England who had acquired a reputation for his widespread appeal, Dawson popularized the writings and ideas of Emerson and Carlyle.[72] When, in the next dispatch, Fuller discusses British intellectuals such as Wordsworth and De Quincey, she introduces them as instances of a "past dynasty in the progress of thought" (*SGD,* 88). While they are brilliant intellectuals, these artists are not yet able to overcome "the shocking inhumanity of exclusiveness" which prevented the "treasures created by English genius" from being "used for the benefit of all" (*SGD,* 88). Dawson, by contrast, may be intellectually and creatively inferior to these Romantic geniuses, but he represents a new generation of intellectuals who seek to popularize literary excellence as a source of inspiration. Fuller finds here united what remains asunder in America. None of the British reformers can match William Henry Channing's eloquence or his ability to communicate "spiritual beauty," nor can they reach Theodore Parker's "fullness and sustained flow." But "in power of practical and homely adaptation of their thought to common wants, they are superior to the former, and all have more variety, finer perceptions and are more powerful in single passages than Parker" (*SGD,* 86). Their popularization of Romanticism resonated with Fuller's desire to reconcile literary excellence with the wide distribution of learning.

Dawson and the English reformers captured Fuller's attention because they translated intellectual brilliance and broad public appeal into a form of popular Romantic education. But it was Giuseppe Mazzini who would epitomize the organic Romantic intellectual. Mazzini was the role model, but also the narrative mediator, who enabled Fuller to theorize Romantic reform. Fuller's ninth dispatch was published on February 19, 1847. Just like the first dispatch, the essay commences with the observer's position. Fuller is no longer on the ship that brought her to Europe, but writing in a lonely chamber, from which she can set her "mind [. . .] to *action*" (*SGD*, 93; emphasis added). As the narrative continues, Fuller transforms the meaning of "action" from intellectual activity into cultural and political work. Starting once more with a discussion of art in London, she works her way from cultural life in England to more political territory. She complains that German revolutionary (and intellectual) Ferdinand Freiligrath leads a dire existence in his English exile, then observes that "here returns naturally to my mind one of the most interesting things I have seen here or elsewhere" (*SGD*, 98), Mazzini's school for children. Equally exiled from his native country, Mazzini's school opened in London in November 1841. Whereas Freiligrath leads a comparatively miserable life in exile, Fuller argues, "the misfortunes" of Mazzini's Italy "have only widened the sphere of his instructions" (*SGD*, 99).

When Fuller presents Mazzini as the preliminary hero of her narrative, she also introduces class as an analytical category. The redefinition of Romanticism as a class-inflected practice manifests most clearly when Fuller depicts Mazzini's school as the epitome of Romantic reform, an attempt to realize "an individuality which might exist, if it does not yet" (*SGD*, 48). Contrary to all predictions that such a school would not attract hard-working youths who had been "sold by their families into virtual slavery," more than 200 students voluntarily enrolled in Mazzini's school.[73] The curriculum ranged from Italian, geography, arithmetic, and drawing to English, chemistry, and mechanics. The project was funded by the British public, among them prominent figures such as Lord Shaftesbury and the Carlyles. Besides Fuller, by then an established public figure, such notables as Charles Dickens also visited the school.[74] As a result, not only did Mazzini become an increasingly well-known public figure, he also forced the Catholic Church to open a rival school to counter the impression that it lacked interest in the poor.[75] Fuller presents the successful Mazzini as the embodiment of the engaged, organic intellectual: he is an "educator of the people" (*SGD*, 85) who connects idealism, education, and reform.

The more concrete her depictions of education become, the more pronounced her emphasis on class. Fuller introduces class as a seminal category not only related to educational and social reform but also for assessing the role of the cultural critic who is economically separated from those he or she seeks to teach. Moreover, the poor increasingly receive an active role in the reform process. She is impressed by the teachers' voluntary efforts to dedicate their "minds capable of great thoughts, large plans and rapid progress" to redeem the boys (and the few girls who attended the school) "from bondage and gross ignorance" (*SGD*, 99). But it is the "poor Italian boys" whom she envisions as "the leaven that leavens the whole mass" (*SGD*, 99). Mazzini does not speak for the poor, she emphasizes, but he creates a space in which they can find and articulate their own voices, thereby enabling them to help "this universal interest in all nations and place where Man, understanding his inheritance, strives to throw off an arbitrary rule and establish a state of things where he shall be governed as becomes a man by his own conscience and intelligence" (*SGD*, 98).

Fuller presents Mazzini's school as the realization of Romanticism's egalitarian impulse; it is the logical, class-conscious continuation of the Romantic conversational model, a class-conscious Temple School for the masses. If Mazzini serves Fuller as the prototypical Romantic educator, he also becomes a vehicle for rewriting the genealogy of Transcendentalism. In the same dispatch, she contrasts Mazzini's egalitarian approach with Thomas Carlyle's authoritarian conversational style. Fuller turns from Mazzini's school to an evening with Carlyle, who dominates what should have been a hierarchy-free conversational space: "Carlyle allows no one a chance, but bears down all opposition. [. . .] He does not converse—only harangues" (*SGD*, 101). The two episodes seem to coincidentally occur around the same time; but of course Fuller has a strategic reason for placing them next to each other. The dispatch constitutes a watershed moment in Fuller's reassessment of Romanticism, as Mazzini and his egalitarian school supersede the authority of one of the forefathers of New England Transcendentalism. Emerson had offered a similar, at least implicit, critique when he "democratized Carlyle's elitist claim that outstanding individuals possess power inaccessible to the common man, who should be content to be ruled by them given their superiority."[76] But Fuller not only criticizes Carlyle; she replaces him with Mazzini, and hence exchanges what she considers an elitist version of Romanticism with an egalitarian one. By doing so, Fuller brings the Romantic rebellion against tradition to its logical conclusion.

Fuller's dispatches conceptualize how social class affects the ideal of self-reliance. The politicization of her Romanticism is most evident in her dispatch from March 1848. Fueled by the worker's revolution in France that dethroned Louis Philippe, and encouraged by the successful revolutions in Milan and Venice, Fuller not only includes a poem by fellow transcendentalist Christopher Cranch, thereby thematically linking poetic prophecy and history, but inscribes history and politics into the Romantic subject's bodily constitution. The apparently innocuous dispatch establishes a structural link between Fuller, the intellectual, Italy's winter climate, and the people's revolutionary agency. "It is long since I have written; my health entirely gave way beneath the Roman Winter," Fuller writes (*SGD*, 209). Of course, the reason for this illness was her pregnancy; but the private experience becomes a type of a larger historical cycle. This winter now "seems past" and "Nature seems in sympathy with the great events that are transpiring" (*SGD,* 209). Interiority, nature, and politics are interdependent. Romantic typology no longer simply refers to the individual's ability to read nature's signs as an occasion to experience beauty; it now refers to a promise that awaits historical realization.

The difference between individual constitution and historical development collapses here. The intellectual can no longer stand apart from political affairs that reflect a class structure on which his or her authority rests. But as with Mazzini's school, the teacher does not simply instruct his students. While Fuller declares her solidarity with the Italian revolution, and while she stresses that she wants to convince her American audience of the necessity to embrace a class-based socialism, she also turns the intellectual into a cultural worker reliant on the agency of the people. One key passage illuminates her thinking:

> It is vain to cry Peace, peace, when there is no peace. The news from France, in these days, sounds ominous, though still vague; it would appear that the political is being merged in the social struggle: it is well; whatever blood is to be shed, whatever altars cast down. Those tremendous problems MUST be solved, whatever be the cost! That cost cannot fail to break many a bank, many a heart in Europe, before the good can *bud* again out of a mighty corruption. To you, people of America, it may perhaps be given to look on and learn in time for a preventive wisdom. You may learn the real meaning of the words FRATERNITY, EQUALITY: you may, despite the apes of the Past, who strive to tutor you, learn the needs of a true Democracy. You may in time learn to reverence, learn to guard, the true aristocracy of a nation, the only really noble—the LABORING CLASSES. (*SGD,* 211)

Fuller articulates the revolution in Romantic terms—the blossoming of the bud into a flower promises a social revolution. The image also evokes her earlier dispatch, in which she stated that Mazzini's school planted "a grain of mustard-seed" (*SGD* 100), a seed that contains a promise that will now "bud again out of a mighty corruption." Scholarship has not yet grasped the complexity of this seminal passage. Although critics have frequently emphasized Fuller's radical comments on the laboring classes, it is at least misleading to state that she "would not really return to this final statement [on the laboring classes] in a pronounced way," or to declare that "class questions [. . .] would largely remain the blind spot in Fuller's view of the Risorgimento."[77] Jeffrey Steele, by contrast, has taken the passage more seriously and remarked that this commentary is a "startling declaration of a new class consciousness."[78]

Indeed, once we ask about the carrier of this consciousness, the passage becomes fundamentally important for understanding the potential and limits of popular Romantic education.

In this precise case, Fuller's target audience needed little political persuasion, as progressive Americans generally viewed the Italian Revolution favorably, and in her final dispatch Fuller comments on how "it is refreshing to read how cordially America sympathized" (*SGD,* 316).[79] Conversely, Fuller did not assume that she spoke for, or even represented, the laboring classes. Such an imagined alliance between middle-class intellectuals and laboring classes would simply be a false reconciliation of the tensions built into popular reform journalism.[80] Fuller consciously writes in the literary mode, as opposed to Marx and Engels, for instance, whose *Communist Manifesto* explicitly urges workers to unite and thus seeks to intervene in the period's political struggles. Fuller develops a class-conscious assessment of the intellectual's role as a cultural worker. Consequently, she sees as her dispatches' true provocation not so much her defense of the revolution, but her affiliation with the "brigands" and "vagabonds" who help forward the Italian Revolution (*SGD,* 305): "I know that many 'respectable' gentleman would be surprised to hear me speak in this way" (*SGD,* 305). While she affirms that intellectuals can provide a valuable form of consciousness-raising, she acknowledges that education cannot solve a socioeconomic problem, although it can certainly help educate the poor to become self-reliant and acquire a form of political agency, as Mazzini's comprehensive Romantic efforts illustrate. Popularization, however, ultimately means that the educators accept their dependency on the subject they represent. True mutuality means surrendering agency to a collectively created political Romanticism.

Fuller's literary conversations, then, bring the logic of Romantic education, the great project of "mutual education," full circle. Her connection between literary complexity and popular appeal is precisely the journalistic aesthetics which Greeley saw at the heart of effective nineteenth-century journalism. In her final dispatch, written sometime after the fall of the Roman Republic, Fuller reconnects Romanticism, the individual, and history, distinctively linking class condition and Romantic idealism: "Nature again sympathizes with this injured people, though, I fear me, many a houseless wanderer wishes she did not" (*SGD,* 321). Where, in "Our City Charities," nature simply reflected the abysmal conditions of New York's tenements as well as the intellectual's brooding concern, here Fuller affirms the mutual relationship linking nature, the intellectual, and the people. Nature remains fundamentally incomplete without a political revolution that enables everyone to appreciate its aesthetic qualities. The fact that this contradiction between aesthetic promise and social reality exists casts a shadow on the intellectual work Fuller performs in the dispatches. While the intellectual can read nature for signs of historical regeneration, the poor simply suffer in the wake of revolutionary defeat.

Fuller does not act as a political journalist—something which Brownson could credibly do—but as a Romantic intellectual incorporating class and revolution into her literary education. Her final metaphor is therefore a thoroughly Romantic one, the fantasy of a universal literary conversation, "[a] congress of great, pure, loving minds, and not a congress of selfish ambitions, shall preside" (*SGD*, 322). Fuller's European writings therefore do not so much signal a movement away from New England Transcendentalism but rather demarcate the limits of intellectual activity and education.[81] Her experience of the revolutionary situation in Rome clearly pushed her to redefine intellectual activity as political practice. Larry Reynolds and Susan Belasco Smith have argued that "when Fuller arrived in Italy in 1847, her radicalism was still a state of mind rather than a course of action."[82] This is true for her political views. But she did not move "from theory to practice";[83] in fact, her educational efforts had always been practical. The move was from a concrete audience to an anonymous public. Fuller could not translate the literary practice of her European dispatches into an American context. On her journey back to New York, she died in a shipwreck. But her reconceptualization of American Romanticism showed the inevitability of reform if Romanticism should be realized as a generative principle of society.

The *Dial*, the *Boston Quarterly Review*, and the *New-York Tribune* tried to change the conditions of the intellectual field. By reconnecting the differentiated fields of modernity through a popular form of education the Transcendentalists (willingly or unwillingly) became aware of the exclusionary social mechanisms underlying intellectual activity and education. Driven by their popular medium, the Transcendentalists reconceptualized the role of the intellectual as involved in the world, thus countering the tendency of a modern, differentiated society to separate education from the world it seeks to explore. As Pierre Bourdieu has pointed out, because intellectuals strive for, or seek to maintain, a privileged status, they tend to "feel entitled to perceive the world as a representation, a spectacle, to survey it from above and from afar and organize it as a whole designed for knowledge alone."[84] But the *Boston Quarterly Review* advocated popular reform in the name of a Romantic social vision; the *Dial* established the Transcendentalists as a public movement, therefore moving Romanticism into the center of intellectual discussions; and Fuller, finally, asked progressive intellectuals and a broad literate audience alike to reconsider their role in the perpetuation of class privilege. The audience was no longer a spectacle to be observed and instructed; it had now been theorized as integral part of the Romantic reform project. This intense reconsideration of Romanticism was the result of the logic of popularity inherent in Romantic education.

## NOTES

1. David Dowling, "Publishers," 221.
2. Emerson, *Selected Letters,* 213.
3. John Sullivan Dwight, "The Religion of Beauty," *Dial,* July 1840, 18–9.
4. Orestes Brownson, "Conversations with a Radical," *Boston Quarterly Review* 4, no.1 (1841): 14–5.
5. See Sterling F. Delano, *Brook Farm: The Dark Side of Utopia* (Cambridge, MA: Harvard University Press, 2004), 14–38; Amy Hart, *Fourierist Communities of Reform: The Social Networks of Nineteenth-Century Female Reformers* (Basingstoke: Palgrave Macmillan, 2021), 172–3.
6. "Education," *Harbinger,* July 25, 1846, 111.
7. *Harbinger* July 24, 1847, 108.
8. Orestes Brownson, "Union and Progress." *Boston Quarterly Review*, April 1838, 195–6.
9. George Ripley, "Brownson's Writings," *Dial,* July 1840, 30.
10. Clarence Louis Frank Gohdes, *The Periodicals of American Transcendentalism* (Durham: Duke University Press, 1931), 33.
11. See also Patrick Carey, *Orestes A. Brownson: American Religious Weathervane* (Grand Rapids: W. B. Eerdmans, 2004), 68.
12. Orestes Brownson, *A Discourse on the Wants of the Times, Delivered in Lyceum Hall, Hanover Street, Boston, Sunday, May 29, 1836* (Boston: James Munroe and Co., 1836), iv.
13. Orestes Brownson, "American Literature," *Boston Quarterly Review*, January 1839, 16.
14. Catherine Maria Sedgwick, *Means and Ends; Or, Self-Training* (New York: Harper and Harper, 1842), 269, 7.
15. Orestes Brownson, "Literary Notices," *Boston Quarterly Review,* July 1839, 389.
16. Orestes Brownson, "Alcott on Human Culture," *Boston Quarterly Review,* October 1838, 432.
17. Brownson, "Alcott on Human Culture," 418–9.
18. Brownson, "The Laboring Classes," 395.
19. Brownson, "The Laboring Classes," 364–5.
20. Brownson, "The Laboring Classes," 365.
21. Scott Henkel, *Direct Democracy: Collective Power, the Swarm, and the Literatures of the Americas* (Jackson: University Press of Mississippi, 2017), 18.
22. Brownson, "The Laboring Classes," 363.
23. Channing, *Works,* 2:390.
24. David P. Edgell, *William Ellery Channing: An Intellectual Portrait* (Boston: Beacon Press, 1955), 130.
25. On Channing's engagement with labor issues, see Jack Mendelsohn, *Channing, the Reluctant Radical* (Westport: Greenwood Press, 1980), 208–10.
26. Channing, *Works* 2:350, 386, 400.

27. Brownson, "The Laboring Classes," 375.
28. Brownson, "Education," 156.
29. Orestes Brownson, "American Literature," 8.
30. Merrill D. Peterson, *The Great Triumvirate: Webster, Clary, and Calhoun* (New York: Oxford University Press, 1987), 339.
31. Stewart Davenport, *Friends of the Unrighteous Mammon: Northern Christians and Market Capitalism, 1815-1860* (Chicago: University of Chicago Press, 2008), 139.
32. Brownson, "The Laboring Classes," 388–9.
33. Gohdes, *The Periodicals of American Transcendentalism*, 13.
34. Joel Myerson, *The New England Transcendentalists and the Dial* (Rutherford: Farleigh Dickinson Press, 1980), 37–8.
35. Ralph Waldo Emerson, "The Editors to the Reader," *Dial*, July 1840, 1–3.
36. Glenn Wallach, *Obedient Sons: The Discourse of Youth and Generations in American Culture, 1630-1860* (Amherst: University of Massachusetts Press, 1997).
37. Adam Tuchinsky, *Horace Greeley's New-York Tribune: Civil War-Era Socialism and the Crisis of Free Labor* (Ithaca: Cornell University Press, 2009), 70.
38. Emerson, *Selected Letters*, 213.
39. Amos Bronson Alcott, "Orphic Sayings," *Dial*, January 1841, 357.
40. Elizabeth Peabody, "A Glimpse of Christ's Idea of Society," 227.
41. How broadly the term "education" was understood can be seen from a book that was advertised in the *Dial*. John Dunmore Lang's book carried the sprawling title *Religion and Education in America; with Notices of the State and Prospects of American Unitarianism, Popery, and African Colonization* (London: Thomas Ward, 1840).
42. The caricature features a stanza from Carline Sturgis Tappan's poem "Life," which had been published in the *Dial* in October 1840: "Why for work art thou striving, / Why seek'st thou for aught? / To the soul that is living / All things shall be brought." Of course, this is not the gist of Tappan's poem, whose speaker actually states that she cannot be "[w]ithout labor or love" (195). Cranch therefore, in the tradition of parody, isolates a cliché to make a specific, problematic point about a subject.
43. Qtd. in Frederick De Wolfe Miller, *Christopher Pearse Cranch and His Caricatures of New England Transcendentalism* (Cambridge: Harvard University Press, 1951), 37.
44. Matthew Philpotts, "The Role of the Periodical Editor: Literary Journals and Editorial Habitus," *Modern Language Review* 107, no.1 (2012): 42.
45. Joel Myerson, *The New England Transcendentalists and the Dial*, 50.
46. Qtd. in Myerson, *The New England Transcendentalists and the Dial*, 49.
47. See Joel Myerson, "'In the Transcendental Emporium': Bronson Alcott's 'Orphic Sayings' in the *Dial*," *English Language Notes* 10 (1972): 31–8.
48. Christopher Green, "The Dial," *Plain Speaker*, January 30, 1841, 3.
49. Steven Fink, "Thoreau and His Audience," *The Cambridge Companion to Henry David Thoreau*, ed. Joel Myerson (Cambridge: Cambridge University Press, 1995), 74.

50. Tuchinsky, *Horace Greeley's,* 70–1.
51. Qtd. in De Wolfe Miller, *Christopher Pearse* Cranch, 489.
52. Tuchinsky, *Horace Greeley's,* 70.
53. Horace Greeley, "Literary Notices," *New-York Daily Tribune,* April 27, 1844, 1.
54. Fuller, *Papers on Literature and Art* 2: 140.
55. Fuller, *Papers on Literature and Art* 2: 137–8; my emphasis.
56. Charles Capper describes Fuller's early educational practice as that of a cultural reformer with little interest in addressing social privilege: "There is no evidence to suggest that Fuller had in mind using her classes to alter power relations between men and women, much less the political institutions upon which the two-spheres cultural ideology rested." Capper, "Margaret Fuller as Cultural Reformer," 522.
57. Qtd. in Frederic Hudson, *Journalism in the United States, from 1690-1872* (New York: Harper & Brothers, 1873), 523.
58. While demanding constant production from his writers, Greeley simultaneously encouraged them to carefully construct and revise their articles. As he comments in a *Tribune* editorial: "If you send us word that you 'have written in great haste, and have no time to correct,' we shall put your manuscript quietly in the fire." Horace Greeley, "To Correspondents," *New-York Daily Tribune,* February 10, 1845, 2.
59. David Robinson, "Margaret Fuller, New York, and the Politics of Transcendentalism," *ESQ: A Journal of the American Renaissance* 52, no. 4 (2006): 284.
60. Jeffrey Steele, "Sympathy and Prophecy: The Two Faces of Social Justice in Fuller's New York Writing," *Margaret Fuller and Her Circles,* ed. Brigitte Bailey, Katheryn P. Viens, and Conrad Edick Wright (Durham: University of New Hampshire Press, 2013), 162.
61. Robert Hudspeth, "Margaret Fuller and Urban Life," *Margaret Fuller and Her Circles,* ed. Brigitte Bailey, Katheryn P. Viens, and Conrad Edick Wright (Durham: University of New Hampshire Press, 2013), 187.
62. Margaret Fuller, "Our City Charities," *New-York Daily Tribune,* March 19, 1845, 1.
63. Judith Mattson Bean and Joel Myerson, "Introduction," *Margaret Fuller, Critic: Writings from the New-York Tribune, 1844–46,* ed. Judith Mattson Bean and Joel Myerson (New York: Columbia University Press, 2000), xxii.
64. Fuller, "Our City Charities," 1.
65. Monika Elbert, "Urban Reform and the Plight of the Poor in Women's Journalistic Writing," *Philanthropic Discourse in Anglo-American Literature, 1850–1920,* ed. Frank Q. Christianson and Leslee Thorne-Murphy (Bloomington: Indiana University Press, 2017), 88.
66. Margaret Fuller, "Christmas," *New-York Daily Tribune,* December 25, 1844, 1.
67. Paula Kopacz, "Feminist at the 'Tribune': Margaret Fuller as Professional Writer," *Studies in the American Renaissance* (1991): 124.

68. Qtd. in Bell Gale Chevigny, *The Woman and the Myth: Margaret Fuller's Life and Writings*, rev. ed. (Boston: Northeastern University Press, 1994), 300.

69. Fuller's personal situation is still too often the center of discussions about her later writings. While it is certainly true that "the story of how her own personal revolution paralleled the Italian revolution" (Kopacz, "Feminist at the 'Tribune,'" 135), the focus on Fuller's private life as a cause for the hopes and doubts expressed in these letters tends to prevent acknowledging Fuller's dispatches as works of art

70. The dispatches—marked only by an asterisk or star, which readers (among them Edgar Allan Poe) would recognize as her trademark—were also reflections on her intellectual status. See Edgar Allan Poe, "The Literati of New York City—No. IV," *Godey's Lady's Book* 33 (August 1846): 72; Anon., "Death of Margaret Fuller," *Southern Literary Messenger* 16 (August 1850): 519.

71. Ian Balfour, *The Rhetoric of Romantic Prophecy* (Stanford: Stanford University Press, 2002), 18.

72. See Martin Hewitt, "Ralph Waldo Emerson, George Dawson, and the Control of the Lecture Platform in Mid-Nineteenth-Century Manchester." *Nineteenth-Century Prose* 25, no. 2 (1998): 1–23.

73. Denis Mack Smith, *Mazzini* (New Haven: Yale University Press, 1994), 38.

74. Dickens was introduced to Mazzini through a fake letter seeking funding, to which he responded. Dickens testified against the imposter before court and became involved with Mazzini's school afterward; see Shannon 89.

75. Mack Smith, *Mazzini*, 38.

76. David Dowling, *Emerson's Protégés*, 297n.60.

77. Adam Tuchinsky, "Margaret Fuller, Self-Culture, and Associationism," *Margaret Fuller and Her Circles*, ed. Brigitte Bailey et al. (Durham: University of New Hampshire Press, 2013), 115; Capper, *Fuller*, 2:423.

78. Jeffrey Steele, *Transfiguring America: Myth, Ideology, and Mourning in Margaret Fuller's Writing* (Columbia: University of Missouri Press, 2001), 278.

79. Walt Whitman would publish a laudatory poem on the Roman Revolution, "Resurgemus," in the *New-York Tribune* on June 21, 1850, 3.

80. Fuller, *Papers on Literature and Art* 2:2.

81. If we understand Fuller's later dispatches as logically addressing Romanticism's tensions, such a reassessment also questions strict distinctions between Emersonian individualism and political reform. This supposed contradiction still shapes the discussion over whether Fuller's socialist years indicate a break with her earlier Transcendentalism. On the one hand, David Robinson and others have presented the case for continuity by arguing that Fuller's radical writings, beginning with *Woman in the Nineteenth Century*, reflect her growing awareness that "the ideal demands embodiment while the process of social transformation must have the guidance of an ideal," David M. Robinson, "Margaret Fuller and the Transcendental Ethos: Woman in the Nineteenth Century," *PMLA* 97, no. 1 (1982): 95–6. On the other hand, Bell Gale Chevigny refutes what she considers "the simple clarity of this formula." Chevigny argues that Fuller's European radicalism required an epistemological break with her earlier Transcendentalism. She takes the Transcendentalists' "refusal of her radical meanings" as evidence for this break; Bell Gale Chevigny, "To the Edges of

Ideology: Margaret Fuller's Centrifugal Evolution," *American Quarterly* 38, no. 2 (1986): 199, n. 16. Similarly, Larry Reynolds has argued that "it was her experience in Europe during 1846–49 that led her farthest away from Emersonian individualism and gave her new values, new concerns, and new forms of expression," Larry J. Reynolds, *European Revolutions and the American Renaissance* (New Haven: Yale University Press, 1988), 58. More recent assessments have rightly pointed to the rhetorical and ideological continuities between Fuller's New England writing and her later dispatches as well as her consistent cultural cosmopolitanism. See for example Dorri Beam, *Style, Gender, and Fantasy in Nineteenth-Century American Women's Writing* (Cambridge: Cambridge University Press, 2010); Christina Zwarg, *Feminist Conversations*; and *Leslie Eckel, Atlantic Citizens: Nineteenth-Century American Writers At Work in the World* (Edinburgh: Edinburgh University Press, 2013).

82. Larry J. Reynolds and Susan Belasco Smith, Introduction, *"These Sad but Glorious Days": Dispatches from Europe, 1846–1850*, ed. Larry J. Reynolds and Susan Belasco Smith (New Haven: Yale University Press, 1991), 18.

83. Howe, *Making the American Self*, 224.

84. Bourdieu, *Pascalian Meditations*, 21.

*Chapter 4*

# Public Intellectuals

## *The Romantic Lecture, Professionalization, and Politics*

The Romantic lecture was a form of popular education. Its practice was inextricably linked to the lyceum movement, which was an integral part of the nineteenth-century educational landscape. Josiah Holbrook proposed his plan for the establishment of a lecture platform "to diffuse rational and useful information through the community generally" in the *American Journal of Education*.[1] Holbrook's idea was to create a loose network of educational venues which would contribute to the "elevation of character among the agricultural and mechanic classes" and prevent "those insidious inroads of vice, which are ever ready to be made on hours of leisure." The lyceum's purpose was "to procure for youths an economical and practical education, and to diffuse rational and useful information through the community generally." This practical mission was underscored by Holbrook's demand to "apply the science and the various branches of education to the domestic and useful arts, and to all the common purposes of life."[2]

Lyceums were generally perceived as public discussion forums in the tradition of New England's townhall meetings. Their voluntary character enabled a dialogic exchange. The lyceum constituted an alternative discussion platform potentially open to everyone and certainly one that projected its idea of education beyond the cultural elite. As Angela G. Ray has shown, "[t]he lyceum ideal implied a popular audience—a cross-section of 'the public'—even if actual lyceum audiences may have been more narrowly circumscribed. For that popular audience, the term *lyceum* implied that what was heard was meant to be useful, by provoking thought and discussion or a better understanding of human experience."[3] During its heyday in the 1840s, lyceums in the North and West had "a weekly total public of about four-hundred thousand, mostly native-born, lower-middle-class, and in their early twenties or thirties."[4] The movement's public influence grew so strong that historians retrospectively defined the significance of their town's cultural history in terms of its involvement with the lyceum movement. In his *History of Southbridge*, Moses Plimpton wrote: "In literature there is nothing worthy of particularly notice in our history, more than has been related in the notice of our common schools, except that in Oct. 1826, the Southbridge Lyceum was established, being among the first associations of the kind in this state."[5] From Southbridge and other towns, the lyceum movement spread across Massachusetts. These platforms enabled the emergence of the Boston Lyceum, which was instrumental in popularizing the works of some of the most important nineteenth-century intellectuals.

Romantic lectures were often presented to lyceum audiences but also at other, popular public venues, which required equally complex rhetorical strategies. Ronald Wesley Hoag has argued that "[i]mportant and underacknowledged is the blurred distinction between lyceums, the lecture circuit, and other lecture venues."[6] But as Hoag also points out, Alcott referred to a Young Men's Institute in Connecticut simply as "Lyceum,"[7] so that lyceum had become synonymous with public lecturing for the Transcendentalists. Most importantly, the lyceum set the tone for the public nineteenth-century lecture when it merged popular education, accessible style, and intellectual autonomy. Even if they addressed specific associations, the Transcendentalists understood their lectures as a popular form of education. In the course of the 1840s and 1850s, from which the lectures discussed in this chapter stem, for the Transcendentalists "[l]yceums and sponsored lectures converged, with 'lyceum' attaching to all."[8] This convergence coincided with a professionalization and politicization of public lecturing. As such, the genre posed new challenges to the Romantics: lectures became more performance-oriented just as lecturing in general became a profession in which words needed to be carefully chosen with regard to their potential public reception.

This chapter explores how the public lecture forced the Transcendentalists to reconsider Romanticism's practical implications for everyday life. Conversely, although the lyceum was originally designed as a platform to convey scientific knowledge to a broad audience, speakers like Emerson, Thoreau, and Douglass soon broadened the lecture circuit's scope. By introducing philosophy, literature, and, eventually, politics into the discourse, they redefined what "practical" meant. Although the lyceum was initially most interested in a utilitarian form of education, the public conversational platform appealed to the Romantic reformers and curators proved flexible enough to accommodate their form of literary education. But the lyceum's popular appeal also posed a challenge for the Romantic lecturer. Because of the platform's increasing popularity and professionalization, lectures were a hybrid medium for the Romantics. The audiences in attendance consisted of laborers, artisans, intellectuals, and, later, white and African American reformers, whose interests had to be carefully balanced, particularly as soon as speakers received salaries for their talks and were dependent on favorable reception. In addition, as soon as the lyceum and other lecture venues became more widely noticed, the lecturer also had to address a future, intended audience. The lectures were attended by an interested, literate general audience from various social spectrums, while the printed versions that often resulted from these speeches were read and reviewed primarily by professional journalists, theologians, and intellectuals. This tension intensified with the professionalization and politicization of the lecture circuit in antebellum America.

Lecture venues provided the stage for a symbiotic relationship between philosophy, rhetoric, and politics, a relationship which created a genre full of tensions emblematic of Romantic education. But they also promised to fulfill a deep-seated desire to reconnect education and the public. The metaphor of the street held a permanent appeal to the Romantic lecturer. In 1846, Ralph Waldo Emerson defined the teacher's role as follows:

> The teacher should be the complement of the pupil; now for the most part they are earth's diameters wide of each other. A college professor should be elected by setting all the candidates loose on a miscellaneous gang of young men taken at large from the street. He who could get the ear of the youths after a certain number of hours, or of the greatest number of these youths should be professor. (*JMN* 9: 249)

Thoreau insisted that "[t]his discipline [education], which we allow to be the end of life, should not be one thing in the schoolroom, and another in the street."[9] That both Emerson and Thoreau use vague, generalizing terms rather than denoting a specific social group illustrates how "the street" symbolized an ambition to reach out to a general public rather than simply referring to an alternative group of learners. The street, therefore, comes to signify an alternative space of education, one in which, at least ideally, the conversation was the determining principle of interaction. Frederick Douglass's arrival on the lecture circuit permanently altered the landscape of popular education. For Douglass the street had a much more concrete meaning: it was the place where he had received his early education and where he educated poor white boys and turned himself into a teacher. In "American Slavery, American Religion" (1846), Douglass spoke about carrying the "denunciations against slavery uttered in London" into "the streets of Boston."[10] Douglass transformed the meaning of the street into a much more concretely political arena and, as we will see, accordingly transformed the way popular public lectures functioned. Slavery and racism became a public issue for the lyceum with the appearance of Frederick Douglass because he redeployed, as did Emerson and Thoreau, the established language of selfhood only to turn it into a call for political change.

## EMERSON'S AUDIENCES

Ralph Waldo Emerson was hesitant to embrace institutions; but he was also aware that institutionalized alternatives were necessary to spread the practice of self-reliance, "for you cannot talk with any intelligent company without presently hearing expressions of regret & impatience whose scope affects the whole order of *good* institutions."[11] Emerson wanted to remain as aloof from institutions and movements as possible. But he was also the Romantic most astutely familiar with self-promotion, marketing, and the use of literary networks.[12] The lyceum's open organizational form appealed to Emerson, particularly since it contrasted with his previous educational venue, the church.

Emerson's career as a public speaker logically resulted from his break with Unitarianism in 1832. While his dedication to a religion and philosophy of intuitive truth did not drastically alter after he abandoned his ministry, his position in the intellectual field did. David Robinson has argued that Emerson's break with the church was the result of an "essentially professional, or vocational, dissatisfaction" which, according to Robinson, must not obscure the intellectual continuities between his ministry and his later career.[13] As Peter Field has put it, Emerson "proceeded to preach his pantheistic vision of God-in-the-world where it belonged—in the street." According to Field, for Emerson "the lecture hall promised to serve as that great step, as well as a bridge, from the artificial and exclusive isolation of the pulpit and church toward a congregation of each and all."[14] The lyceum was supposed to become a democratic substitute for the church. Most importantly, the lyceum put Emerson in conversation with an audience again.

Emerson began lecturing publicly in 1833. His main venue was the Masonic Temple in Boston, but Emerson soon became a public figure in New England. After spending a year in Europe, he began to "carve out a speaking career on the newly formed lyceum circuit."[15] The lyceum's immediate communicational situation combined with its public appeal promised an institutional situation where Emerson could realize the Romantic ideal of sympathetic communication: "I take pleasure only in coming near to people. What avails any conversation but the sincere? Uncover thy face, uncover they heart to me, be thou who thou may, & the purpose of purposes is answered to us both" (*JMN* 8:17). To achieve this end, Emerson approached the lyceum strategically. Peter S. Field has argued that "[p]erhaps no other American intellectual in the nineteenth century so consciously and effectively endeavored to have an impact upon both contemporary thought and public behavior as Emerson."[16] Indeed, Emerson took care of organizational matters from the outset as he organized other lyceum lectures and sold tickets for his own. Emerson's strategic approach of the lyceum was part of his attempt to free education from its institutional constraints: "The object of Education should be to remove all obstructions & let this natural force have free play & exhibit it peculiar product" (*JMN* 4:378).

The lyceum allowed Emerson to actively shape the conditions of his educational mission. Emerson's involvement with the lyceum helped transform it into a platform that allowed lecturers to be relatively free from institutional constraints, while also providing a secure livelihood. But the lyceum's openness and intended popularity also proved a challenge. As a minister, Emerson could target a specific, consistent, and usually predictable audience. The lecturer, however, had to account for shifting audiences and regional differences, and he had to make sure to secure a reputation for himself. As Emerson learned with his Divinity School Address, which was intended for sympathetic Harvard graduates but was attacked by the literary establishment in the aftermath, lectures did not only address those in attendance but also a projected audience who would respond to his lectures in the periodicals of the time. For him, this did not mean compromise: "I design not to utter any speech, poem or book that is not entirely and peculiarly my work. I will say at public lectures, and the like, those things which I have meditated for their own sake, and not for the first time with a view to that occasion" (*JMN* 4:335). Emerson continuously asserted his integrity and the purity of his educational vision: "remember that you are not to say, What must be said in a Lyceum? but what discoveries or stimulating thoughts have I to impart to a thousand persons? not what they will expect to hear but what is fit for me to say" (*JMN* 4:372). Still, after the heated response his Divinity School Address drew, Emerson realized that he had to be careful about his rhetoric if he wanted to establish himself as a successful public speaker.

Emerson paradigmatically discusses and enacts the relationship between intellectual, audience, and literary institutions in "Man the Reformer," a lecture presented before the Mechanics' Apprentices' Library Association in Boston on January 25, 1841. As Sylvia J. Cook has stated, "the Apprentices were an anomalous audience for Emerson's appeal to the wealthy, advantaged, and privileged to permit the power of love to induce them to share and encourage the aspirations of the laboring class."[17] But it was precisely this audience which forced him to outline the tension between daily routine and a "clearer communication with the spiritual nature" (*CW* 1:145). In his speech, Emerson defines the reformer as a "mediator between the spiritual and the actual world" (*CW* 1:159). "Man the Reformer" has all the characteristics of a typical lyceum lecture, but is addressed to a more specific audience. As David Robinson has suggested, the speech "illustrates Emerson's desire to translate individualist self-culture into a workable ethical praxis."[18] In his diagnosis of nineteenth-century society, Emerson advocates the necessity to reconcile manual and intellectual labor. The crass utilitarianism characteristic of modern capitalism affects the conditions of spiritual education:

> We must have a basis for our higher accomplishments, our delicate entertainments of poetry and philosophy, in the work of our hands. [. . .] Is it possible that I who get indefinite quantities of sugar, hominy, cotton, buckets, crockery ware, and letter paper, by simply signing my name once in three months to a cheque in favor of John Smith and Co. traders, get the fair share of exercise to my faculties by that act, which nature intended for me in making all these far-fetched matters important to my comfort? It is Smith himself, and his carriers, and dealers, and manufacturers, it is the sailor, the hide-drogher, the butcher, the negro, the hunter, and the planter, who have intercepted the sugar of the sugar, and the cotton of the cotton. They have got the education, I only the commodity. (*CW* 1:150)

The passage exemplifies the tensions inherent in Emerson's attempt to popularize Romanticism. As a counterpoint to a detached intellectuality, and in a manner typical for the Romantics, Emerson understands manual labor as organic simplicity, the work of a "sincere learner" (*CW* 1:152).[19] While Emerson assigns manual labor (and thus the work of his audience) a high educational value, he also conflates educational value and material wealth: "Why needs any man be rich? Why must he have horses, fine garments, handsome apartments, access to public houses, and places of amusement? Only for want of thought" (*CW* 1:154). Despite the fact that he elevates his audience's spirituality, Emerson's romanticization of labor occasionally lapses into an involuntary cynicism that sounds rather absurd given his audience.

But Emerson's remarks must also be understood as a reflection about the possibilities, necessities, and limits of Romantic education directed at the intellectual class that was not present. Given his experience as the editor of the *Dial*, Emerson must have been aware of how these literary works had an afterlife in print. In fact, besides the publication as a single volume at the request of the Mechanics' Apprentices' Library Association, the speech was printed in the *Dial* in 1841. Accordingly, some of the lecture's sentences seem to address the *Dial*'s readership rather than the mechanic apprentices in the audience: "See this wide society of laboring men and women. We allow ourselves to be served by them, we live apart from them, and meet them without a salute in the streets" (*CW* 1:158). The nexus between labor, work, and education which Emerson establishes in "Man the Reformer" therefore reaches across the audiences. One of the lessons of his speech is clearly directed at the literate class: "I doubt not, the faults and vices of our literature and philosophy, their too great fineness, effeminacy, and melancholy, are attributable to the enervated and sickly habits of the literary class. Better that the book should not be quite so good, and the bookmaker abler and better, and not himself often a ludicrous contrast to all that he has written" (*CW* 1:152). Emerson speaks to, but also functionalizes, his audience of apprentices. In this moment, the audience present at the lecture is transformed into a normative horizon for his implied readership.

Emerson's lecture importantly links education to social philosophy. Ultimately, however, he remains undecided about how far to push the issues of class and privilege. Emerson proclaims that if Romanticism is to become society's generative principle reform is needed:

> We are to revise the whole of our social structure, the state, the school, religion, marriage, trade, science, and explore their foundations in our own nature; we are to see that the world not only fitted the former men, but fits us, and to clear ourselves of every usage which has not its roots in our own mind. What is a man born for but to be a Reformer, a Remaker of what man has made; a renouncer of lies; a restorer of truth and good, imitating that great Nature which embosoms us all, and which sleeps no moment on an old past, but every hour repairs herself, yielding us every morning a new day, and with every pulsation a new life? (*CW* 1:155–56)

Emerson evokes a collectivity when he speaks of the "men transfigured and raised above themselves by the power of principles" (*CW* 1:157) as those who will enact the necessary social transformations. Unsure about how much authority to grant his audience in this reform process, Emerson describes the needed rebel as a Carlylean Romantic genius (although without the aristocratic notions of genius in Carlyle): "what a house of cards their institutions are, and I see what one brave man, what one great thought executed might effect" (*CW* 1:157). In accordance with this turn to individual reform, Emerson eventually clings to the idealistic vision of charity that underlay Fuller's early New York writings: "The state must consider the poor man, and all voices must speak for him. Every child that is born must have a just chance for his bread. Let the amelioration in our laws of property proceed from the concession of the rich, not from the grasping of the poor" (*CW* 1:159).

Continuing to struggle with the problem of popular education, Emerson addressed the divide between lecturer, audience, and educational mission again in "The Young American," which he read to the Mercantile Library Association in Boston on February 7, 1844: "A gulf yawns for the young American between his education and his work" (*CW* 1:222). Emerson advocates the same practicality as in "Man the Reformer," and the lecture was read to a similar audience of young men (*CW* 1:217). In "The Young American," however, Emerson dissolves the class tensions in a vision of national unity. His cultural nationalism shows when he complains that America's curriculum is European, while the practical tasks at hand are genuinely American: "We are sent to feudal school to learn democracy" (*CW* 1:222). The questioning, rebellious tone of "Man the Reformer" is replaced with an affirmative exceptionalism. The lecture's introduction compares American education to a banker's daughter who cannot help her father after bankruptcy because of a lack of practical skills. The "all-accomplished banker's daughter" could "waltz, and cut rice-paper, and paint velvet, and transfer drawings, and make satin stitch, and play on the clavichord, and sing German songs, and act charades, and arrange tableaux, and a great many other equally useful performances" (*CW* 1:222); but she could simply not be of any practical assistance to her father. Emerson's strangely anti-aesthetic and paternalistic tone is directed at a European aristocratic tradition which does not fit democratic America.

This is not to reduce Emerson to a conformist or nationalist speaker. As Eric Keenaghan has put it, "The Young American" exemplifies how "lecture culture played on the often contradictory interaction between cosmopolitan and nationalist impulses."[20] For our purposes, it is important to understand how Emerson's rhetoric illustrates his underlying insecurity about how far he was willing to link education, class, and politics, a connection that was literally embodied by his lecture's audience. His rhetoric resembles that of the anti-intellectual populist workingmen's periodicals, accompanied by nationalist overtones. Emerson here easily dissolves the tensions of Romantic education and the problem of how to unite manual and intellectual labor in a model of exemplary nationhood. Intention, subject matter, and audience easily merge in the national cause. The American Scholar is no longer presented as an ideal to which a conflicted present aspires. Instead, questions of education, audience, and popularity are collapsed into a fantasy of the reconciliation between intellectual and manual labor: "The land, with its tranquilizing, sanative influences, is to repair the errors of a scholastic and traditional education, and bring us into just relations with men and things" (*CW* 1:336).

But the lecture also hails international political events as harbingers of the golden age. Emerson ultimately combines a trust in the progressive forces of history with a rhetoric of political radicalism. This becomes particularly evident in his discussion of trade, a topic immediately relevant to his audience. While it is true that "trade planted America and destroyed Feudalism; that it makes peace and keeps peace, and it will abolish slavery," it also threatens to "bring every kind of faculty of every individual that can in any manner serve any person, *on sale*" (*CW* 1:233–4). Despite its historical significance, then, trade, for Emerson, is already in need of replacement. Indeed, there are already "signs of that which is the sequel of trade." He sees these signs in nineteenth-century reform movements and popular education: "All this beneficent socialism is a friendly omen, and the swelling cry of voices for the education of the people, indicates that Government has other offices than those of banker and executioner" (*CW* 1:235). The lecturer here evokes a new commonality, a collective that forms in the lyceum circuit, acknowledging that "in the scramble of parties for the public purse, the main duties of government were omitted—the duty to instruct the ignorant, to supply the poor with work and with good guidance" (CW 1:235). Emerson's progressive message and its populist tone was not lost on Horace Greeley, who reprinted "The Young American" in the April 23, 1844, issue of the *New-York Tribune*. The lecture circuit's multiple audiences, however, caused a reconsideration of his Romanticism.

Eric Keenaghan has suggested that Emerson "seems to go out of his way to suggestively link the common with a political futurity embedded in the very term used to distinguish some of his nation's states from others: *commonwealth*."[21] In the end, however, Emerson collapses any potential differences between groups and classes, which need to be addressed and resolved, in an American cultural exceptionalism. Rejecting the "English press," he dissolves the tensions of his lecture in America's sublime nature: "If only the men are employed in conspiring with the designs of the Spirit who led us hither, and is leading us still, we shall quickly enough advance out of all hearing of other's censures, out of all regrets of our own, into a new and more excellent social state than history has recorded" (*CW* 1:237). Robert Milder has pointed out that "[t]he question of Emerson's radicalism need not and assuredly cannot be settled."[22] "Man the Reformer" and "The Young American" illustrate how Emerson was very much willing to use the lecture circuit to popularize his Romanticism, in the process linking it to questions of public education and progressive politics. But politics remained an abstract consideration. The tensions embodied by Emerson's divergent audiences were silenced by an abstract vision of unity.

The question of audience is particularly important as it also determines the lyceum's limits as a platform for Romantic education. Emerson's speeches operated through multiple channels. Their accessible, but also enigmatic style appealed to his various audiences. Mary Kupiec Cayton has pointed out how Emerson engaged his audience through a familiar rhetoric: "Emerson meant to inculcate moral reformation through his lecture topics, and he proposed to draw in his audience through a choice of topics that seemed familiar and practical."[23] But their open, aphoristic style could also be readily appropriated by a mercantile elite looking for cultural legitimation.[24] In this context, Richard Teichgraeber has argued that from the 1830s "Emerson commanded attention less for what he wrote or said than for the extraordinary ways in which he wrote and spoke."[25] While it is true that Emerson's style was a commodity that he carried to market, he did so in order to gain a platform for his educational provocations. As Luke Philip Plotica has argued, "what distinguishes Emerson from the enlightened bourgeoise to which he is often assimilated by his critics and commentators is precisely the restless striving for self-culture he depicts, carried out within an institutional, practical context that is both opportunity and adversary, and that cannot realistically be avoided."[26] Emerson's lectures were always a form of practice and as such mediated form, style, and content through the institutional conditions in which these necessarily manifest as cultural practice. If he remained insecure about the relationship between Romanticism, education, and reform, he still publicly proclaimed the importance of Romanticism as an organizing social principle.

## THOREAU'S PRACTICALITY

Just like the institutional conditions of the lecture circuit were inscribed into Emerson's speeches, Thoreau's works cannot be separated from his career as a lecturer. Thoreau presented crucial sections of his books, such as the "Economy" chapter of *Walden*, as lectures before they were prepared for publication. He lectured at a variety of venues from the Concord Lyceum to the Masonic Temple, which could accommodate 150 to 200 listeners. Thoreau's national and international reputation as a lecturer was insignificant when compared to Emerson's: "Away from Concord, Emerson lectured far, wide, profitably, and to international acclaim. Thoreau, away from Concord, just fifty-two lectures in almost twenty-three years, with only five beyond England and none outside the United States."[27] But Thoreau rose to regional fame with his lectures, and it was through his public appearances that he confronted the possibilities and limits of his educational method. Thoreau intended to "make education a pleasant thing both to the teacher and the student."[28] While the lyceum enabled him to establish such a sympathetic relationship, its immediate, practical nature also imposed several institutional restrictions on him that influenced the way this sympathetic relationship was realized.[29]

As we have seen with Emerson, public lectures promised the perfect balance between intellectual autonomy and engagement. In 1837, Thoreau had assumed and quickly resigned a teaching position at a Concord school. Eventually, Thoreau left the school because he refused to administer corporeal punishment. Thoreau saw the lyceum not only as an alternative, more inclusive educational platform, but also as an extension, rather than a repudiation of his earlier teaching efforts.[30] The institution had accompanied Thoreau since his earliest youth. But as much as it liberated Thoreau from the constraints of the school curriculum and from violent disciplinarian acts such as administering corporeal punishment, lecturing imposed a different set of institutional requirements and restrictions on him. Bradley P. Dean and Ronald Wesley Hoag have meticulously established a picture of the circumstances and settings of Thoreau's lectures. Their scholarship shows that public lectures were a complex institutional affair. As a curator of the Concord Lyceum, Thoreau became steeped in organizational matters. He was "charged with preparing programs, arranging lectures, and securing the lighted and heated hall,"[31] and he experienced how literary networks were required to recruit speakers for the educational platform. Hoag states that Thoreau's personality embodied characteristics of the semiprofessional lyceum culture: "In an era before specialization, with an Enlightenment regard for the practical polymath, the lyceum's cornucopia was embodied in 'handy' Henry Thoreau and his encyclopedic writings."[32]

For Thoreau, just like for Emerson, lectures were intermediate steps between original thought and published essay: "From all points of the compass from the earth beneath and the heavens above have come these inspirations and been entered duly in such order as they came in the Journal. Thereafter when the time arrived they were winnowed into Lectures—and again in due time from Lectures into Essays" (*PJ* 2:205). The history of one of Thoreau's most frequently delivered lectures, "Economy," helps us understand how his lectures and his published works were part of the same attempt to institutionalize a poetic education. "Economy—Illustrated by the Life of a Student," for instance, was presented in Gloucester's town hall on December 20, 1848. One reviewer "praised the entertainment value of the lecture but pronounced it educationally worthless."[33] But what the reviewer found educationally worthless was Thoreau's intended provocation. Thoreau's economy didn't produce any value that could be carried to market. In "Life Without Principle," he asks his audience to reconsider economy as economic justice: "it would be economy for a town to pay its laborers so well that they would not feel that they were working for low ends, as for a livelihood merely, but for scientific, or even moral ends."[34] This process of the literary reforming of language is Thoreau's idea of popular education. For Thoreau, a proper education first required the unlearning of habitualized practices: "When any real progress is made, we unlearn and learn anew, what we thought we knew before" (*PJ* 1:24).

Thoreau's writing reflects his lectures' rhetorical strategies and his constant interaction with his audience. In *Walden* (1854), Thoreau equally transformed the meaning of "economy." It no longer refers to the nineteenth-century market aiming at profit maximization but now denotes a principle of self-reliance and natural relations. In accordance with this rhetorical strategy, Thoreau's temporary withdrawal becomes a form of education: "Every man has to learn the points of compass again as often as he awakes, whether from sleep or any abstraction. Not till we are lost, in other words not till we have lost the world, do we begin to find ourselves, and realize where we are and the infinite extent of our relations" (*W* 171). Solitude is the temporary result of an attempt to unlearn social conventions. It prepares the individual for a redefinition of social relations. The "infinite extent of our relations" that we discover in our solitude is therefore also firmly rooted in the practices that necessitate this solitude in the first place. Thoreau's solitude is not one of withdrawal; rather it is the reflected distancing from a society in whose name that distancing ultimately occurs.

*Walden*, and its "Economy" chapter in particular, can be read as the logical continuation of the lyceum's educational mission. *Walden* displays how Thoreau forces the reader to unlearn conventions by explicitly translating existing literary conventions into a new, aesthetic form of education. As Leonard Neufeldt has shown, Thoreau's *Walden* must be read in the context of the various nineteenth-century moral guides for young men. Not only did Thoreau's personal library include these guidebooks, they also enjoyed "an infinitely greater authority of presence in the homes of moderately and well-educated families at Harvard." These books blended "school, church, lecture hall, reading room, and private library"—in other words, they connected all branches of nineteenth-century education.[35] *Walden* resembles the guidebooks in its attempt to establish an alternative education: they, too, rejected rote learning, instead of propagating moral education, and they, too, addressed the young generation as the group which would determine New England's future. But Thoreau ultimately rejected conventions and accordingly rewrites the literary tradition he draws on into a form of education that is categorically different from the young man's manuals' utilitarianism. In *Lectures to Young Men* (1828), one of the books on which Thoreau modeled *Walden*, Joel Hawes writes: "The various departments of business and trust, the pulpit and the bar, our course of justice and halls of legislation; our civil, religious, and literary institutions; all, in short, that constitutes society and goes to make life useful and happy, are to be in your hands and under your control." Hawes places a strong emphasis on duty and tradition ("venerable fathers"). Education served to maintain the "social order."[36] Thoreau, of course, would be appalled by precisely such an adherence to tradition, competition, and self-interest instead demanding "a poetic or divine life" (*W* 90).

Amidst all strategic consideration, then, Thoreau sought to advocate the poetic life for all. On November 29, 1843, Thoreau delivered a lecture on "The Ancient Poets" in front of the Concord Lyceum. A shorter version of the lecture was published in the *Dial* as "Homer. Ossian. Chaucer" in January 1844, making sure it gained wider circulation. Ultimately, the lecture would become part of *A Week on the Concord and Merrimack Rivers* (1849). On October 25, 1843, Emerson had told Thoreau to "bring something that will serve for Lyceum lecture—the craving thankless town!"[37] Thoreau decided to lecture on Homer, Ossian, Chaucer, and the poetic life. Poetry, he proclaims, is "as if nature spoke"; it is "so universally true and independent of experience."[38] In the printed version, Thoreau concludes with a provocation of the reader which he probably also directed at his audience during the lecture: "The reader easily goes within the shallowest contemporary poetry [. . .] but it will have to speak to posterity, traversing these deserts through the ruins of its outmost walls, by the grandeur and beauty of its proportions." He not only proclaims the transhistorical value of art but also stresses that its completion occurs through reception and practice: "The true finish is the work of time and the use to which a thing is put."[39] Thoreau's advocacy of practicality and relevance show the influence of the lyceum's mission. Conversely, his insistence on the aesthetic experience also shows how the Romantic tried to broaden the lyceum's practical aspirations by arguing that literature could indeed be of relevance to everyday life.

The question of practice and practicality was not only present in Thoreau's lectures and writings, it also crucially influenced the public's view of Thoreau and his works. Thoreau's reception in the *New-York Tribune* serves particularly well as an example of how important the question of practice was for his educational project. In a review of the *Dial* in the January 25, 1844, *New-York Tribune*, Horace Greeley praised the printed version of Thoreau's lecture:

> We deeply desire to quote many pages, by different writers, from this number [of the *Dial*], but must be content for to-day with the following extracts from a Lecture on Poetry, by H. D. Thoreau, a young disciple and companion of Emerson, in whom the true spirit of the author's philosophy is reproduced, without the egotism and indifference to practical life which we have regretted to see it cherish in less genial natures.[40]

Greeley's emphasis on practicality is remarkable, as Thoreau was often perceived as the epitome of impracticality. While Greeley acknowledges that Transcendentalism can lead to retreat and self-centeredness ("in less genial natures"), he insists that Thoreau's philosophy is a form practical education.

Greeley repeatedly defended Thoreau against charges of esotericism. Five years later, he printed a letter by one Timothy Thorough, who saw Thoreau's Walden experiment as the epitome of self-centeredness, the outrageous deeds of "a whimsy or else a good-for-nothing." Greeley's sarcastic response is printed below the letter: "Mr. Thorough is indeed in a fog—in fact, we suspect there is a mistake in his name, and that he must have been changed at nurse for another boy whose true name was Shallow." Greeley then outlines *Walden*'s educational mission, rightly identifying "a large class of young men who aspire to Mental Culture through Study, Reading, Reflection, &c."

as the book's target audience. Those, Greeley claims, *Walden* can teach a "lesson" about how "by chastening their physical appetites, they may preserve their proper independence without starving their souls."[41] Greeley captures the book's gist. *Walden* was intended as an alternative to self-help books such as Hawes's, which promoted education as a means of financial success. But with his defense, Greeley also consecrates Thoreau's educational project and simultaneously establishes his reputation as a practical reformer.

The question of how practical Romanticism could and should be would assume center stage with Thoreau's later lectures. Thoreau's lectures and writings were educational from the outset, with Thoreau bragging "as lustily as *chanticleer* in the morning, standing on his roost, if only to wake my neighbors up" (*W* 84). With his lectures on John Brown, however, Thoreau approached the limit case of literary education. Thoreau's "A Plea for Captain John Brown" (1859) was written at a time when the lecture circuit became increasingly politicized. Brown's appearance on the political and intellectual scene contributed to this politicization. In fact, Brown's presence was woven into the lecture circuit. Brown himself had lectured in Concord to raise money for the abolitionist movement. Thoreau met and talked to Brown on this occasion.[42] The Transcendentalists were all impressed by Brown's rhetorical force, and his rhetoric shows in Thoreau's fervent defense of the rebel. Thoreau's lecture was not an abstract political consideration but discussed a character who was linked to the Transcendentalists and politics alike.

In 1859, after John Brown's raid on Harpers Ferry and his subsequent execution, Thoreau became involved in a heated political discussion. According to Dean and Hoag, Thoreau was "the first person in the country to speak out publicly on behalf of Brown."[43] In Concord, Thoreau met a mostly sympathetic audience. The true test occurred when Thoreau gave the same lecture in Boston, where newspapers had broadly condemned Brown's actions, and where he was confronted with an audience that was more involved with the local periodical culture. Thoreau was invited to give one of the Fraternity Course lectures, which were organized by Theodore Parker's congregation. The Benevolent Fraternity of Churches had originally been founded in response to Boston's growing poverty and as such was home to political discourse.[44] But the setting was especially politically charged because Thoreau had replaced Frederick Douglass as speaker. Douglass was rumored to have participated in the Harpers Ferry raid and escaped to Canada. The *Tribune* noted only briefly: "A larger audience converged at Syracuse on Friday evening to bear the lecture from Frederick Douglass on 'Self-Made Men,' but the lecturer failed to appear."[45] The *Liberator*'s correspondent wrote, "Mr. Douglass, however, did not appear, and the explanation of his absence by the Committee gave us to understand that he does not now consider himself safe in any part of the United States, in consequence of his alleged implication in the Harper's Ferry invasion."[46]

As Hoag has shown, the lyceum and other discussion forums increasingly converged in the 1840s, undergoing lasting changes in participation and audience structure. Besides its growing professionalization, the lyceum was increasingly politicized: "an early lyceum standard of nonpartisan, uncontroversial lectures educating all and offending none made way for pointed speeches on women's rights, abolitionism, and other social issues, some from female or black lecturers, including the formidable Frederick Douglass."[47] The lyceum's politicization also visibilized its mechanisms of exclusion and discrimination. In the 1840s, African Americans were frequently denied access to lyceum lectures and membership. In 1845, the curators of the New Bedford Lyceum had decided to seat African Americans separately. Informed by Mary Brooks, Emerson cancelled his scheduled lecture in protest.[48] Five months earlier, Emerson and Thoreau witnessed the Concord Lyceum's unwillingness to host abolitionist speakers. The lyceum's conservative section sought to prevent the invitation of abolitionist Wendell Philipps and, when they failed, eventually resigned in protest. The curators had hoped that this blatant attempt at racial segregation would simply be ignored by the lyceum's white audience. However, the progressive lyceum members prevailed, and Emerson and Thoreau accepted positions as curators.[49]

In "A Plea for Captain John Brown" (1859), Thoreau embraced the politicized platform, linking Douglass's fate to his speaker position and the topic of his lecture: "The reason why Frederick Douglass is not here is the reason why I am."[50] In his lecture, Thoreau reconsiders Romanticism in light of the struggle against slavery. His rhetoric is precise, aiming at effect. Thoreau presents Brown as a Romantic, "a transcendentalist above all."[51] Steeped in manual labor, as Emerson envisioned the true Romantic, Brown was also a man of "original observations": "He was by descent and birth a New England farmer, a man of great common-sense, deliberate and practical as that class is, and tenfold more so" (*RP* 112–3). Preparing his critique of the cultural elite, Thoreau presents Brown in contradistinction from Harvard as a man who "went to the great university of the West, where he sedulously pursued the study of Liberty" (*RP* 113). Thoreau doesn't openly criticize Harvard, to which he refers as "good old Alma Mater," but still foregrounds the contrast between an intellectual elite and the man of political action. When he addresses his "foes," they sound remarkably like graduates of the good old Alma Mater: "So they proceed to live their sane, and wise, and altogether admirable lives, reading their Plutarch a little, but chiefly pausing at that feat of Putnam, who was let down into a wolf's den; and in this wise they nourish themselves for brave and patriotic deeds some time or other" (*RP* 119–20). Brown, by contrast, was a "man of rare common-sense and directness of speech, as of action; a transcendentalist above all, a man of ideas and principles,—that was what distinguished him" (*RP* 115). Thoreau applauds Brown's principles and integrity. But more importantly, Brown figures as a verification of Transcendentalist ideas. His actions become the practical, if pointed, manifestation of Romantic principles.

Thoreau's drastic rhetoric and his sincere support of Brown's actions push the limits of popular education. Thoreau argues against the widespread opinion that Brown was insane, someone who acted in a wave of frenzy. According to Thoreau, Brown's rebellion was a principled, if drastic form of action: "I hear many condemn these men because they were so few. When were the good and the brave ever in a majority? Would you have had him wait till that time came?—till you and I came over to him?"[52] If the state fails to act according to principles and if waiting for the majority to turn to reform is futile, a "Vigilant Committee" is necessary. Thoreau is at pains to involve his audience in his quest, seeking to educate them in the need for principled action. But as opposed to Thoreau's earlier efforts, there is no subtle cognitive realignment through humor and provocation. Michael Stoneham has demonstrated that John Brown led many New England intellectuals to adopt a style of "literary confrontation": "Insightful, intelligent, manipulative, and extremely characteristic, John Brown was able to inspire some of the most enlightened men and women in his society to express their approval of dramatic and arbitrary violence in the name of morally justified social change."[53] The lecture is characterized by a tension between democratic discourse and the temporary support of political violence. It is true that Thoreau provocatively, but also genially, creates a space in which an imagined audience can take shape: "The newspapers seem to ignore, or perhaps are really ignorant of the fact, that there are at least as many as two or three individuals to a town throughout the North who think much as the present speaker does about him and his enterprise" (*RP* 117). But ultimately, Thoreau simply assumes that his audience supports radical change; and if they don't, they are simply part of the erring majority. The abolition of slavery becomes the horizon of a now political education: "Then, and not till then, we will take our revenge" (*RP* 138).

"A Plea for Captain John Brown" redefined Romanticism not only as a practical but also as a political affair. As Laura L. Mielke writes, "Thoreau offered himself as an eloquent spectacle in the interest of restaging John Brown as a noble idealist rather than a bloodthirsty terrorist, a sacrificial hero rather than a deranged murderer."[54] The staged spectacle elicited conflicted responses from Boston's intellectual public. The lecture was broadly advertised and reported on by most major Boston periodicals. Newspapers printed long excerpts.[55] Prominent periodicals attacked the lecture's aggressive attack on the press as self-congratulatory. Ironically, it was the *New-York*

*Tribune*'s Boston correspondent who would single out "A Plea for Captain John Brown" as a particularly irrelevant, impractical form of general education, with little to no political consequences. On November 9, 1859, Greeley's correspondent reviewed Thoreau's John Brown lectures at the Tremont Temple. He found "some just and striking remarks in it, and many foolish and ill-natured ones." He was particularly outraged by Thoreau's sneering remarks at Republicans, who, "while the lecturer was cultivating beans and killing woodchucks on the margin of Walden pond, made a public opinion strong enough on Anti-Slavery grounds to tolerate a speech from him in defense of insurrection." The correspondent was not willing to accommodate the rage of "the upstart Abolitionist of the day."[56] This is a remarkable critique as the *Tribune* had supported the Transcendentalists from the *Dial* to Thoreau's Walden project.

The *Liberator* equally criticized Thoreau, but mostly for what they considered his misrepresentation of Garrison's and the *Liberator*'s stance on John Brown. Mostly, however, the *Liberator* found praise for Thoreau's "real enthusiasm" and his informative lecture on Brown. Although the *Liberator* approached the lecture from a different angle, they similarly referred to Thoreau's image as an impractical philosopher: the events of Harper's Ferry "seemed to have awakened 'the hermit of Concord' from his usual state of philosophic indifference."[57] Feminist and abolitionist Caroline Healey Dall, by contrast, agreed on Thoreau's supposedly exaggerated rhetoric, but applauded his lecture's practical message: "Many of the sharpest things he said were in very bad taste—but it was on the whole a grand tribute to the truest American who has lived since George Washington. I was surprised for I had thought Mr. Thoreau *only* a philosopher."[58] All of the reviews, however, shared the sense that before this political lecture, Thoreau had essentially been a detached, impractical intellectual.

But Thoreau had never been an unpolitical person nor were his educational projects unpractical. His careful self-fashioning in *Walden* was an attempt to wake up his neighbors in the spirit of Emerson's dictum that teaching is "not instruction, but provocation" (*CW* 1:80). What changed was that Thoreau now linked Romanticism to political activism. Thoreau's radical rhetoric redefined the public position of an educator whose ideas of self-reliance and aesthetic experience needed redefinition in a time of political crisis. Accordingly, instead of advocating a national identity, as Emerson had done in "The Young American," thereby essentially circumventing politics, Thoreau ties Romanticism's educational mandate to a particular form of political action. His point is that there is no time and place for subtlety when human lives are at stake. The fact that Thoreau describes Brown as an idealist is not a contradiction. It is rather the attempt to reconcile intellectual practice and political activism at a time when such an alliance seemed necessary.

By linking his public personality to principled political action, Thoreau inadvertently suggests the limits of public education. Thoreau relies on Brown's authority, abandoning the conversational tone of his earlier lectures. But while Fuller in her European dispatches meticulously differentiated between her cultural work and the political action of Italian revolutionaries, Thoreau collapses this difference. The moment of solitude necessary for unlearning is no longer present in "A Plea for Captain John Brown." The lecture's openness retires in the name of a political activism which threatens to obliterate the popular lecture's educational function altogether. Thoreau's lecture marks a moment when popular education gives way to politics.

## DOUGLASS'S REPRESENTATIVITY

Frederick Douglass's emergence as a public speaker helped transform lecture platforms into political arenas just as much as his rise to fame was enabled by nineteenth-century lecturing platforms. Douglass emerged as one of the most powerful nineteenth-century speakers. He gave his first lyceum speech in 1854. As Angela Ray has shown, Douglass's later lyceum lectures "created transformational possibilities within highly assimilationist discourse."[59] In his later lyceum lectures, Douglass used the lyceum's principles, "the value of ordinary experiential observation, the importance of learning via models, and the unique role of the United States in world progress—and then adapted them to correspond to the lived experience of black Americans, changing the foundation of these premises in the process."[60] This strategy already shows in his early lectures, which were embedded in New England's popular educational culture. His conflicted situation as a public speaker, caught between various audiences and demands, is firmly in place in his early lectures and allows us to understand how for Douglass a Romantic emphasis on self-reliance was influenced by the speaker's position.

Douglass commenced his career as a lecturer in New Bedford, Massachusetts. Having established his local reputation as a preacher, he quickly drew the attention of larger audiences, finally being hired as a speaker by the American Anti-Slavery Association. An accomplished speaker, Douglass was also adept at using the mechanisms of the literary market and hence capable of positioning himself successfully in an increasingly professionalized intellectual field. But Douglass's relationship with public lecture forums was ambivalent. On the one hand, they were often controlled by patrons who had little interest in radical abolitionism and who frequently discouraged and even prevented abolitionist lectures. On the other hand, Douglass's meteoric rise to fame was also enabled by the public lecture forum's more progressive branches. Douglass was looking for a public outlet of his educational endeavors that sought to reach both a white, middle-class abolitionist audience and African Americans. The North's various lecture platforms provided such a space despite the racism that still pervaded them.

As we have seen with Thoreau's John Brown lectures, Douglass's sheer presence caused a tectonic shift in public lecturing. But although a child of the public lecture circuit, Douglass was also profoundly estranged from it. In a letter to William Lloyd Garrison, Douglass discusses his conflicted role as a public speaker. Writing from the Victoria Hotel, Belfast, on January 1, 1846, he addresses how his role as public educator lacks a direction:

> I have no end to serve, no creed to uphold, no government to defend; and as to nation, I belong to none. I have no protection at home, or resting-place abroad. The land of my birth welcomes me to her shores only as a slave, and spurns with contempt the idea of treating me differently. So that I am an outcast from the society of my childhood, and an outlaw in the land of my birth.[61]

In his letter, Douglass describes a Romantic "rapture" which is readily interrupted by the existence of slavery:

> In thinking of America, I sometimes find myself admiring her bright blue sky—her grand old woods—her fertile fields—her beautiful rivers—her mighty lakes, and star-crowned mountains. But my rapture is soon checked, my joy is soon turned to mourning. When I remember that all is cursed with the infernal spirit of slaveholding, robbery and wrong,—when I remember that with the waters of her noblest rivers, the tears of my brethren are borne to the ocean, disregarded and forgotten, and that her most fertile fields drink daily of the warm blood of my outraged sisters, I am filled with unutterable loathing, and led to reproach myself that any thing could fall from my lips in praise of such a land.

Douglass's experience in England, by contrast, with "the entire absence of every thing that looked like prejudice against me, on account of the color of my skin" provides a glimpse of true freedom. As he points out, this is particularly paradoxical since for African Americans, European monarchy may be a more humane system than American democracy: "Instead of a democratic government, I am under a monarchical government. Instead of the bright blue sky of America, I am covered with the soft grey fog of the Emerald Isle. I breathe, and lo! the chattel becomes a man." Douglass then explicitly relates these observations to various occasions on which he was denied access to public events because of his skin color, among them an incidence in New Bedford.[62] Douglass's paradoxical transatlantic position contrasts sharply with Emerson's confident vision of national unity in "The Young American."

Throughout his career Douglass would grapple with the contradictory position of the nineteenth-century African American intellectual.

As Gregory P. Lampe has shown, "Douglass's success on the lecture circuit was instantaneous."[63] To secure this success, Douglass's rhetorical and educational strategies tapped into nineteenth-century lyceum discourses of selfhood and self-improvement.[64] Indeed, Douglass was not simply reduced to his experience as a slave but perceived as a philosophical speaker proclaiming the value of self-culture and individuality. The *Liberator*'s review of Thoreau's John Brown lecture presented Douglass first of all as a self-reliant intellectual. Douglass, the reviewer writes, was to lecture on "Self-Made Men, a subject on which he is well qualified to speak."[65] Others celebrated him as "Representative American man," the product of a successful education, one to be emulated by other Americans.[66] Because these two dimensions of his public persona were intimately connected, Douglass could appropriate the discourse of selfhood for his political aims. As John Stauffer has it, "Douglass became an American icon through art. He brilliantly used the power of the word, voice, and image to write himself into public existence and remake himself while seeking to reform his nation."[67] Carefully gauging his rhetoric would soon become part of lecturing for Douglass.

Douglass's rhetoric and method could fall on fertile ground because he linked himself to an established Romantic position of selfhood but he also transformed these positions by doing so. Ethan Kytle has argued that although Douglass's "call for black self-help was born in African American communities that had few direct ties to Boston's elite Unitarian circles, it resembled the romantic vision of gradual self-culture embraced in the latter."[68] This is not to say that his call for self-help was merely strategic. Waldo E. Martin, Jr. has shown that "Frederick Douglass's view of the self-made men drew upon the religious, economic, and combined personal and social aspects of self-improvement and success in America," displaying a "deep-seated belief in the Protestant-capitalist work ethic."[69] But in his lectures, Douglass manipulated existing tropes so as to inscribe his own position into the intellectual field. He emerged as a representative man, as a public voice that testified to the potential of African Americans.

In the beginning of his career, however, Douglas was not yet the public representative of self-culture. His earliest speeches illustrate an important transitional moment in the history of the popular lecture. While Emerson and Thoreau chose to redefine their positions as intellectuals, Douglass's speaker position was politically determined from the very beginning of his career. He was forced to address and conceptualize his unprecedented position in the field. His early speech "I Have Come to Tell You Something About Slavery" (1841) was delivered in Lynn, Massachusetts, where Douglass had moved in 1841, and reprinted in the *Pennsylvania Freeman* in 1841. Lynn was not only a Quaker town, it was also a safer place for a runaway slave than Boston.[70] But the speaker's platform was already determined by the numerous expectations projected on the runaway slave so that Douglass had to carefully balance his political message with an attempt to establish himself as a public speaker.

"I Have Come to Tell You Something About Slavery" shows how Douglass had to balance popular appeal, self-promotion, and abolitionist education. In the beginning of the speech, Douglass establishes a speaker position that emphasizes experience as the ground of truth: "My friends, I have come to tell you something about slavery—what I *know* of it, as I have *felt* it."[71] While white abolitionists understand the struggle against slavery, they "cannot refer you to a back covered with scars." Douglass's emphasis on experience is not only meant to reinforce his abolitionism. It is also intended to counter the prejudice that African Americans show a lack of incentive to achieve their own freedom: "A larger portion of the slaves know that they have a right to their liberty.—It is often talked about and read of, for some of us know how to read, although all our knowledge is gained in secret." This rhetorical trope not only creates a relatable public persona,[72] it also introduces a categorical difference between his white middle-class audience and the speaker. In this context, Douglass's opening remark that he feels "greatly embarrassed when I attempt to address an audience of white people" because he has "always looked up to them with fear,"[73] also decenters questions of the self into structural issues of slavery and racism. While Douglass probably didn't believe himself to be inferior to his audience, as a subject he was denied education and self-realization. His supposed fear, then, stands symbolically for the structural oppression slavery had produced.

Through his rhetorical strategies, Douglass successfully established a sympathetic relationship with his audience. But he simultaneously addressed the gap that separated them from each other. For Douglass, popular appeal did not simply mean a favorable reception from the audience; it meant moving his audience to political activism. Feeling compassion was insufficient without proper action. As the audience tended to get wrapped up in the affective responses to Douglass's speech,[74] he had to accentuate the necessity of structural change rather than just trying to elicit his audience's compassionate sympathy. It is in the speech's conclusion where Douglass adds his final twist, one that provokes his audience in the best Romantic sense. While racist Southerners deny slaves education because they acknowledge and fear their intelligence, it is the paternalistic Northerners who do not believe in racial equality:

> My friends, we are not taught from books; there is a law against teaching us, although I have heard some folks say we could not learn if we had a chance. The northern people say so, but the south do not believe it, or they would not

have laws with heavy penalties to prevent it. The northern people think if slavery were abolished, we would all come north. They may be more afraid of the free colored people and the runaway slaves going South. We would all seek our home and our friends, but, more than all, to escape from northern prejudice, would we go to the south. Prejudice against color is stronger north than south; it hangs around my neck like a heavy weight. It presses me out from among my fellow men, and, although I have met it at every step the three years I have been out of southern slavery, I have been able, in spite of its influence, "to take good care of myself."[75]

In this concluding section of his speech, Douglass translates his experience into a structural critique of slavery and racism. In the context of his performance, he underscores the separation of his position from that of his white middle-class audience to pose the question if they are actually willing to be devoted abolitionists. To assert that his liberal white audience is in fact more racist than they are willing to admit certainly prevents any form of easy sympathetic identification with the speaker.

Douglass's final remark was not simply a form of rhetorical self-fashioning in front of a hospitable audience. While large parts of the abolitionist audience were deeply impressed by the spectacular, provocative, and often humorous Douglass, racism still pervaded the lecture halls. Edmund Quincy, an abolitionist attending his lecture in Lynn in 1841, was asked if he had written Douglass's lecture.[76] In fact, one of the main reasons why Douglass published his *Narrative of the Life of Frederick Douglass, an American Slave* (1845) was to settle the discussion once and for all. Accordingly, the title page announces that the text was "written by himself," and in his preface, William Lloyd Garrison found it necessary to emphasize that Douglass did not "employ some one else" to write the autobiography, it being "entirely his own production."[77] What was in question was Douglass's authority as a public intellectual and his ability to educate others.

Written during his time in Lynn, the *Narrative* must be linked to Douglass's experience on the lecture platform. As John Stauffer has argued, the Narrative is "an artistic synthesis of the speeches he had been delivering for over three years."[78] Douglass's autobiographical lectures and writings were always both autobiography proper, the public performances of an intellectual, and political education.[79] Scholarship has demonstrated that Douglass, both in his lectures and his books, masterfully manipulated his own image in order to reach a white middle-class audience.[80] While he emerged as a representative American to his audience, the question of who he represented was more complicated. The complications of the question are most succinctly addressed in Douglass's *Narrative*. Douglass describes education as fundamentally important for the liberation of slaves, and, accordingly, understands his teaching at a Sunday school as his most important work: "The work of instructing my dear fellow-slaves was the sweetest engagement with which I was ever blessed."[81] For Douglass, the school's success exemplifies his students' longing for emancipation: "These dear souls came not to Sabbath school because it was popular to do so, nor did I teach them because it was reputable to be thus engaged. Every moment they spent in that school, they were liable to be taken up and given thirty-nine lashes. They came because they wished to learn." In these moments, Douglass becomes a model that testifies to the abilities of African Americans, asking his audience to finally accept their humanity and abolish slavery.

But there are also moments when Douglass seems to establish an opposition between those slaves passively succumbing to frivolity and those who diligently educate themselves. On Christmas,

> [t]he staid, sober, thinking and industrious ones of our number would employ themselves in making corn-brooms, mats, horse-collars, and baskets; and another class of us would spend the time in hunting opossums, hares, and coons. But by far the larger part engaged in such sports and merriments as playing ball, wrestling, running foot-races, fiddling, dancing, and drinking whisky; and this latter mode of spending the time was by far the most agreeable to the feelings of our masters.

Of course, both are marked as "effective means in the hands of the slaveholder in keeping down the spirit of insurrection." Still, Douglass inscribes a work ethic into this episode which distinguishes between the willing and the unwilling. In accordance with what many white middle-class reformers would expect, Douglass presents education as the product of determination and self-reliance. Accordingly, Douglass describes the students in his Sabbath school as "those of the right sort."[82]

Douglass's remarks on the division between the willing and the unwilling occur in the famous chapter that details his fight with the overseer Edward Covey. This moment of liberation is the result of Douglass's education, his insight that he must fight the circumstances that seek to destroy his humanity; but it is also a moment of physical violence that contrasts with his careful manipulation of public discourse. In the passage quoted above, however, Douglass's distinction and self-fashioning assume priority over collective liberation. Douglass presents himself as part of those willing to work their way out of slavery. His distinction from those unwilling or unable to educate themselves primarily serves Douglass's self-authorization as an intellectual who had been publicly questioned. But these moments also prevent him from imagining the full force of educated resistance. As David Leverenz has suggested, "Douglass argued vehemently and repeatedly that a vigorous self-reliance was the only way for freed blacks to prosper." According to Leverenz, "Douglass's unswerving advocacy of middle-class individualism and hard work blocked his awareness of lower-class black experience in a great many ways."[83] Similarly, as Kenneth Warren has demonstrated for Douglass's later writings, "[t]he intelligent, articulate spectator, while attempting to reveal the details of these mute, silenced lives, distances himself from those he represents, making them other than himself, and confines them to a realm outside of that inhabited by the spectator."[84] Education, in these cases, functions as a means of prestige and differentiation which maintains the status quo.

Of course, as opposed to the Transcendentalists, who even when under public attack could rely on the support of a cultural movement, Douglass had to address different groups to none of which he completely belonged. As part of the lecture circuit, and particularly after the mid-nineteenth-century shifts in the lyceum's audience, he addressed a white middle class, many of whom were uncertain about how to deal with African Americans. On the one hand, Douglass's mission, as he constantly emphasized, was to show that African Americans had the same intellectual abilities as white men and women and therefore had to be immediately liberated. On the other hand, Douglass staged himself as an extraordinary intellectual. As Waldo Martin has claimed, Douglass's "middle-class strategy of racial elevation—illustrative of the mainstream cast of his mind—betrayed certain telling intellectual and tactical limitations." In his moments of self-fashioning, Douglass's success could be perceived as a display of "black ability" while, reassuringly, most were still able to see "such black achievement as the exception proving the rule of black inability."[85] In these instances, the necessity to cater to his white middle-class audiences affected his message of equality. For Douglass, the lyceum's audience proved an opportunity as much as a problem. He presented himself in a way that risked downplaying the collective resistance of uneducated African Americans in his quest for representativity and authority. At the same time, it was such a strategy that opened the lyceum platform for African American speakers like himself who advocated the necessity of abolitionism. And it was the success of his strategies that changed the lecture circuit permanently.

Paradoxically, the more the lecture circuit became a forum for urgent political questions, the more it became a middle-class institution. The more the lyceum tended toward professionalization, the more it institutionalized the gap between teacher and learner, becoming part of the self-perpetuating educational system it had set out to challenge. As Hoag outlines, in the 1840s, the time of Douglass's emergence, the lyceum had failed to attract the lower classes, hence essentially becoming a forum for a white middle-class audience and, what was more problematic for both the movement's original mission and the Romantic educational ideal, for the "professional strata."[86]

The tension between popularity, professionalism, and educational ideal built into the genre of the lecture itself intensified. At the same time, these tensions combined with the political events of the time shifted the emphasis from educational ideas to the social conditions that need to be changed in order for true education to be possible, hence enabling or forcing speakers to address these conditions more openly.

In antebellum America, and with the increasing involvement of the Romantics in political affairs from abolitionism to the Italian Revolution, Romantic education productively reached its limits. Nathan Crick has argued that the "individual Transcendentalists each articulated a unique rhetoric and politics that applied their philosophical reflections and poetic practices to affairs of persuasive eloquence and social justice."[87] In "The Last Days of John Brown," Thoreau draws out the tensions and potential underlying Romantic education:

> We seem to have forgotten that the expression "a liberal education" originally meant among the Romans one worthy of free men; while the learning of trades and professions by which to get your livelihood merely was considered worthy of slaves only. But taking a hint from the word, I would go a step further, and say that it is not the man of wealth and leisure simply, though devoted to art, or science, or literature, who, in a true sense, is liberally educated, but only the earnest and free man. In a slaveholding country like this, there can be no such thing as a liberal education tolerated by the State; and those scholars of Austria and France who, however learned they may be, are contented under their tyrannies have received only a servile education.[88]

Thoreau connects questions of empowerment, accessibility, and literary expression. When in her European dispatches Fuller had argued that Romanticism cannot be truly realized as a principle of social organization without the necessary political struggle for social and economic equality, she had not only limited the claims of Romantic education but also related them to political action. In this passage, Thoreau makes the success of Romantic education contingent on the abolition of slavery. Much earlier, in his *Narrative*, Douglass had proclaimed that "education and slavery were incompatible with each other."[89] For Thoreau, it is precisely Romantic education which can enlist his audience in the struggle against slavery.

Alcott had stressed that education needed to become practical: "Means of Reform. Our plans of influence, to be successful, must become more practical. We must be more faithful. We must deal less in abstractions; depend less on precepts and rules. We must fit the soul for duty by the practice of duty."[90] The lyceum promised to fulfill these aspirations. Its self-description certainly sounded very Romantic. On April 9, 1829, the *Boston Recorder and Religious*

*Telegraph* printed an article by the Boston Lyceum's newly elected chairman on its title page. In almost the same terms that Fuller would use to define the educational nature of her popular journalism, he described the lyceum as a forum of "mutual instruction" that was aimed at "the friends of popular education."[91] The more education became politicized because of changes in the lecture circuit and because of the rise of abolitionism as a movement, the more it had to align itself with political activism, and the more it became professionalized, the more speakers had to carefully balance their potential audiences. The Transcendentalists realized that Romanticism needed to rely on political reform to fulfill its promise as a generative principle of society. But importantly, none of them abandoned their Romantic principles for popularity and influence. Even in his most political moment, Thoreau would still try to portray John Brown as a Transcendentalist. The point was to make the Romantic practice of self-reliance and self-realization available to a larger audience and to connect it to the social and political movements of the day. While Romantic popular education remained conflicted about its constituencies, at this point it found itself dedicated to changing the social conditions that prevented the realization of the comprehensive Romantic project.

## NOTES

1. Josiah Holbrook, "Associations of Adults for Mutual Instruction," *American Journal of Education* 1 (1826): 595.

2. Holbrook, "Associations," 594–5.

3. Angela G. Ray, "How Cosmopolitan Was the Lyceum, Anyway?" *The Cosmopolitan Lyceum: Lecture Culture and the Globe in Nineteenth Century*, ed. Tom F. Wright (Amherst: University of Massachusetts Press, 2013), 28.

4. Ronald J. Zboray, *A Fictive People: Antebellum Economic Development and the American Reading Public* (Oxford: Oxford University Press, 1993), 107.

5. Moses Plimpton, *History of Southbridge* (Southbridge: Journal Steam Book Print, 1882), 39.

6. Ronald Wesley Hoag, "Odd Man In: Thoreau, the Lyceum Movement, and the Lecture Circuit," *Henry David Thoreau in Context*, ed. James S. Finley (Cambridge: Cambridge University Press, 2017), 147. Tom F. Wright has suggested that the lyceum was a complex "international and cross-media phenomenon" with which scholarship has yet to come to terms: "uncertainty about how to approach the scope and conflicts of lecture culture has helped perpetuate a continuing scholarly disregard for a fundamental expressive form of the period." Tom F. Wright, *Lecturing the Atlantic: Speech, Print, and an Anglo-American Commons 1830–1870* (Oxford: Oxford University Press, 2017), 3.

7. Hoag, "Odd Man In," 147.

8. Hoag, "Odd Man In," 149.

9. Thoreau, *Correspondence*, 1:37.

10. Frederick Douglass, *The Speeches of Frederick Douglass: A Critical Edition*, ed. John R. McKivigan (New Haven: Yale University Press, 2018), 47.

11. Emerson, *The Letters of Ralph Waldo Emerson,* 2:88.

12. See Dowling, "Publishers."

13. David M. Robinson, *Apostle of Culture: Emerson as Preacher and Lecturer* (Philadelphia: University of Pennsylvania Press, 1982), 44.

14. Peter S. Field, *Ralph Waldo Emerson: The Making of a Democratic Intellectual* (Lanham: Rowman and Littlefield, 2003), 135.

15. Kenneth Sacks, *Understanding Emerson: "The American Scholar" and His Struggle for Self-Reliance* (Princeton: Princeton University Press, 2003), 7.

16. Field, *Ralph Waldo Emerson,* 210.

17. Sylvia J. Cook, *Working Women, Literary Ladies: The Industrial Revolution and Female Aspiration* (Oxford: Oxford University Press, 2008), 95.

18. David M. Robinson, *Emerson and the Conduct of Life: Pragmatism and Ethical Purpose in the Later Thought* (New York: Cambridge University Press), 1993.

19. As in many of the Transcendentalists' discussions of poverty, Emerson displays a tendency to naturalize poverty: "Hence it happens that the whole interest of history lies in the fortunes of the poor. Knowledge, Virtue, Power are the victories of man over his necessities, his march to the dominion of the world" (*CW* 1:151).

20. Eric Keenaghan, "Reading Emerson, in Other Times: On a Politics of Solitude and an Ethics of Risk," *The Other Emerson,* ed. Cary Wolfe and Branka Arsić (University of Minnesota Press, 2010), 171.

21. Wright, *Lecturing the Atlantic*, 5

22. Robert Milder, "The Radical Emerson?" *Cambridge Companion to Ralph Waldo Emerson*, ed. Joel Porte and Saundra Morris (Cambridge: Cambridge University Press, 1999) 73.

23. Mary Kupiec Cayton, "The Making of an American Prophet: Emerson, His Audiences, and the Rise of the Culture Industry in Nineteenth-Century America," *American Historical Review* 92, no. 3 (1987): 613.

24. See Cayton, "Making of an American Prophet," 613.

25. Richard F. Teichgraeber, *Sublime Thoughts, Penny Wisdom* (Baltimore: Johns Hopkins University Press, 1995), 209.

26. Luke Philip Plotica, *Nineteenth-Century Individualism and the Market Economy: Individualist Themes in Emerson, Thoreau, and Sumner* (Basingstoke: Palgrave Macmillan, 2018), 117.

27. Bradley P. Dean and Ronald Wesley Hoag, "Thoreau's Lectures Before 'Walden': An Annotated Calendar," *Studies in the American Renaissance* (1995): 130.

28. Thoreau, *Correspondence* 1:31.

29. Once Thoreau had finalized his lecture in written form, he never used it as a lecture again. Before that, however, the lecture was work-in-progress. Records of Thoreau's early lectures must therefore be gathered from his final essays and journal entries of those in attendance. In most cases, however, the lectures came very close to the final, published form.

30. See Hoag, "Odd Man In," 144; Laura Dassow Walls. *Henry David Thoreau: A Life* (Chicago: University of Chicago Press, 2017), 54–6.

31. Hoag, "Odd Man In," 146.
32. Hoag, "Odd Man In," 145.
33. Dean and Hoag, "Thoreau's Lectures Before 'Walden'," 162.
34. Henry David Thoreau, *Collected Essays and Poems,* ed. Elizabeth Hall Witherell (New York: Library of America, 2001), 351.
35. Leonard N. Neufeldt, *The Economist: Henry Thoreau & Enterprise* (New York: Oxford University Press, 1989), 105.
36. Joel Hawes, *Lectures to Young Men; on the Formation of Character &c.* (Hartford: Cooke and Co. 1832), 1–12, 83.
37. Thoreau, *Correspondence,* 149.
38. Henry David Thoreau, "Homer. Ossian. Chaucer," *Dial,* January 1844, 293.
39. Thoreau, "Homer. Ossian. Chaucer," 305.
40. Horace Greeley, "'The Dial' for January," *New-York Daily Tribune,* January 25, 1844, 1.
41. Horace Greeley, "Reply," *New-York Daily Tribune,* April 7, 1849, 5.
42. Bradley P. Dean and Ronald Wesley Hoag, "Thoreau's Lectures After 'Walden': An Annotated Calendar." *Studies in the American Renaissance Studies in the American Renaissance* (1996): 309.
43. Dean and Hoag, "Thoreau's Lectures After 'Walden'," 312.
44. See Dean Grodzins, *American Heretic: Theodore Parker and Transcendentalism* (Chapel Hill: University of North Carolina Press, 2002), 416.
45. *New-York Daily Tribune,* October 25, 1859, 7.
46. C.K.W., "Fifth Fraternity Lecture," *The Liberator,* November 4, 1859, 174.
47. Hoag, "Odd Man In," 148.
48. Sandra Harbart Petrulionis, *To Set this World Right: The Antislavery Movement in Thoreau's Concord* (Ithaca: Cornell University Press, 2006), 54–5.
49. Robert D. Richardson, Jr., *Henry Thoreau: A Life of the Mind* (Berkeley: University of California Press, 1986), 151.
50. Dean/Hoag, "Thoreau's Lectures After 'Walden'," 312.
51. Henry David Thoreau, *Reform Papers,* ed. Wendell Glick (Princeton: Princeton University Press, 1973), 115; hereafter cited parenthetically as *RP*.
52. Thoreau, *Reform Papers,* 131.
53. Michael Stoneham, *John Brown and the Era of Literary Confrontation* (New York: Routledge, 2009), 9.
54. Laura L. Mielke, *Provocative Eloquence: Theater, Violence, and Antislavery Speech in the Antebellum United States* (Ann Arbor: University of Michigan Press, 2019), 188.
55. Dean and Hoag, "Thoreau's Lectures After 'Walden'," 317.
56. Anon., "From Boston," *New-York Daily Tribune,* November 9, 1859, 3.
57. C.K.W., "Fifth Fraternity Lecture," 174.
58. Caroline Healey Dall, *Daughter of Boston: The Extraordinary Diary of a Nineteenth-Century Woman* (Boston: Beacon Press, 2005), 286.
59. Angela G. Ray, "Frederick Douglass on the Lyceum Circuit: Social Assimilation, Social Transformation?" *Rhetoric and Public Affairs* 5, no. 4 (2002): 626.
60. Ray, "Frederick Douglass on the Lyceum Circuit," 640.

61. Frederick Douglass, *The Frederick Douglass Papers, Series Three: Correspondence, vol. 1*, ed. John R. McKivigan (New Haven: Yale University Press, 2009), 73.

62. Douglass, *The Frederick Douglass Papers*, 73–4.

63. Gregory P. Lampe, *Frederick Douglass: Freedom's Voice, 1818-184* (East Lansing: Michigan State University Press, 2012), 66.

64. Carefully gauging his rhetoric would soon become part of lecturing for Douglass. During his Garrisonian, for instance, he had toned down his rhetoric to prevent marginalization. John R. McKivigan et al., Introduction, *The Speeches of Frederick Douglass: A Critical Edition*, ed. John R. McKivigan et al. (New Haven: Yale University Press, 2018), xxvii.

65. C.K.W., "Fifth Fraternity Lecture," 174.

66. Qtd. in John Stauffer, "Frederick Douglass's Self-Fashioning and the Making of a Representative American Man," *Cambridge Companion to the African American Slave Narrative*, ed. Audrey A. Fisch (Cambridge: Cambridge University Press, 2007), 201.

67. Stauffer, "Fredrick Douglass's Self-Fashioning," 201.

68. Ethan Kytle, *Romantic Reformers and the Antislavery Struggle in the Civil War Era* (New York: Cambridge, 2014), 87.

69. Waldo E. Martin, Jr., *The Mind of Frederick Douglass* (Chapel Hill: University of North Carolina Press, 1984), 255–6.

70. William S. McFeely, *Frederick Douglass* (New York: Norton, 2017), 99.

71. Douglass, *Speeches of Frederick Douglass*, 5.

72. Terry Baxter, *Frederick Douglass's Curious Audiences: Ethos in the Age of the Consumable Subject* (New York: Routledge, 2004), 92.

73. Douglass, *Speeches of Frederick Douglass*, 5.

74. See Vincent Lloyd, "The Affect of God's Law," *A Political Companion to Frederick Douglass*, ed. Neil Robert (Lexington: University of Kentucky Press, 2018), 311–2.

75. Douglass, *Speeches of Frederick Douglass*, 7–8.

76. See David W. Blight, *Frederick Douglass Prophet of Freedom* (New York: Simon and Schuster, 2018), 113.

77. Frederick Douglass, *Autobiographies* (New York: Library of America, 1994), 7.

78. Stauffer, "Frederick Douglass's Self-Fashioning," 203.

79. See Stauffer, "Frederick Douglass's Self-Fashioning," 201–17.

80. Kenneth Warren, "Frederick Douglass's Life and Times: Progressive Rhetoric and the Problem of Constituency," *Renewing Black Intellectual History: The Ideological and Material Foundations of African American Thought*, ed. Adolph Reed, Jr., Kenneth Warren (New York: Routledge, 2010), 4.

81. Douglass, *Autobiographies*, 71.

82. Douglass, *Autobiographies*, 71.

83. David Leverenz, "Frederick Douglass's Self-Refashioning," *Criticism* 29, no. 3 (1987): 361.

84. Warren, "Frederick Douglass's Life and Times," 6.

85. Martin, *The Mind of Frederick Douglass*, 281.

86. Hoag, "Odd Man In," 148.

87. Nathan Crick, *The Keys of Power: The Rhetoric and Politics of Transcendentalism* (Columbia: University of South Carolina Press, 2017), 9.

88. Thoreau, *Reform Papers,* 151.

89. Douglass, *Autobiographies*, 40.

90. Alcott, *Doctrine and Discipline,* 21.

91. Asa Rand, "Education," *Boston Recorder and Religious Telegraph*, April 9, 1829, 57.

# Conclusion

It is not a coincidence that with the increasing commercialization of education in the twenty-first century there has been a growing interest in alternative forms of education.[1] Teachers and students alike are confronted with the logic of profit and competition. In many cases, education, as Megan Erickson argues in *Class War*, is about acquiring prestige from the earliest childhood on. Employing a word choice that illustrates just how important the Romantic tradition remains, Erickson demands that "American schools must be transformed to integrate the human love of play—making meaning through building with blocks, experimenting with words, listening to music, dancing." According to Erickson, "work should be revised and restructured around both basic human needs (like caring for friends and family) and complex needs, like being creative—instead of around the relentless drive for profit."[2] Erickson's claims, drawn from her experiences as a teacher, show how the Romantic vision needs to be unearthed and refunctionalized in the name of an education that fosters collective creativity and individual development.

Erickson's remark also points out that pedagogical principles are instrumental in reproducing the prestige necessary to maintain the status quo. In this sense, Romanticism was not simply an idea; it was a practice which positioned itself in a discourse about the future of universal education. The Romantic reformers worked through the institutional conditions of education. Their belief that Romanticism should become the organizing principle of social interaction prompted them to move into the public. The popularization of Romanticism, in turn—Alcott's publication of his school records, Fuller's tenure with the *New-York Tribune*, Emerson's and Thoreau's political speeches, Brownson's political journalism—forced them to consider the exclusionary mechanism on which education and intellectual practice rested. With the literary and educational institutions undergoing an increasing professionalization in the 1830s and 1840s, the desire for universal access to an aesthetic education was more and more at odds with a differentiated modern society driven by profit and competition. The vision to reconnect collective creativity and social totality, however, persisted and drove the Transcendentalists to engage the paradoxes of universal education in a liberal capitalist society.

It is precisely these questions about the possibilities and limits of aesthetic education and agency that have received renewed attention in recent critical works such as Gayatri Spivak's *An Aesthetic Education in the Era of Globalization*. Spivak's re-reading of Schiller shows how there is an impetus to re-activate the idea of aesthetic education at a time where the Humanities are in crisis everywhere. The Transcendentalists forced themselves to develop a practical Romanticism which may very well aid that project. Romantic education instituted concrete oppositional spaces, whether in schools and conversational circles or by carving out these spaces in the dominant institutions of the time. Accepting the limits of education was an essential part of turning their educational projects into an effective practice. The modern educational system is built on exclusion—in fact, as has been frequently argued, exclusion and the preservation of privilege are one of the system's major purposes. Reform, however, can still take shape in these confines. At the very least, the Transcendentalists engaged in an act of consciousness-raising. They inserted a core of aesthetic critique into a system that frequently served the preservation of an elite under attack and a new comprehensive market capitalism. This important episode in nineteenth-century education allows us to gauge the possibilities and limits of literary education which is particularly relevant in a global educational system increasingly invested in the accumulation of prestige and profit.

The Transcendentalists' educational practices were interventions. Speaking of practices as interventions (or at least possible conscious attempts at intervention) qualifies sociological accounts in the wake of Pierre Bourdieu's theories which mostly see practice as inherited, habitualized forms of behavior. In *Reproduction in Education, Society and Culture,* a book that has set the standard for contemporary sociological analyses of education, Bourdieu and Passeron suggest a correspondence between ruling ideology and educational practice. In the wake of this book and Bourdieu's other work, Bourdieu-inspired studies have productively studied how education has reproduced class structures and how the increasingly specialized field of literature represents the ruling ideologies of a particular class formation. And yet, it is often forgotten that for Bourdieu the empirical study of education served the larger purpose of transforming the field. For Bourdieu, the fact that the modern educational system rests on a stratified social system necessitates an awareness of, and a struggle against, the stratification that prevents large parts of the world from realizing the "universal anthropological possibility" of education. It is the sociologist's task to break "the enchanted circle of collective denial" that prevents "the world of knowledge" from admitting that the autonomy of the scholastic field is "favoured by economic separation."[3]

The Transcendentalists didn't need a sociologist to reveal the contradictions of the educational system to them. Their writings are remarkably clear on the reproductive function of education. This is not to say that they stood outside the conditions of education. American Romanticism stands as an episode in American educational history that outlines a practical, yet idealistic education, a movement that created progressive spaces of education from within the restrictions of an increasingly professionalized and competitive educational system. With the Transcendentalists, perhaps for the last time, education could be perceived as a comprehensive social practice rooted in self-realization and aesthetic sensibility. Their educational reform efforts sought to reintegrate the fields of an increasingly differentiated modernity. Confronted with the task of how to project their educational practice into comprehensive reform projects, the Transcendentalists developed a complex, and sometimes contradictory, understanding of how social practice was linked to the reproduction of socioeconomic privilege. But it was also the historical moment when the end of such a form of education needed to be imagined.

In order to make its history available for the present, it is important to acknowledge that Romantic education was a conflicted and sometimes inconsequential endeavor, even in the nineteenth century, whose dynamic education field was so permissive of reform. Walter Benn Michaels's fundamental critique of education brings into focus the conflicted nature of educational reform more generally. In an essay called "Dude, Where's My Job?", Michaels has argued that "economic inequality is the business we're in. It's only because we exclude lots of students that we can plausibly sell the students we admit on the economic advantages of having a college degree since if everybody had one, those advantages would disappear."[4] Brownson would agree. As I have tried to show in this book, the popularization of education led the Romantics to accept its limits. They realized that self-culture could become universal only if accompanied by social reform. But that realization could occur only because they uncompromisingly followed their ideal of a Romanticized world in the first place.

Orestes Brownson insisted that the practical purpose of education is the cultivation of the self, not the functioning of the individual under liberal capitalism. Brownson arrives at a question that resonates with a twenty-first-century audience: "But what is meant by *practicalness*; who is practical man?" Following traditions, orders, and reproducing the system through habitualized practice is a "waste of the resources of society" as it makes impossible the "social progress" for the development of all individuals according to their potential. Progress and improvement are "the constant obligation of man's being, individually and socially." Only thus is it possible to "draw out into free activity the whole faculties of the mind."[5] As a utopian vision, Romanticism drove the Transcendentalists to institutionalize and popularize their literary education. The history of Romantic education shows not only how complicated and contradictory that project was but also how an uncompromising insistence on a non-reifiable aesthetic experience is necessary to imagine alternative forms of social interaction.

## NOTES

1. Classic studies such as Christopher Newfield's *Unmaking the Public University* have addressed the commercialization and economization of higher education in the United States; see Christopher Newfield, *Unmaking the Public University: The Forty-Year Assault on the Middle Class* (Cambridge: Harvard University Press, 2010). There is a plethora of literature on the commodification of education. Suffice it to say that this phenomenon is a function of neoliberalism. See, for instance, Richard Münch, *Akademischer Kapitalismus: Über die politische Ökonomie der Hochschulreform* (Frankfurt Suhrkamp, 2011).

2. Megan Erickson, *Class War: The Privatization of Childhood* (London: Verso, 2015), 21.

3. Bourdieu, *Pascalian Meditations*, 5, 9, 15.

4. Walter Benn Michaels, "Dude, Where's My Job?" *PMLA* 127, no. 4 (2012): 1007.

5. Brownson, "Education," 155–7, 145.

# Bibliography

Abbott, Jacob. *The Little Scholar Learning to Talk: A Picture Book for Rollo*. Boston: John Allen, 1835.
Albert, Judith Strong. "Margaret Fuller's Row at Green Street School: Early Female Education in Providence, 1837–1839." *Rhode Island History* 42 (1983): 43–55.
Alcott, Amos Bronson. Amos Bronson Alcott Papers. MS Am 1130.12. Houghton Library, Harvard University.
———. *Conversations with Children on the Gospels*. 2 vols. Boston: James Munroe and Co., 1836–37.
———. "Days from a Diary." *Dial*, April 1842, 409–37.
———. *The Doctrine and Discipline of Human Culture*. Boston: James Munroe and Co., 1836.
———. *The Journals of Bronson Alcott*, edited by Odell Shepard. 2 vols. Boston: Little, Brown, and Co., 1938.
———. *The Letters of A. Bronson Alcott*, edited by Richard L. Herrnstadt. Ames: Iowa State University Press, 1969.
———. *Observations on the Principles and Methods of Infant Instruction*. Boston: Carter and Hendee, 1830.
———. "Orphic Sayings." *Dial*, Jan 1841, 351–61.
———. "Primary Education." *American Journal of Education* 3, no. 1 (1828): 26–31.
Anon. "About Mr. Alcott's School." *Parley's Magazine* 4 (1836): 131–2.
———. "A. Bronson Alcott," *American Journal of Education* 6 (1877): 225–36.
———. "Alcott's *Conversations on the Gospels*." *Christian Examiner* 5, no. 2 (1837): 252–61
———. "Boston Public Schools," *Boston Courier,* December 7, 1832, 1.
———. "Common Schools—Education in Philadelphia," *Philadelphia Inquirer*, Apr. 24, 1838, n.p.
———. "Death of Margaret Fuller." *Southern Literary Messenger* 16 (1850), 519.
———. "Education." St. Louis *Daily Commercial Bulletin*, Aug. 10, 1837, 2
———. "Education in Massachusetts," *Mississippian*, March 3, 1837, 1.

———. "From Boston." *New-York Daily Tribune*, November 9, 1859, 3.
———. *Mind and Matter; or Familiar Conversations on the Body and Soul; Designed for Children at Home and at School*. Boston: Benjamin H. Greene, 1833.
———. "New England Free Schools," *Scioto Gazette*, April 11, 1832, 1.
———. "To Fathers and Mothers." *Boston Courier*, 30 Mar. 1837: 1.
———. "Universal Education: The Great European Movement," *Vermont Chronicle*, Jan 31, 1838, 18.
Bailyn, Bernard. *Education in the Forming of American Society*. New York: Norton, 1972.
Balfour, Ian. *The Rhetoric of Romantic Prophecy*. Stanford: Stanford University Press, 2002.
Bancroft, George. "Correspondence," *The Globe*, November 13, 1834, 2.
Bankston, III, Carl L., and Stephen J. Caldas. *Public Education: America's Civil Religion. A Social History*. New York. Teachers College Press, 2009.
Baxter, Terry. *Frederick Douglass's Curious Audiences: Ethos in the Age of the Consumable Subject*. New York: Routledge, 2004.
Beadie, Nancy. *Education and the Creation of Capital in the Early American Republic*. Cambridge: Cambridge University Press, 2010.
Beam, Dorri. *Style, Gender, and Fantasy in Nineteenth-Century American Women's Writing*. Cambridge: Cambridge University Press, 2010.
Bean, Judith Mattson, and Joel Myerson. "Introduction." In *Margaret Fuller, Critic: Writings from the New-York Tribune, 1844–46*, edited by Judith Mattson Bean and Joel Myerson, 1–35. New York: Columbia University Press, 2000.
Beiser, Frederick C. *The Romantic Imperative: The Concept of Early German Romanticism*. Cambridge, MA: Harvard University Press, 2003.
Bellin, Roger. "Argument: The American Transcendentalists and Disputatious Reasons." PhD diss., Princeton University, 2011.
Beneke, Chris. "The Idea of Integration in the Age of Horace Mann." In *Inequity in Education: A Historical Perspective*, edited by Debra Meyers, Burke Miller, 101–14. Lanham, MD: Lexington Books, 2009.
Bergmann, Hans. *God in the Street: New York Writing from the Penny Press to Melville*. Philadelphia: Temple University Press, 1995.
Bickman, Martin. *Minding American Education: Reclaiming the Tradition of Active Learning*. New York: Teachers College Press, 2003.
Bledstein, Burton. *The Culture of Professionalism: The Middle Class and the Development of Higher Education in America*. New York: Norton, 1976.
Blight, David W. *Frederick Douglass Prophet of Freedom*. New York: Simon and Schuster, 2018.
Bourdieu, Pierre. *The Field of Cultural Production*. New York: Columbia University Press, 1993.
———. *Pascalian Meditations*. Stanford: Stanford University Press, 2000.
Bourdieu, Pierre, and Jean-Claude Passeron. *Reproduction in Education, Society and Culture*. London: Sage, 1990.
Brownson, Orestes. "Alcott on Human Culture," *Boston Quarterly Review*, Oct. 1838, 417–32.

———. "American Literature," *Boston Quarterly Review*, Jan. 1839, 1–26.
———. "Conversations with a Radical," *Boston Quarterly Review*, Jan. 1841, 1–41.
———. *A Discourse on the Wants of the Times, Delivered in Lyceum Hall, Hanover Street, Boston, Sunday, May 29, 1836.* Boston: James Munroe and Co., 1836.
———. "Education." *Boston Quarterly Review*, April 1840, 137–65.
———. "The Laboring Classes." *Boston Quarterly Review*, July 1840, 358–95.
———. "Literary Notices," *Boston Quarterly Review,* July 1839, 389–90.
———. "Observations and Hints on Education," *Boston Quarterly Review,* April 1840, 137–66.
———. "Union and Progress." *Boston Quarterly Review*, April 1838, 192–9.
Buckingham, Joseph T. "Alcott's Conversations on the Gospels." *Boston Courier*, May 11, 1837: 1.
———. Postscript to "To Fathers and Mothers," *Boston Courier*, 30 Mar. 1837, 1.
Buckminster, Joseph. "Discourse on the Dangers and Duties of Men of Letters." *The Works of Joseph Stevens Buckminster; with Memoirs of His Life.* Vol.2. 339–62. Boston: James Munroe and Co., 1839.
Buehrens, John A. *Conflagration: How the Transcendentalists Sparked the American Struggle for Racial, Gender, and Social Justice.* Boston: Beacon Press, 2020.
Buell, Lawrence. *Literary Transcendentalism: Style and Vision in the American Renaissance.* Ithaca: Cornell University Press, 1973.
Burkholder, Robert. "Emerson, Kneeland, and the Divinity School Address." *American Literature* 58, no. 1 (1986): 1–14.
Capper, Charles. *Margaret Fuller: An American Romantic Life.* 2 vols. New York: Oxford University Press, 1992, 2007.
———. "Margaret Fuller as Cultural Reformer: The Conversations in Boston." *American Quarterly* 39, no. 4 (1987): 509–28.
Carey, Patrick. *Orestes A. Brownson: American Religious Weathervane.* Grand Rapids: W. B. Eerdmans, 2004.
Carlson, Larry A. "Bronson Alcott's "Journal for 1837" (Part One)." *Studies in the American Renaissance* (1981): 27–132.
———. "Bronson Alcott's "Journal for 1837" (Part Two)." *Studies in the American Renaissance* (1982): 53–167.
———. "Bronson Alcott's "Journal for 1838" (Part One)." *Studies in the American Renaissance* (1993): 161–244.
———. "Bronson Alcott's "Journal for 1838" (Part Two)." *Studies in the American Renaissance* (1994): 123–93.
———. "'Those Pure Pages of Yours': Bronson Alcott's Conversations with Children on the Gospels." *American Literature* 60, no. 3 (1988): 451–60.
Cavell, Stanley. *The Senses of Walden,* exp. ed. Chicago: University of Chicago Press, 1992.
Cayton, Mary Kupiec. *Emerson's Emergence: Self and Society in the Transformation of New England, 1800-1845.* Chapel Hill: University of North Carolina Press, 1989.

———. "The Making of an American Prophet: Emerson, His Audiences, and the Rise of the Culture Industry in Nineteenth-Century America," *American Historical Review* 92, no. 3 (1987): 597–620.

Channing, William Ellery. *The Works of William E. Channing, D. D.* 2nd ed. 6 vols. Boston: James Munroe and Co., 1843.

Chevigny, Bell Gale "To the Edges of Ideology: Margaret Fuller's Centrifugal Evolution." *American Quarterly* 38, no. 2 (1986): 173–201.

———. *Woman and the Myth: Margaret Fuller's Life and Writings*, rev. ed. Boston: Northeastern University Press, 1994.

C.K.W., "Fifth Fraternity Lecture," *The Liberator*, 4 Nov. 1859, 174.

Clarke, James Freeman. *The Letters of James Freeman Clarke to Margaret Fuller*, edited by John Wesley Thomas. Hamburg: Cram, De Gruyter, 1957.

———. "Mr. Alcott's Book and the Objections Made to It." *Western Messenger* 3, no. 4 (1837): 678–83.

Cohoon, Linda. "Susanna Rowson and Early Romantic Pedagogies." In *Romantic Education in Nineteenth-Century America*, edited by Monika Elbert and Lesley Ginsberg, 75–88. New York: Routledge, 2015.

Cook, Sylvia J. *Working Women, Literary Ladies: The Industrial Revolution and Female Aspiration*. Oxford: Oxford University Press, 2008.

Crick, Nathan. *The Keys of Power: The Rhetoric and Politics of Transcendentalism*. Columbia: University of South Carolina Press, 2017.

Dall, Caroline Healey. *Daughter of Boston: The Extraordinary Diary of a Nineteenth-Century Woman*. Boston: Beacon Press, 2005.

Davenport, Stewart. *Friends of the Unrighteous Mammon: Northern Christians and Market Capitalism, 1815–1860*. Chicago: University of Chicago Press, 2008.

Dean, Bradley P. and Ronald Wesley Hoag. "Thoreau's Lectures After 'Walden': An Annotated Calendar." *Studies in the American Renaissance* (1996): 241–362.

———. "Thoreau's Lectures Before 'Walden': An Annotated Calendar." *Studies in the American Renaissance* (1995): 127–228.

Delano, Sterling F. *Brook Farm: The Dark Side of Utopia*. Cambridge, MA: Harvard University Press, 2004, 14–38.

De Wolfe Miller, Frederick. *Christopher Pearse Cranch and His Caricatures of New England Transcendentalism*. Cambridge: Harvard University Press, 1951.

Douglass, Frederick. *Autobiographies*. New York: Library of America, 1994.

———. *The Frederick Douglass Papers, Series Three: Correspondence*, vol. 1, edited by John R. McKivigan. New Haven: Yale University Press, 2009.

———. *The Speeches of Frederick Douglass: A Critical Edition*, edited by John R. McKivigan. New Haven: Yale University Press, 2018.

Dowling, David. *The Business of Literary Circles in Nineteenth-Century America*. New York: Palgrave, 2011.

———. *Emerson's Protégés: Mentoring and Marketing Transcendentalism's Future*. New Haven: Yale University Press, 2014.

———. "Publishers." In *Ralph Waldo Emerson in Context*, edited by Wesley Mott. 221–9. New York: Cambridge University Press, 2014.

Dwight, John Sullivan. "The Religion of Beauty," *Dial,* July 1840, 17–22.

Eckel, Leslie. *Atlantic Citizens: Nineteenth-Century American Writers at Work in the World.* Edinburgh: Edinburgh University Press, 2013.

Edgell, David P. *William Ellery Channing: An Intellectual Portrait.* Boston: Beacon Press, 1955.

Elbert, Monika. "Urban Reform and the Plight of the Poor in Women's Journalistic Writing." In *Philanthropic Discourse in Anglo-American Literature, 1850–1920,* edited by Frank Q. Christianson and Leslie Thorne-Murphy. 85–113. Bloomington: Indiana University Press, 2017.

Elbert, Monika and Lesley Ginsberg, ed., *Romantic Education in Nineteenth-Century America.* New York: Routledge, 2015.

Emerson, Ralph Waldo. *The Collected Works of Ralph Waldo Emerson.* 8 vols. to date, edited by Robert E. Spiller, Alfred E. Ferguson, Joseph Slater, Jean Ferguson Carr, Wallace E. Williams, and Douglas Emory Wilson. Cambridge, Mass.: Harvard University Press, 1971-.

———. "The Editors to the Reader," *Dial,* July 1840, 1–4.

———. *The Journals and Miscellaneous Notebooks of Ralph Waldo Emerson,* edited by William H. Gilman et al. 16 vols. Cambridge, MA: Belknap Press of Harvard, 1960–82.

———. *The Letters of Ralph Waldo Emerson,* edited by Ralph L. Rusk and Eleanor M. Tilton. 10 vols. New York: Columbia University Press, 1939–1995.

———. *Selected Lectures,* edited by Ronald A. Bosco and Joel Myerson. Athens: University of Georgia Press, 2005.

———. *Selected Letters,* edited by Joel Myerson. New York: Columbia University Press, 1997.

Erickson, Megan. *Class War: The Privatization of Childhood.* London: Verso, 2015.

Fergenson, Laraine R. "Margaret Fuller in the Classroom: The Providence Period." *Studies in the American Renaissance* (1987): 131–42.

Field, Peter S. *The Crisis of the Standing Order: Clerical Intellectuals and Cultural Authority in Massachusetts, 1780-1833.* Amherst: University of Massachusetts Press, 1998.

———. *Ralph Waldo Emerson: The Making of a Democratic Intellectual.* Lanham: Rowman and Littlefield, 2003.

Fink, Steven. "Thoreau and His Audience." In *The Cambridge Companion to Henry David Thoreau,* edited by Joel Myerson, 71–91. Cambridge: Cambridge University Press, 1995.

Frothingham, Octavius Brooks. *Transcendentalism in New England: A History.* Philadelphia: University of Pennsylvania Press, 1972 [1876].

Fuller, Margaret. "Christmas." *New-York Daily Tribune,* December 25, 1844, 1.

———. "Emerson's Essays," *New-York Daily Tribune,* December 7, 1844, 1.

———. *Letters of Margaret Fuller,* edited by Robert N. Hudspeth. 6 vols. Ithaca: Cornell University Press, 1983–94.

———. *The Memoirs of Margaret Fuller Ossoli,* edited by Ralph Waldo Emerson, William Henry Channing, and James Freeman Clarke. 2 vols. Boston: Philips, Sampson and Co., 1852.

———. "Our City Charities." *New-York Daily Tribune,* March 19, 1845, 1.

———. *Papers on Literature and Art*. 2 vols. New York: Wiley and Putnam, 1846.

———. *"These Sad but Glorious Days": Dispatches from Europe, 1846–1850*, edited by Larry J. Reynolds and Susan Belasco Smith. New Haven: Yale University Press, 1991.

———. "Woman in the Nineteenth Century." In *The Essential Margaret Fuller*, edited by Jeffrey Steele, 243–378. New Brunswick: Rutgers University Press, 1992.

Gann, Kyle. *Charles Ives's Concord: Essays After a Sonata*. Urbana: University of Illinois Press, 2017.

Ganter, Granville, and Hani Sarji. "'May We Put Forth Our Leaves': Rhetoric in the School Journal of Mary Ware Allen, Student of Margaret Fuller, 1837–1838." *Proceedings of the American Antiquarian Society* 117 (2007): 61–142.

Geiger, Roger L. *The History of American Higher Education: Learning and Culture form the Founding to World War II*. Princeton: Princeton University Press, 2015.

Gilmore, William J. *Reading Becomes a Necessity of Life: Material and Cultural Life in Rural New England, 1780-1835*. Knoxville: University of Tennessee Press, 1989.

Gohdes, Clarence Louis Frank. *The Periodicals of American Transcendentalism*. Durham: Duke University Press, 1931.

Goodrich, Samuel Griswold. *The Tales of Peter Parley About America*. Rev. ed. Philadelphia: Thomas, Cowperthwait & Co., 1847.

Gramsci, Antonio. *Selections from the Prison Notebooks*, edited by Quintin Hoare and Geoffrey Nowell Smith. New York: International Publishers, 2008.

Greeley, Horace. "To Correspondents," *New-York Daily Tribune*, Feb. 10, 1845, 2.

———. "'The Dial' for January," *New York Tribune*, January 25, 1844, 1.

———. "Literary Notices," *New-York Daily Tribune*, April 27, 1844, 1.

———. "Reply," *New-York Daily Tribune*, April 7, 1849, 5.

Green, Christopher. "The Dial," *Plain Speaker*, January 30, 1841, 3.

Grodzins, Dean. *American Heretic: Theodore Parker and Transcendentalism*. Chapel Hill: University of North Carolina Press, 2002.

Gross, Robert N. *Public vs. Private: The Early History of School Choice in America*. New York: Oxford University Press, 2018.

Gustafson Sandra M. "Choosing a Medium: Margaret Fuller and the Forms of Sentiment." *American Quarterly* 47, no. 1 (1995): 34–65.

Habich, Robert D. "Emerson's Reluctant Foe: Andrews Norton and the Transcendental Controversy." N*ew England Quarterly* 65. no. 2 (1992): 208–37.

Hart, Amy. *Fourierist Communities of Reform: The Social Networks of Nineteenth-Century Female Reformers*. Basingstoke: Palgrave Macmillan, 2021.

Hawes, Joel. *Lectures to Young Men; on the Formation of Character &c*. Hartford: Cooke and Co. 1832.

Hayward, John. *The New England Gazetteer: Containing Descriptions of All the States, Counties and Towns in New England*, 6th ed. Concord, NH: Israel S. Boyd and William White, 1839.

Hegel, Georg Wilhelm Friedrich. "Oldest System Program of German Idealism." Trans. Andrew Bowie. In *Aesthetics and Subjectivity: From Kant to Nietzsche*,

edited by Andrew Bowie. 2nd ed. 334–5. Manchester: Manchester University Press, 2003.
Henkel, Scott. *Direct Democracy: Collective Power, the Swarm, and the Literatures of the Americas*. Jackson: University Press of Mississippi, 2017.
Hewitt. Martin. "Ralph Waldo Emerson, George Dawson, and the Control of the Lecture Platform in Mid-Nineteenth-Century Manchester." *Nineteenth-Century Prose* 25, no. 2 (1998): 1–23.
Hiner, N. Ray. "Children in American History." In *Rethinking the History of American Education*, edited by William J. Reese, John L. Rury, 161–85. New York: Palgrave Macmillan, 2008.
Hoag, Ronald Wesley. "Odd Man In: Thoreau, the Lyceum Movement, and the Lecture Circuit." In *Henry David Thoreau in Context*, edited by James S. Finley, 141–51. Cambridge: Cambridge University Press, 2017.
Hogan, David. "Modes of Discipline: Affective Individualism and Pedagogical Reform in New England, 1820-1850." *American Journal of Education* 99, no. 1 (1990): 1–56.
Holbrook, Josiah. "Associations of Adults for Mutual Instruction." *American Journal of Education* 1 (Oct. 1826): 594–7.
Howe, Daniel Walker. *Making the American Self: Jonathan Edwards to Abraham Lincoln*. Oxford: Oxford University Press, 1997.
———. *The Unitarian Conscience: Harvard Moral Philosophy, 1805-1861*. 2nd ed. Middletown: Wesleyan University Press, 1988.
———. *What Hath God Wrought: The Transformation of America*, 1815–1848. Oxford: Oxford University Press, 2007.
Hudson, Frederic. *Journalism in the United States, from 1690-1872*. New York: Harper & Brothers, 1873.
Hudspeth, Robert. "Margaret Fuller and Urban Life." In *Margaret Fuller and Her Circles*, edited by Brigitte Bailey, Katheryn P. Viens, and Conrad Edick Wright, 179–205. Durham: University of New Hampshire Press, 2013.
John, Richard R. *Spreading the News: The American Postal System from Franklin to Morse*. Cambridge: Harvard University Press, 1995.
Kaestle, Carl F. and Maris A. Vinovskis. *Education and Social Change in Nineteenth-Century Massachusetts*. Cambridge: Cambridge University Press, 1980.
Keenaghan, Eric. "Reading Emerson, in Other Times: On a Politics of Solitude and an Ethics of Risk." In *The Other Emerson*, edited by Cary Wolfe and Branka Arsić, 167–99. University of Minnesota Press, 2010.
Kneeland, Abner. *National Hymns, Original and Selected, for the Use of Those Who Are "Slaves to No Sect."* Boston: Boston Investigator, 1836.
Kopacz, Paula. "Feminist at the 'Tribune': Margaret Fuller as Professional Writer," *Studies in the American Renaissance* (1991): 119–39.
Kytle, Ethan. *Romantic Reformers and the Antislavery Struggle in the Civil War Era*. New York: Cambridge, 2014.
Labaree, David F. "Citizens and Consumers: Changing Visions of Virtue and Opportunity in U.S. Education, 1841-1954." In *Schooling and the Making of*

*Citizens in the Long Nineteenth Century*, edited by Daniel Tröhler, Thomas Popkewitz, and David F. Labaree, 168–83. New York: Palgrave Macmillan, 2011.

Lampe, Gregory P. *Frederick Douglass: Freedom's Voice, 1818-1845*. East Lansing: Michigan State University Press, 2012.

Lane, Charles. *The Law and Method in Spirit-culture: An Interpretation of A. Bronson Alcott's Idea and Practice at the Masonic Temple, Boston*. Boston: James Munroe, 1843.

Lang, John Dunmore. *Religion and Education in America; with Notices of the State and Prospects of American Unitarianism, Popery, and African Colonization*. London: Thomas Ward, 1840.

LaPlante, Eve. *Marmee & Louisa: The Untold Story of Louisa May Alcott and Her Mother*. New York: Simon and Schuster, 2012.

Lefebvre, Henri. *The Critique of Everyday Life*. London: Verso, 1991.

Leverenz, David. "Frederick Douglass's Self-Refashioning." *Criticism* 29, no. 3 (1987): 341–70.

Lloyd, Vincent. "The Affect of God's Law." In *A Political Companion to Frederick Douglass*. edited by Neil Robert. Lexington: University of Kentucky Press, 2018. 305-23.

Loeffelholz, Mary. *From School to Salon: Reading Nineteenth-Century American Women's Poetry*. Princeton: Princeton University Press, 2004.

Maas, Christel-Maria. *Margaret Fullers transnationales Projekt: Selbstbildung, feminine Kultur und amerikanische Nationalliteratur nach deutschem Vorbild*. Göttingen: Universitätsverlag Göttingen, 2006.

Machor, James L. *Reading Fiction in Antebellum America: Informed Response and Reception Histories, 1820-1865*. Baltimore: Johns Hopkins University Press, 2011.

Mack Smith, Denis. *Mazzini*. New Haven: Yale University Press, 1994.

Marble, Annie Russell. "Margaret Fuller as Teacher." *Critic* 43 (October 1903): 334–45.

Marshall, Megan. *Margaret Fuller: A New American Life*. Boston: Houghton Mifflin Harcourt, 2013.

Martin, Jr., Waldo E. *The Mind of Frederick Douglass*. Chapel Hill: University of North Carolina Press, 1984.

Matteson, Frank, *The Lives of Margaret Fuller: A Biography*. New York: Norton, 2012.

May, Samuel Joseph, *Memoir of Samuel Joseph May*, edited by Thomas James Mumford. Boston: American Unitarian Society, 1876.

Mayrl, Damon. *Secular Conversions: Political Institutions and Religious Education in the United States and Australia, 1800–2000*. Cambridge: Cambridge University Press, 2016.

McFeely, William S. *Frederick Douglass*. New York: Norton, 2017.

McKivigan, John R. et al. "Introduction." In *The Speeches of Frederick Douglass: A Critical Edition*, edited by John R. McKivigan et al., xix–xxxix. New Haven: Yale University Press, 2018.

Mendelsohn, Jack. *Channing, the Reluctant Radical*. Westport: Greenwood Press, 1980. First published 1971 by Little, Brown.

Meyer, Thomas J. "The Great Rebellion of 1823." Accessed August 3, 2021. http://www.thecrimson.com/article/1982/2/17/the-great-rebellion-of-1823-pii/.

Michaels, Walter Benn. "Dude, Where's My Job?" *PMLA* 127, no. 4 (2012): 1006–1009.

Mielke, Laura L. *Provocative Eloquence: Theater, Violence, and Antislavery Speech in the Antebellum United States.* Ann Arbor: University of Michigan Press, 2019.

Milder, Robert. "The Radical Emerson?" In *Cambridge Companion to Ralph Waldo Emerson*, edited by Joel Porte and Saundra Morris, Cambridge: Cambridge University Press, 1999. 49–75.

Miller, John P. *Transcendental Learning: The Educational Legacy of Alcott, Emerson, Fuller, Peabody and Thoreau.* Charlotte: Information Age Publishing, 2011.

Miller, Perry. *The Transcendentalists: An Anthology.* 1950. Reprint, Cambridge, MA: Harvard University Press, 2001.

Miller Solomon, Barbara. *In the Company of Educated Women: A History of Women and Higher Education in America.* New Haven: Yale University Press, 1985.

Mitchell, Catherine C., ed. *Margaret Fuller's New York Journalism: A Biographical Essay and Key Writings.* Knoxville: University of Tennessee Press, 1995.

Moran, Gerald F.; Maris A Vinovskis. "Literacy, Common Schools, and High Schools in Colonial Antebellum America." In *Rethinking the History of American Education*, edited by William J. Reese and John L. Rury, 17–46. New York: Palgrave Macmillan, 2008.

Morrow, John. *Thomas Carlyle.* London: Continuum, 2006.

Mott, Wesley. "Education." In *The Oxford Handbook of Transcendentalism*, edited by Joel Myerson et al. 153–71. Oxford: Oxford University Press, 2010.

Münch, Richard. *Akademischer Kapitalismus: Über die politische Ökonomie der Hochschulreform.* Frankfurt Suhrkamp, 2011.

Myerson, Joel. "'In the Transcendental Emporium': Bronson Alcott's 'Orphic Sayings' in the Dial." *English Language Notes* 10 (1972): 31–8.

———. *The New England Transcendentalists and the Dial.* Rutherford: Farleigh Dickinson Press, 1980.

Nash, Margaret A. *Women's Education in the United States, 1780-1840.* New York: Palgrave, 2005.

Nehring, James. *The Practice of School Reform: Lessons from Two Centuries.* Albany: State University of New York Press, 2009.

Neufeldt, Leonard N. *The Economist: Henry Thoreau & Enterprise.* New York: Oxford University Press, 1989.

Newfield, Christopher. *Unmaking the Public University: The Forty-Year Assault on the Middle Class.* Cambridge: Harvard University Press, 2010.

Newman, Lance. *Our Common Dwelling: Henry Thoreau, Transcendentalism, and the Class Politics of Nature.* New York: Palgrave, 2005.

Norton, Andrews. *A Discourse on the Latest Form of Infidelity.* Cambridge: John Owen, 1839.

———. *Speech Delivered Before the Overseers of Harvard.* Boston: Cummings, Hilliard, & Co., 1825.

Pacheco, Derek. *Moral Enterprise: Literature and Education in Antebellum America.* Columbus: Ohio State University Press, 2013.

Packer, Barbara. "The Transcendentalists." In *The Cambridge History of American Literature*, vol. 2: 1820–1865, edited by Sacvan Bercovitch, 329–604. Cambridge: Cambridge University Press, 1995.

Parille, Ken and Anne Mallory. "Romantic Reform and Boys: Bronson. Alcott's Materialist Pedagogy." In *Romantic Education in Nineteenth-Century America*, edited by Monika Elbert and Lesley Ginsberg, 15–30. New York: Routledge, 2015.

Parkhurst, J. L., ed. *Teacher's Guide and Parent's Assistant*, vol. 1. Portland: Shirley and Hyde Printers, 1827.

Peabody, Elizabeth Palmer. "A Glimpse of Christ's Idea of Society," *Dial*, Oct. 1841, 227.

———. *Record of a School: Exemplifying the General Principles of Spiritual Culture.* Boston: James Munroe, 1835.

Peterson, Merrill D. *The Great Triumvirate: Webster, Clary, and Calhoun.* New York: Oxford University Press, 1987.

Petrulionis, Sandra Harbart. *To Set this World Right: The Antislavery Movement in Thoreau's Concord.* Ithaca: Cornell University Press, 2006.

Philpotts, Matthew. "The Role of the Periodical Editor: Literary Journals and Editorial Habitus." *Modern Language Review* 107, no. 1 (2012): 39–64.

Pierpont, John. *The American First Class Book, or, Exercises in Reading and Recitation.* Boston: William B. Fowle, 1823.

Plimpton, Moses. *History of Southbridge.* Southbridge: Journal Steam Book Print, 1882.

Plotica, Luke Philip. *Nineteenth-Century Individualism and the Market Economy: Individualist Themes in Emerson, Thoreau, and Sumner.* Basingstoke: Palgrave Macmillan, 2018.

Poe, Edgar Allan. "The Literati of New York City—No. IV." *Godey's Lady's Book* (Aug. 1846): 72–724.

Power, Edward J. *A Legacy of Learning: A History of Western Education.* Albany: SUNY Press, 1991.

Quincy, Josiah. *Speech of Josiah Quincy, President of Harvard University, Before the Board of Overseers of that Institution, February 25, 1845, on the Minority Report of the Committee of Visitation, Presented to that Board by George Bancroft, Esq., February 6, 1845.* Boston: Charles C. Little, Brown, and Co., 1845.

Ramble, Robert. *The Table Book: Comprising the Tables Necessary to Be Committed to Memory at an Early Age.* Philadelphia: Desilver, Thomas & Co., 1836.

Rand, Asa. "Education." *Boston Recorder and Religious Telegraph*, April 9, 1829. 57.

Ray, Angela G. "Frederick Douglass on the Lyceum Circuit: Social Assimilation, Social Transformation?" *Rhetoric and Public Affairs* 5, no. 4 (2002): 625–647.

———. "How Cosmopolitan Was the Lyceum, Anyway?" In *The Cosmopolitan Lyceum: Lecture Culture and the Globe in Nineteenth Century*, edited by Tom F. Wright. 23–41. Amherst: University of Massachusetts Press, 2013.

Reynolds, Larry J. *European Revolutions and the American Renaissance.* New Haven: Yale University Press, 1988.
Reynolds, Larry J. and Susan Belasco Smith. "Introduction." In *"These Sad but Glorious Days": Dispatches from Europe, 1846–1850*, edited by Larry J. Reynolds and Susan Belasco Smith. 1–35. New Haven: Yale University Press, *1991*.
Richardson, Alan. Lit*erature, Education, and Romanticism: Reading as Social Practice, 1780–1832.* Cambridge: Cambridge University Press, 1994.
Richardson, Robert D., Jr. *Henry Thoreau: A Life of the Mind.* Berkeley: University of California Press, 1986.
Ripley, George. "Brownson's Writings," *Dial*, July 1840, 22–46.
Robinson, David M. *Apostle of Culture: Emerson as Preacher and Lecturer.* Philadelphia: University of Pennsylvania Press, 1982.
———. *Emerson and the Conduct of Life: Pragmatism and Ethical Purpose in the Later Thought.* New York: Cambridge University Press, 1993.
———. "Margaret Fuller, New York, and the Politics of Transcendentalism." *ESQ: A Journal of the American Renaissance* 52, no. 4 (2006): 271–99.
———. "'A Religious Demonstration': The Theological Emergence of New England Transcendentalism." In *Transient and Permanent: The Transcendentalist Movement and Its Contexts*, edited by Charles Capper and Conrad Edick Wright, 49–72. Boston: Massachusetts Historical Society, 1999.
Ronda, Bruce. *Elizabeth Palmer Peabody: A Reformer on Her Own Terms.* Cambridge, Mass.: Harvard University Press, 1999.
Rose, Anne C. *Transcendentalism as a Social Movement, 1830-1850.* New Haven: Yale University Press, 1981.
Rowson, Susanna. *A Spelling Dictionary.* Boston: John West, 1807.
Rury, John L. *Education and Social Change: Contours in the History of American Schooling*, 5th ed. New York: Routledge, 2016.
Rush, Benjamin. *A Plan for the Establishment of Public Schools and the Diffusion of Knowledge in Pennsylvania; to Which Are Added Thoughts Upon the Mode of Education, Proper in a Republic.* Philadelphia: Thomas Dobson, 1786.
Ryan, Mary. *Women in Public Between Banners and Ballots, 1825-1880.* Baltimore: Johns Hopkins University Press, 1990.
Sacks, Kenneth. *Understanding Emerson: "The American Scholar" and His Struggle for Self-Reliance.* Princeton: Princeton University Press, 2003.
Sanborn, Frank B. *A. Bronson Alcott: His Life and Philosophy.* V.1. Cambridge, MA: John Wilson and Son, 1893.
Sánchez-Eppler, Karen. *Dependent States: The Child's Part in Nineteenth-Century American Culture.* Chicago: University of Chicago Press, 2005.
Schlegel, Friedrich. "Fragmente," *Athenaeum* 1, no. 2 (1798): 3–146.
Schlicht, Rüdiger C. *Die pädagogischen Ansätze amerikanischer Transzendentalisten: Erziehungswissenschaftliche Studien zu Amos Bronson Alcott, Ralph Waldo Emerson und Henry David Thoreau, 1830-1840.* Frankfurt: Lang, 1977.
Schmid, Franziska. *Educating New England: The Pedagogical Experiments of the American Transcendentalists.* Heidelberg: Winter, 2018.

Sedgwick, Catherine Maria. *Means and Ends; Or, Self-Training*. New York: Harper and Harper, 1842.

Sellers, Charles. *The Market Revolution: Jacksonian America, 1815–1846*. New York: Oxford University Press, 1991.

Shannon, Mary L. *Dickens, Reynolds, and Mayhew on Wellington Street: The Print Culture of a Victorian Street*. Milton Park: Routledge, 2016.

Shepard, Odell. *Pedlar's Progress: The Life of Bronson Alcott*. Boston: Little, Brown, and Co. 1938.

Shuffelton, Frank. "Margaret Fuller at the Greene Street School: The Journal of Evelina Metcalf." *Studies in the American Renaissance* (1985): 29–46.

Sigourney, Lydia Howard. *Poems for Children*. Harford: Canfield & Robins, 1836.

Simmons, Nancy Craig. "Margaret Fuller's Boston Conversations: The 1839–1840 Series." *Studies in the American Renaissance* (1994): 195–226.

Spahr, Clemens. *Radical Beauty: American Transcendentalism and the Aesthetic Critique of Modernity*. Paderborn: Schöningh, 2011.

Spivak, Gayatri. *An Aesthetic Education in the Era of Globalization*. Cambridge, MA: Harvard University Press, 2012.

Stauffer, John. "Frederick Douglass's Self-Fashioning and the Making of a Representative American Man." In *The Cambridge Companion to the African American Slave Narrative,* edited by Audrey A. Fisch. 201–17. Cambridge: Cambridge University Press, 2007.

Steele, Jeffrey. "Sympathy and Prophecy: The Two Faces of Social Justice in Fuller's New York Writing." In *Margaret Fuller and Her Circles*, edited by Brigitte Bailey, Katheryn P. Viens, and Conrad Edick Wright, 161–78. Durham: University of New Hampshire Press, 2013.

———. *Transfiguring America: Myth, Ideology, and Mourning in Margaret Fuller's Writing*. Columbia: University of Missouri Press, 2001.

Stoehr, Taylor. *Nay-Saying in Concord: Emerson, Alcott, and Thoreau*. Hamden: Archon Books, 1979.

Stokes, Melvyn and Stephen Conway. *The Market Revolution in America*. Charlottesville: University of Virginia Press, 1996.

Stoneham, Michael. *John Brown and the Era of Literary Confrontation*. New York: Routledge, 2009.

Story, Ronald. *The Forging of an Aristocracy: Harvard and the Boston Upper Class, 1800-1870*. Middletown, CT: Wesleyan University Press, 1980.

Taylor, George. *The Transportation Revolution, 1815–60*. London: Routledge, 1951.

Taylor, Nikki Marie. *America's First Black Socialist: The Radical Life of Peter H. Clark*. Lexington: University of Kentucky Press, 2013.

Teichgraeber, Richard F. *Sublime Thoughts, Penny Wisdom*. Baltimore: Johns Hopkins University Press, 1995.

Thoreau, Henry David. *Collected Essays and Poems,* edited by Elizabeth Hall Witherell. New York: Library of America, 2001.

———. *Correspondence*, vol. 1: 1834–1848, edited by Robert N. Hudspeth. Princeton: Princeton University Press, 2013.

———. *Early Essays and Miscellanies*, edited by Joseph J. Moldenhauer et al. Princeton: Princeton University Press, 1975.

———. "Homer. Ossian. Chaucer." *Dial,* Jan. 1844, 290–305.

———. *Journal.* edited by John C. Broderick, Robert Sattelmeyer, Elizabeth Hall Witherell et al. 8 vols. Princeton: Princeton University Press, 1981–2009.

———. *Reform Papers*, edited by Wendell Glick. Princeton: Princeton University Press, 1973.

———. *Walden*, edited by J. Lyndon Shanley. Princeton: Princeton University Press, 1971.

Tuchinsky, Adam. *Horace Greeley's New-York Tribune: Civil War-era Socialism and the Crisis of Free Labor.* Ithaca: Cornell University Press, 2009.

———. "Margaret Fuller, Self-Culture, and Associationism." In *Margaret Fuller and Her Circles,* edited by Brigitte Bailey et al. 100–27. Durham: University of New Hampshire Press, 2013.

Urbas, Joseph. *Emerson's Metaphysics: A Song of Laws and Causes.* Lanham: Lexington Books, 2016.

Vásquez, Mark G. *Authority and Reform: Religious and Educational Discourses in Nineteenth-Century New England Literature.* Knoxville: University of Tennessee Press, 2003.

Wallach, Glenn. *Obedient Sons: The Discourse of Youth and Generations in American Culture, 1630-1860.* Amherst: University of Massachusetts Press, 1997.

Wallerstein, Immanuel. *World-Systems Analysis: An Introduction.* Durham: Duke University Press, 2004.

Walls, Laura Dassow. Henry David Thoreau: A Life. Chicago: University of Chicago Press, 2017.

Warren, Kenneth. "Frederick Douglass's Life and Times: Progressive Rhetoric and the Problem of Constituency." In *Renewing Black Intellectual History: The Ideological and Material Foundations of African American Thought*, edited by Adolph Reed, Jr. and Kenneth Warren, 3–18. New York: Routledge, 2010.

Wayne, Tiffany K. *Woman Thinking: Feminism and Transcendentalism in Nineteenth-Century America.* Langham: Lexington, 2005.

Wright, Tom F. *Lecturing the Atlantic: Speech, Print, and an Anglo-American Commons 1830-1870.* Oxford: Oxford University Press, 2017.

Zboray, Ronald J. *A Fictive People: Antebellum Economic Development and the American Reading Public.* Oxford: Oxford University Press, 1993.

Zwarg, Christina. *Feminist Conversations: Fuller, Emerson, and the Play of Reading.* Ithaca: Cornell University Press, 2018.

# Index

Aborn, Frances, 58
Alcott, Amos Bronson, 2, 6–7, 12, 17–20, 27–29, 38–57, 75–76, 86, 92, 102, 125, 131; Cheshire school, 17, 44–45; *Conversations with Children on the Gospels*, 27–28, 38, 40, 50–56; *Doctrine and Discipline of Human Nature*, 40; and Fruitlands, 63; journals, 42–44; *Observations on the Principles and Methods of Infant Instruction*, 46, 48; "Orphic Sayings", 80, 83; and Temple School, 2, 12, 17–20, 29, 38–39, 46–58, 86, 92
Alcott, Louisa May, 43
Allen, Mary Ware, 59–60
*American Journal of Education*, 4, 17, 38, 44–46, 55, 101
Associationism, 72
Austin, James, 53

Bancroft, George, 23
Benevolent Fraternity of Churches, 114
*Boston Courier*, 4, 19, 22, 52–53
*Boston Investigator*, 23–24
*Boston Quarterly Review*, 12, 71–79, 84, 95
*Boston Recorder (and Telegraph)*, 19, 45, 56

Bourdieu, Pierre, 6–7, 25–26, 95, 132
British Romanticism, 3
Brook Farm, 72–73, 86
Brown, John, 21, 114–20, 125–26
Brownson, Orestes, 3, 6, 9, 12, 20, 27–30, 53, 72–79, 84, 95, 131, 133; on Alcott, 75–76; "American Literature", 74; *Boston Quarterly Review*, 12, 72–79, 84; on Carlyle, 76–78; *Discourse on the Wants of the Times*, 74; as editor, 73–76; "The Laboring Classes", 3, 74–78; *New Views of Christianity, Society, and the Church*, 74; "Union and Progress", 73
Bruce, Georgiana, 86
Buckingham, Joseph T.: review of Amos Bronson Alcott's *Conversations*, 53–54
Buckminster, Joseph: "Discourse on the Dangers and Duties of Men of Letters", 5

Carlyle, Thomas, 90, 92, 107; on Chartism, 29, 76
Cavell, Stanley, 5
Channing, William Ellery: "Address on Self-Culture", 77; "Likeness to God", 62

Channing, William Henry, 10, 90
Chantrey, Francis Legatt, 89
*Christian Examiner*, 52, 83–84
Christianity, 21, 42–44
*Christian Register*, 53
Clarke, James Freeman, 10, 37–38, 53, 82
class, 12, 22–24, 28–31, 39, 62–63
conversation, 2, 7, 12, 27, 37–63, 83, 95, 103–5; conversational circles for women, 61–63; conversation and literary journalism, 85–86; and Romanticism, 37–38; and schoolbooks, 40–42
Cranch, Christopher: and *Dial*, 81–83
Crandall, Prudence: and educational reform, 43–44
cult of the child, 39

Dawson, George, 90
*Dial*, 3, 12, 71–74, 78–86, 90, 95, 106, 112–13, 117; avant-gardism, 82–86; populism, 83–84
Dickens, Charles, 91
domestic-tutelary complex, 39
Douglass, Frederick, 12–13, 31, 102–4, 114–15, 118–26; "American Slavery, American Religion", 103–4; "I Have Come to Tell You Something About Slavery", 120–21; letter to William Lloyd Garrison, 119–20; and lyceum, 118; in Lynn, 120–22; *Narrative of the Life of Frederick Douglass, an American Slave*, 122–24; in New Bedford, 118–20; and Protestant-capitalist work ethic, 120; and Romantic self-culture, 120
Dwight, John Sullivan, 71

education: in nineteenth-century textbooks, 40–42, 45, 50–51, 57. *See also* literary education; popular education; private schools; public education; universal education
Edwards, Jonathan, 44
*The Emancipator*, 23

Emerson, Ralph Waldo, 3, 5, 9–10, 12, 18–20, 24–32, 50, 60–62, 90, 92, 115, 117, 119–20, 131; "The American Scholar", 29; and the *Dial*, 71–73, 79–83; Divinity School Address, 44, 55; inaugural speech at Greene Street School, 57–58; "Man the Reformer", 105–8; and ministry, 104; *Nature*, 52; "The Poet", 49; as public speaker, 102–10; on sympathy, 37; on Temple School, 50, 53; "The Young American", 108–10
Engels, Friedrich, 94

Fourierism, 72
Freiligrath, Ferdinand, 91
Fruitlands, 63
Fuller, Hiram, 47, 56–60
Fuller, Margaret, 1–4, 7, 9–12, 20, 25–30, 37–40, 42, 71, 107, 118, 125–26, 131; "American Literature", 85–86; Boston conversations, 61–63; and class, 62–63; and the *Dial*, 79–85; "The Great Lawsuit", 84–85; at Greene Street School, 55–61; and literary journalism, 85–95; on newspaper writing, 7, 85; at *New-York Tribune*, 85–95; "Our City Charities", 87, 94–95; *Summer on the Lakes, in 1843*, 30, 39; *Woman in the Nineteenth Century*, 30, 39

Garrison, William Lloyd, 119, 122
genre, literary, 1–2, 8, 11–12, 41, 51–52, 80, 88–89, 102–3, 125
German Romanticism, 62–63
Goodrich, Samuel Griswold, 50; *The Tales of Peter Parley*, 50
Greaves, James Pierrepont, 55
Greeley, Horace, 83–88, 94, 109; on the *Dial*, 85; and *New-York Tribune*, 86–88; On Thoreau, 113–13
Greeley, Mary, 63
Greene Street School, 37, 39, 47, 55–61, 86

*Harbinger*, 72
Harvard Divinity School, 9, 27
Harvard University, 50, 52, 59, 112, 115
Hawes, Joel, 112; *Lectures to Young Men*, 112
Holbrook, Josiah, 101; and lyceum, 101

Kneeland, Abner, 23–25, 28

laboring classes, 9–10, 20–21, 24, 76–78, 93
Lancastrian School, 5, 18, 22, 47, 50
lectures, 12–13, 25, 28–29, 79, 101–26
Lefebvre, Henri, 26
*The Liberator*, 31, 43, 115, 117, 120
literary education, 3–4, 7–8, 10, 12–13, 31, 46, 49, 55, 78, 80, 95, 102–3, 114, 132–34
literary journalism, 2, 7, 11–12, 21, 58, 85–95; Fuller and literary journalism, 85–95
Liverpool's Mechanics' Institute, 89
lyceum: Boston Lyceum, 102; Concord Lyceum, 110–13; Southbridge Lyceum, 102

Mann, Horace, 6–7, 18, 22
market revolution, 21, 27
Martineau, Harriett, 50
Marx, Karl, 94
Masonic Temple, 48, 104, 110
Massachusetts Board of Education, 17, 75
Massachusetts school system, 19–20
May, Samuel Joseph, 43–44
Mazzini, Giuseppe, 88–93; Mazzini's boy school, 91–93
*Mechanic and Farmer*, 23
Metcalf, Evelina, 60
*Mississippian*, 19
Munroe, James, 19–20, 50–52

National Teachers Association, 18
*New England Gazetteer*, 43
*New-York Tribune*, 10, 12, 30, 63, 71–72, 84–95, 109, 113, 131

Nias, Georgianna, 58
*North American and Daily Advertiser*, 19
*North American Review*, 52
Norton, Andrews, 25–28, 54

Parker, Theodore, 84, 90, 114
Peabody, Elizabeth, 9, 47, 53, 56–57, 61, 81; and Fuller, 61; *Record of a School*, 50
*Pennsylvania Inquirer*, 19
periodicals, 4–5, 12, 19, 23–24, 28, 46–47, 71–95, 105, 108, 116
Pestalozzi, Johann Heinrich, 22
Pierpont, John: *American First Class Book*, 41
Plimpton, Moses, 102
popular education, 1, 4, 6, 10–13, 21, 23–24, 29–30, 63, 71–95, 101–4, 107, 109, 111, 116–18, 126, 131, 133
print market, 12, 18–19, 71, 83, 86
private schools, 17–18, 23, 47, 56, 76
professionalization: of education, 17–18; of lecture circuit, 101–4, 115, 124, 132
public education, 21–22, 31, 109

Quincy, Josiah, 10; on education as drilling, 26

Ramble, Robert: *Table Book*, 41
Republican education, 20–22
Ripley, George, 27, 73; *Discourses on the Philosophy of Religion*, 52
Ripley, Sophia, 56, 62
Romantic reform, 55, 73, 85, 91–96
rote learning, 7, 12, 26–27, 40, 48, 53, 59, 112
Rowson, Susanna, 59
Rush, Benjamin, 21
Russell, William, 17–18

*Scioto Gazette*, 19
Sedgwick, Catherine Maria: and sentimentalism, 75–76

sentimentalism, 51, 75–76
social reform: and education, 5, 8, 23, 30, 42, 46, 48, 51–52, 61, 87–91
specialization, 2, 111
Sumner, Charles, 31
swarm, 76–77
sympathy, sympathetic relations, 37–40

Temple School. *See* Alcott
Thoreau, Henry David, 3–4, 12–13, 30–31, 101–4, 110–21, 125–26; "The Ancient Poets", 112–13; and Concord Lyceum, 111–13; "Economy—Illustrated by the Life of a Student"; "Homer. Ossian. Chaucer", 112–13; on John Brown, 21, 114–18; "Life Without Principle", 111; "A Plea for Captain John Brown", 114–18; *Walden*, 4, 110–14
Transcendental Club, 37, 52, 73, 79, 82

Unitarianism, 5, 28, 53–54, 59, 120
universal education, 17–32, 73, 75–78, 90, 131–32

*Vermont Chronicle*, 19

Wallerstein, Immanuel, 25
*Western Messenger*, 53, 82
Whitefield, George, 44
Wordsworth, William, 90
*Working Man's Advocate*, 23

# About the Author

**Clemens Spahr** is a lecturer of American Studies at Johannes Gutenberg-University Mainz. He is the author of *A Poetics of Global Solidarity: Modern American Poetry and Social Movements* (Palgrave 2015) and *Radical Beauty: American Transcendentalism and the Aesthetic Critique of Modernity* (Schoeningh 2011). He has published in *ESQ: A Journal of Nineteenth-Century American Literature and Culture*, *Nineteenth-Century Prose*, and *NOVEL: A Forum on Fiction*.

www.ingramcontent.com/pod-product-compliance
Lightning Source LLC
Chambersburg PA
CBHW061451300426
44114CB00014B/1928